THOSE MINGLED SEAS

The Poetry of W.B. Yeats,
the Beautiful and the Sublime

Jefferson Holdridge was raised in Connecticut and educated in the United States and Ireland. He is a Fellow in the Department of Anglo-Irish Literature and Drama at University College Dublin, where he obtained his PhD. He lectures regularly on Yeats, including at the Yeats International Summer School. Among his publications are essays on American and contemporary Irish literature as well as on Yeats, Burke and aesthetics. His poetry has appeared in numerous journals.

THOSE MINGLED SEAS

The Poetry of W.B.Yeats, the Beautiful and the Sublime

Jefferson Holdridge

University College Dublin Press
Preas Cholóiste Ollscoile Bhaile Átha Cliath

First published 2000 by University College Dublin Press,
Newman House, 86 St Stephen's Green, Dublin 2, Ireland

© Jefferson Holdridge 2000

ISBN 1 900621 35 5 (hardback)
1 900621 34 7 (paperback)

Cataloguing in Publication data available from the British Library

Typeset in Ireland in 10/12 Sabon and Palatino
by Elaine Shiels, Bantry, Co. Cork
Printed in Ireland by ColourBooks, Dublin

To my mother and in memory of my father,
Anne and Norman F. Holdridge

CONTENTS

ACKNOWLEDGEMENTS

I would first like to thank Declan Kiberd for his unfailing encouragement, provocative insights and consistent enthusiasm. This book would not have proceeded without him. I am also especially indebted to Terence Brown's and Patricia Coughlan's critical insights. Roy Foster likewise honed various points and gave his advice generously. Máire Mhac an tSaoi has been inspiring and appreciative on various fronts. I thank her and her husband, Conor Cruise O'Brien. I am grateful to Jon Stallworthy and Richard Kearney for their time and trouble, and to George Watson and Jonathan Allison for inviting me to lecture in the stimulating atmosphere of the Yeats International Summer School at Sligo in 1999. A deep debt is owed to Anne and Michael B. Yeats for generously allowing me to avail of their father's library, for granting me permission to quote from his work, and to use their uncle's painting on the cover. There are also many Yeatsians whose influence should be noted, but the list, to do justice, would be too long. Barbara Mennell of UCD Press has greatly assisted me throughout the final stages of publication.

Among the lecturers in English and Anglo-Irish literature at University College Dublin, I am very grateful to Brian Donnelly, Gerardine Meaney, Christopher Murray, and Anthony Roche for their sharp engagement at different stages of the writing. Ron Callan, Andrew Carpenter, Danielle Clarke, Catriona Clutterbuck, Lucy Collins, Jerusha McCormack, Gerard Quinn, Philippa Semper, Maria Stuart, Mickey Sweeney, and Norman White have been a pleasure to work with, and have rendered the years of writing much easier and more enjoyable. I would particularly like to thank Anne Fogarty for her concern and commentary throughout the length of the project. I owe a great deal to J.C.C. Mays for supporting me at an early stage of my career, to the late Gus Martin, and my sincere appreciation also goes out to California to Daniel J. Langton who has been supportive for many years.

Past grants and scholarships, as well as the present Fellowship awarded by University College Dublin, have been of both practical and academic aid. I gratefully acknowledge the grants provided by the National University of Ireland and the University College Dublin Academic Publications Scheme in support of this publication. My particular gratitude goes to Dean Fergus D'Arcy and Mary Buckley for their interest and help. I also thank Nicholas Williams and Feargal Murphy for their editorial efforts.

Many colleagues have been an added enjoyment, as have been the literature seminars we shared. Among them are Ashley Gaskin, Derek Hand, Barbara Hughes, P.J. Mathews, Danielle Maze, Sue Norton, Ciara O'Farrell, Ray O'Neill, Stephen O'Neill, Hugh Prior, Moynagh Sullivan, and Betsy Taylor. Other colleagues are from further back, such as María Ángeles Conde Parrilla, Ronan McDonald, Mary McGrath, and Carol Tell. I also remember the late Charlotte Kelleher, while recording the continued interest of her parents, David and Lorraine, in the welfare of their daughter's friends.

I am very grateful to John Holdridge and Ruth Harman for all the trenchant perceptions that they have given over many years. I cannot thank them enough. I also warmly appreciate Penny Tallarini for her life-long support, Matthew Gaddis for our many fertile conversations, James Holdridge for his interest, and Rosa Frigenti *con affetto per tutto*.

I extend my last words of gratitude to Wanda Balzano for all her assistance, excellent advice, and especially for her *alta fantasia*.

J. H.
Dublin, January 2000

The heron-billed pale cattle-birds
That feed on some foul parasite
Of the Moroccan flocks and herds
Cross the narrow Straits to light
In the rich midnight of the garden trees
Till the dawn break upon those mingled seas.

Often at evening when a boy
Would I carry to a friend—
Hoping more substantial joy
Did an older mind commend—
Not such as are in Newton's metaphor,
But actual shells of Rosses' level shore.

Greater glory in the sun,
An evening chill upon the air,
Bid imagination run
Much on the Great Questioner;
What He can question, what if questioned I
Can with a fitting confidence reply.

W.B. Yeats, 'At Algeciras – A Meditation upon Death'

1

INTRODUCTION

My aim in this book is to examine the poetry of W.B. Yeats (1865–1939)[1] in light of current and traditional aesthetic theories. Such a theoretical stance is vital to any understanding of his poetics as a whole, which centre on the relationship between morality and the turbulent sexual world of our subconscious. Except for writing by Frances Ferguson and Christopher Norris, many recent works on aesthetics tend to be materialist readings of the subject that, though valuable, are too reductive for Yeats.[2] There is only one critical work relating to the Yeatsian sublime: Jahan Ramazani's *Yeats and the Poetry of Death*, which admirably avoids some of the worst excesses of highly psychological studies, by consistently and subtly problematising its own psychoanalytical readings with a combination of Heideggerian hermeneutics and attentive politics. Yet it has only one chapter on the sublime and true to its psychoanalytical bearing it is primarily sceptical of Yeats's transcendental deduction. By using Edmund Burke's (1729–1797) empirical and Immanuel Kant's (1724–1804) formal aesthetics as a comparative basis, I shall attempt to show that, for Yeats, the mystery of the aesthetic eludes materialist readings, even if the aesthetic is based in the empirical world.

The central argument of the book is to illustrate the various ways in which Yeats eroticises the idea of the divine. Traditional genderings of the beautiful as feminine and the sublime as masculine are thereby subsumed through an ecstatic vision that may momentarily heal the subject–object divide in human consciousness. For Yeats, the question revolves around whether that moment of illumination has any permanent value. In David Sedley's words, 'Much contemporary debate about the sublime revolves around two positions: the sublime provides either a way out of skepticism or a way into it'.[3] Yeats moves between the two positions. He is not unsceptical of the healing towards which he resolutely aims. He knows that 'profound philosophy must come from terror'.[4] He knows that whether we call it 'grace' or a 'cure', the only proof we have that either will last is in the ecstasy of the experience.

Despite Yeats's conflation of the terms in the phrase 'a terrible beauty',[5] the terrible sublime is historically easily enough defined, and certainly it is easily separated from the beautiful. Yeats conflates the terms in order to hint at the power of the 1916 rebellion to determine the fate of a nation for both ill and good. Such a conflation is indicative of how sublime events distort or redefine the harmonious basis of the beautiful. This disruptive transformation is the reason for which beauty is closely aligned to terror in Modernist literature; it reflects the experience of modernity. The aesthetic conflation is in fact a product of modern history. Since the French Revolution, the Napoleonic Wars, and the second generation of Romantics, beauty has moved towards sublimity, towards modernity, because the underlying *sensus communis* has eroded. The shared experience at the heart of Neo-Classical ideas of beauty provoked the Romantics, like the Poets of Sensibility before them, to find their themes in the more subjective aesthetics of the sublime. The more one looks to the subjective for an aesthetic the more one moves in the terrain of the unconscious and its terror, its death-longing, its symbolic and erotic dreaming. Yet the beautiful is also central to the Romantic aesthetics of William Wordsworth, Samuel Coleridge, Percy Bysshe Shelley and John Keats, though perhaps it is not its most Modernist form. Like Romantic beauty, Yeats's nostalgic conception of the beautiful is a symbol of the harmonious society (from 'Adam's Curse' to the Coole Park poems), of what Yeats calls 'Unity of Culture'. It has its roots in the eighteenth-century idea that the beautiful society reflects the sublime reason of God.

In the eighteenth century, the sublime was seen as an extension of the beautiful and not as its opposite. It was not until the era leading up to the French Revolution that the two terms assumed a dialectical relationship. A major Enlightenment historian of the Revolution and aesthetician of the beautiful and sublime, Burke was the first to characterise the beautiful and the sublime as social harmony and division respectively. In his scheme, evolving from early aesthetic concerns to his political philosophy, violent revolution such as that in France could be viewed only in the frame of the terrible sublime, as an aesthetic experience it was necessary to enjoy from the safe distance of England. Burke was frightened by the opportunists who arose as a consequence of the Revolution in France because he connected them to the rise of the Anglo-Irish in Ireland after its conquest. His emphasis on the terrible sublime at the expense of a more positive example was the result of the experience of it in Ireland. English liberals could watch the happenings in France with sympathy and excitement because they had not personally witnessed Irish history. Burke's chief version of a positive sublime, on the other hand, was not the recognition of a transcendent reality so much as a recognition of a powerful authority justly exerting its might. As he grew older, he found increasingly less occasion to cite this version of sublimity, perhaps because of its absence from the treatment of his native land.

The Burkean sublime is terrible because it ruptures our sense of the beautiful. The terms of the beautiful rely on consensus, a *sensus communis* that seems unreachable, being based on a harmony which no longer seems possible. Burke sees the loss of traditional hierarchies as the cause of these new conditions in India, Ireland and America, thus expressing a point of view which was very important to Yeats. Yeats often laments that the lack of consensus was coincident with the loss of standard-setting privilege; with that loss comes the loss of the beautiful. In striking this note he echoes back through Irish history to the loss of an Irish Parliament, and then to the collapse of the Gaelic order in Ireland. Nevertheless, the relationship between the beautiful and a more positive version of the sublime is not necessarily based on a hierarchical structuring of society, even to Yeats himself. This qualification is just one of many systematic Yeatsian counterpoints. Anyone may experience its religious and psycho-analytical significance; a good hierarchy improves one's chances of doing so, as long as the order is based on the ability to appreciate it, and not merely upon social standing. In the modern age, however, aesthetic experience has become increasingly individualised, found in solitude, and this highly individualised aspect of aesthetics is itself a result of 'a breaking of the soul and world into fragments' as, in true Modernist style, Yeats writes of history since the eighteenth century.[6] Unity of Being is at least still momentarily possible; Unity of Culture, rarely; the modern sublime is characterised by terror and lack of consensus. One of Yeats's main artistic efforts is to understand the nature of this terror and then to subjugate it by moving towards a positive version of sublimity. The historical reason for terror as prerequisite for sublimity is the weakening of the religious sublime in eighteenth-century thought. When the final cause, or God, is no longer behind the sublime encounter, the positive aspects of the sublime become less important than the negative ones.

The terrible sublime, however, is not the only aspect of Romantic or Modernist sublimity; the positive, Kantian sublime is a heightened sense of beauty, seeking its harmony and peace, establishing its morality on a supersensible plane, endeavouring to reconcile subjective and objective truth. In this regard, Kant's concept of the beautiful shares many aspects with previous eighteenth-century ones; he nevertheless separates beauty and sublimity along the lines of object and subject and establishes the aesthetic as bridge between formal metaphysical morals and empirical practical ones. Between these two versions of liminality – Burkean and Kantian – indeed over the abyss, Yeats believed that we offer up our faith. The metaphysical basis of the Yeatsian lyric moves on the distinction between the Burkean and Kantian sublimes. One of the projects of this book is to show how meaningful formal Kantian aesthetic is to Yeats, without losing sight of the significance of the empirical. His poetry derives much of its strength from the tension between the negative and positive sublime, between terror and joy. If profound philosophy comes from terror, as Yeats maintains, profound religion aims to dispel it.

For Yeats, neither extreme of certainty is sufficient – neither beauty without sublimity nor sublimity without beauty. His aesthetic consists of two constellations: positive sublimity and beauty, and terrible beauty and terrible sublimity. He seeks the society that can share the experience of the beautiful as well as the individual mind which in solitude can isolate and therefore better understand the experience of it. If he is a defender of the antithetical[7] dream of Greece, of Friedrich Nietzsche's terrible sublime that defines the Romantic self as antithesis to God, he is also most definitely a devotee of the primary idea of harmony and the ideal of society (occult society or exclusive court) with God as its centre. He is one of Baldesar Castiglione's courtiers, one of the Christian workers in Byzantium. He wants a society in which sublimity and beauty complement one another; he wants a marriage of the beautiful and the sublime as William Blake wants a marriage of Heaven and Hell. Byzantine society is suitable because it is devoted to God; its expression of the beautiful and the terrible find unity in God's reconciliation of sublimity and beauty, of antithetical, masculine knowledge and power and primary, feminine wisdom and love. Through his 'delicate skill' the Byzantine worker expresses the 'murderous madness in the mob' as though it were 'a lovely flexible presence like that of a perfect human body'.[8] Yet, nevertheless, Yeats believed that such unity was rarely achieved. Beauty and positive sublimity more often exist as opposites of the terrible sublime. The divisions in society accentuate this opposition; the more fractious the ideal of beauty becomes the more impossible is any experience of the positive sublime and, consequently, the more powerful is the expression of the terrible sublime. In such an instance, terror is a necessary curative, the stormy threshold of change before any feasible ideas of positive sublimity can be reached. The relationship between these three aesthetics turns on how beauty and sublimity interconnect to find positive expression.

The beautiful is based on a shared perception of reality; during its Neo-Classical inception the beautiful was the embodiment of cultural unity and proof of the universality of taste. The modern predicament, it is well known, allows no easy consensus. Yeats writes of its disunity in 'The Death of Synge':

Our modern public arts, architecture, plays, large decorations, have too many different tastes to please. Some taste is sure to dislike and to speak its dislike everywhere, and then because of the silence of the rest – partly from apathy, partly from dislike of controversy, partly from the difficulty of defence, as compared with the ease of attack – there is general timidity. All creation requires one mind to make and one mind of enjoyment.[9]

On the other hand, Yeats's corrective idea of Unity of Culture and Being, and its artistic correlation, may be summarised as follows:

The old art . . . would have led to the creation of one single type of man, one single type of woman; gathering up by a kind of deification a capacity for all energy and all passion, into a Krishna, a Christ, a Dionysus; and at times a poetical painter, a Botticelli, a Rossetti, creates as his supreme achievement a type of face, known afterwards by his own name.[10]

This is the unifying art of one mind creating something for the reception of a shared taste, creating that taste, even if it is somewhat of an idealisation, uniting quite different godheads as it would unite the beautiful and the sublime. The importance of such an image of unity for the discussion of the erotic and religious basis of the positive sublime, which is passion experienced as both religious suffering and sexual expression, is evident in Yeats's choice of painters, especially Rossetti.

The positive sublime outlined above highlights the religious and erotic basis for the sublime in Yeats. The positive sublime is never absolute, however; it is always haunted by the negative experience. The two aspects of sublimity are like 'those mingled seas' at the edge of the known Classical world in 'At Algeciras – A Meditation upon Death'. The double nature of sublimity is essential to any experience of it. Burke speaks of 'delightful horror', Kant of 'negative pleasure' and Yeats of 'horrible splendour', 'tragic ecstasy' and 'tragic joy'. It is tragic, horrible, etc. because the positive sublime is so difficult to achieve. The unity of the beautiful that underlies it so rarely exists. Yeats reduces this longing for unity to its most intimate and irreducible setting, the longing of one person for another, to what is often tragic longing. This intertwining of religion, eroticism and tragedy in ecstatic experience is vital to an understanding of Yeats's work. The poet's function is to express the power of this figure, the power of ecstasy. There are numerous examples of ecstasy's significance in Yeats's poetry, from early uses such as 'truth's consuming ecstasy' ('To Ireland in the Coming Times') to later ones such as 'the ecstatic waters laugh' ('News for the Delphic Oracle'), and to more direct ones in 'Supernatural Songs' (i.e. part III, 'Ribh in Ecstasy'), in which human sexual passion is seen as directly correspondent to divine passion. Ecstasy is also the subject of much of Yeats's mystical prose. The erotic and religious idea nevertheless goes far beyond the individual uses of ecstasy and finds many forms. To Yeats, we are shaped by successive memories of these moments of exaltation. He thereby tries to bridge the impasse which the aesthetic movement has reached as regards metaphysics or transcendence. The meta-character of the sublime, if it exists, is not the domination of the sensible so much as a transcendent expression of the body – as truly metaphysical as Yeats conceived John Donne to be.[11]

Before presenting a brief synopsis of the book, let us assess the place of Burke and Kant in Yeats's aesthetic vocabulary. One might wonder how and why they are important to him, and how much he studied them. Judging from his library, Yeats did not read that much of Burke's or Kant's works on aesthetics, even though he read a good deal of their other works. Why then discuss him in terms of them? The answer primarily rests on the centrality of the empirical and formal idealist distinction in aesthetic theory, and Burke and Kant are the respective representatives of the distinction. That is the main reason for this discussion, and it remains highly relevant throughout it. Secondly, Yeats was very much influenced both by Burke's political philosophy and by Kant's concept of antinomies, his emphasis on the *a priori*, and his promulgation of the three essentials: 'God, Freedom, and Immortality'.[12] Yeats, however, did own Burke's *Enquiry* (1757) and Kant's *Critique of Judgement* (1790), even if the evidence (the lack of marginalia) shows that he did not study them closely.

In his 1928 copy of the *Critique of Judgement*, there may be no markings, yet the book itself is dedicated to Yeats, both in print and in ink, by the translator James Creed Meredith. Clearly, the concept of the sublime seemed very Yeatsian to one who knew the *Critique of Judgement* intimately. In his lengthy introduction, Meredith uses poetry as his most eloquent example of what he believes is meant by the sublime. Moreover, if we examine Yeats's copy of the *Prolegomena to any Future Metaphysics* (1783), we notice that portions of the 'First Part of the General Transcendental Problem' are either marked or dog-eared. One passage that is marked contains the statement that 'at the basis of their [the senses] empirical intuition lies a pure intuition.'[13] This statement is essential to what Kant is endeavouring to prove in the *Critique of Judgement*. Interestingly, there is also an unattributed article from the *Times Literary Supplement*, 18 April 1929, folded into an envelope and glued to the hardcover of the *Prolegomena*. It is entitled 'Recent Philosophy: The School of Husserl' and itself contains a sentence essential to the present project: 'Consciousness of an object is found to consist . . . in a manifold of "moments" each of which is itself intentional and contributes its intentional quota to the synthesised intentional whole'. The basis of this moment in the Romantic Sublime is obvious. Such moments of intentionality, being, illumination, or otherwise, are also central to Modernism, in Joseph Conrad, Yeats, Virginia Woolf, and T.S. Eliot, precisely because of the philosophical debate over the subjectivity and relativity of experience. In such light, the intellectual context of the Yeatsian sublime reflects a great many twentieth-century preoccupations.

At this point, it is important to note that the scholar's task of detective work is highly problematic. Who put the article there? Could it have been George Yeats, Yeats's wife? Quite likely. She was as avid, if not more avid a reader of philosophy than he was. Perhaps Yeats knew nothing of it. This scepticism throws doubt on all the markings to a certain degree, beyond those that are recognisably Yeats's. All simple marks and folded pages are not necessarily his. Even those that are clearly in his hand may mean less than at first they seem to mean. Is one always influenced most by those passages one highlights? Not necessarily. These questions loom larger when it comes to Burke's *Enquiry*, where most of the pages are still uncut. Is it significant that some of those on 'Terror' and 'Obscurity' have been cut, as have many pages on the relation of the sublime and language? It is difficult to say for certain, but it is not difficult to be sure how central some of the ideas contained therein are to Yeats's poetic. It is worth noting, however, that those early distinctions form part of Burke's later arguments over the French Revolution and 'Irish Affairs', which influenced Yeats more directly. The *Enquiry* provided indispensable metaphors for Burke's political writings, much as *A Vision* later would for Yeats's poetry.

Finally, as regards Burke, there is one small mark, a check, in Yeats's copy of the *Enquiry* not noted by O'Shea in his descriptive catalogue of Yeats's library.[14] It comes in the section on taste, beside a line that reads 'The admirer of Don Bellianis perhaps does not understand the refined language of the Eneid, who, if it was degraded into the style of the Pilgrim's Progress, might feel it in all its energy . . .'.[15] Here we have the question of the style appropriate for the sublime, and the need in Yeats's mind to find one that raises the standard of taste, rather than one that panders to a lower one. We also feel his more egalitarian belief that all people are capable of understanding sublime content, if not sublime style. Still, we must question: how do we know that Yeats made the mark? His daughter Anne Yeats told me she thought it might be his, but could not be certain.[16] As the whole problem of authorship is essential to sublimity, it may be best to leave the question open.

To complete this excursus into Yeats's background in the sublime and the beautiful, it is appropriate to examine Yeats's reactions to William Blake's annotations of Sir Joshua Reynolds's *Discourses*,[17] and then to examine a book from 1902 which Yeats marked extensively: Benedetto Croce's *Aesthetics as Science of Expression and General*

Linguistics. Blake's marginalia on Sir Joshua Reynolds's *Discourses* provide a telling frame for the Yeatsian aesthetic. Reynolds sets forth many of the ideals of eighteenth-century aesthetics, eschewing realistic detail in favour of what are considered eternal, noble qualities. Blake finds that this eschewal leads to vagueness and attacks it vigorously. His comments on Reynolds include some revealing perspectives on Burke as well: 'Burke's treatise on the Sublime and Beautiful is founded on the opinions of Newton and Locke. On this treatise Reynolds has grounded many of his assertions'.[18] In his copy of the edition of Blake's work which he helped to edit, Yeats marks this passage and then a series of others which serve to elucidate Blake's own aesthetic point of view. He underlines Blake's comment on Burke's notion that obscurity is the source of the sublime: 'Obscurity is neither the source of the Sublime nor of anything else'.[19] Yeats also underlines Blake's related idea that 'Without minute neatness of execution the Sublime cannot exist. Grandeur of ideas is founded on precision of ideas'.[20] And he underlines another like opinion: 'All Sublimity is founded on Minute Discrimination'.[21] Throughout the annotations, Yeats agrees with Blake that one must pay attention to Nature in singular detail. For Yeats and Blake, sublimity is in the lineaments of form. Yeats's later approval of Burke is not compromised in this presentation, however. The empirical pragmatism of Burke's political writings balance any sense that he is overly general and vague. The *Enquiry* in fact presented many experiences that made the eighteenth-century Irishman uneasy; sublimity, no less than the notion of metaphysical rights, is entirely too mercurial. The real clues lie in Yeats's attitude towards Blake and their mutual condemnation of Newton and Locke. Blake endeavours to find in particularity a basis for his visionary poetics. The endeavour clearly moves between empirical aesthetics (Blake, it must be remarked, underestimates the subtlety and specificity of Burke's psychological observations) and formal ones. The English poet's concluding statement regarding the connection between Reynolds's *Discourses* and Burke's treatise and his own abhorrence of Locke's and Bacon's epistemology is conclusive: 'Inspiration and Vision was then, and now is, and I hope will always remain, my Element, my Dwelling-place. How can I then hear it condemned without returning Scorn for Scorn?'[22] Taking this passage that Yeats underlines and uniting it with Blake's idea that 'Detail is the Foundation of the Sublime'[23] we have evidence for how the Yeatsian sublime moves between the particularity of the empirical and the visionary quality of the formal.

In Benedetto Croce's *Aesthetics*, one sentence noted by Yeats suffices for the present purpose: 'Art constructs a representation standing midway between the individual and the universal'.[24] Yeatsian poetics continually interrogates this construction between the particular and universal (as well as art's place in similar dualisms between the individual and God, self and soul, the empirical and the formal idealist, etc.) in an effort to find some form of synthesis, however brief it is doomed to be. Any aesthetic synthesis depends upon what Croce himself calls the 'Kantian dualism of the beautiful and the sublime'. In the same passage he asks, 'Did Kant ever think of unifying the beautiful and the sublime and deducing them from a single concept?' And then concludes, 'Apparently not. By his declaration that the principle of beauty must be sought outside ourselves, and that of the sublime within us, he tacitly assumes that the two objects are disparate.'[25] This need to undo Kant's dualities may stem from Croce's belief that 'intuition-expression', or the immediate knowing and transforming of aesthetic impressions, is neither divisible into parts nor subsumable under intellectual categories. Croce dismisses the use of the sublime as an unnecessary category, maintaining that the term 'beauty' is sufficient for 'the image of pain and baseness' as well as 'the pleasing and the good'.[26] Yeats, however, is an intensely dialectical thinker. To understand him, we do well to stay close to the realms of Kantian dualism, even if Yeats himself forces us to problematise them. Beauty and sublimity are not always disparate. Instead, using the constellations of terrible beauty and sublimity and the beautiful and the positive sublime, we shall assess how Yeatsian aesthetics involves an idea of the divine in which traditional concepts of the beautiful and the sublime move towards an epiphanic vision that can momentarily heal the subject–object split in human consciousness. In this way, we may yet see what Croce meant when he wrote that 'intuition is the undifferentiated unity of the perception of the real and of the simple image of the possible'.[27]

*   *   *   *

My central aim is to investigate how the Yeatsian lyric explores the division between empiricist, Burkean aesthetics and formal idealist, Kantian ones and how this exploration continues to unearth objects of critical discussion. For the sake of brevity and interest, and because, historically, the Romantic sublime has a poetic basis, I shall concentrate on the poems and discuss the fiction and drama only when powerful relevance demands (although, of course, a strong case could be made for studying them in light of the sublime). The main reason for such a concentration, in addition to his stature as a poet, is Yeats's own metaphysical conception of the lyric. As this is a discussion of the metaphysical basis of the Yeatsian lyric, there will be a good deal of attention paid to *A Vision*, which is the most concentrated and systematic expression of his metaphysics. Though connections are made between his early poetry and *A Vision* in order to show how the ideas it presents are evident in his early poetry, the specific discussion and explanation of the mystical book, as with the poetry, comes in chronological order. The overall effect should be a straightforward sense of Yeats's maturation coupled with an overarching view of his vast design.

Any discussion of aesthetics must also entail examination of the place of the sublime in various historical attitudes towards revolution, the power and purpose of the state, as well as attitudes towards the highly gendered principles of authority that have been such an imaginative source since their eighteenth-century application. The first section therefore includes critical introductions to Burke's and Kant's ideas on gender and revolution, as well as a detailed comparison of their ideas to Yeats's poetics. The next section outlines Yeats's conception of beauty, its basis in the feminine qualities of nurturing and harmony, and how, through association or marriage, with conventionally masculine qualities such as authority and courage, the beautiful becomes the basis for the positive sublime. The reconciling erotic charge of the beautiful and the positive sublime will also be considered as it aims to conquer death and to give transcendent expression to our sensible portion – to desire.

The third section deals with terrible beauty and the negative sublime. Violent conflict is a necessary aspect of any struggle towards self, societal or religious definition. Yeats's poetic evocations of conflict in the relationship of society to the individual, the individual to society and society to itself, are usually negative ones. Once violence is removed from the realm of the self and the possibilities of transcendence, the workings of the larger society's mechanism most often make it unredeemably destructive. The collective vision and the effects of shared experience impede violence from achieving its transcendent end as the more intimate setting of the relationship with oneself, a lover, and with God, do not. Yeats's evocations of violence both in one's relationship with God and in one's relationship with oneself (or with a lover, that most intimate 'other' version of the self) are therefore usually positive ones; they are creative as well as destructive.

Finally, the last section closes with a vision of the positive sublime as antidote to age, to death, to the age's many deep reasons for disbelief. It then presents the tragedy of the historical search for the antidote. The history of the world is a history of illusions by which cultures have tried to unite subject and object, individual and collective, have tried to create a mythic or fictive world of redemption, to search for a relevant analogy. History therefore reflects the much more intimate, necessary illusion that lovers can unite in sexual ecstasy. The concluding chapter is concerned with alternating visions of sublimity, an alternation which reflects what has always been an uncertain ordering of the negative and positive sublime: the uncertainty before death. Yeats is not sure 'if the last kiss is given to the void'.[28] In order to make the void fruitful, he believes that there must be a female aspect to the deity. Beauty and its social structures give birth to their eternal forms. As though presaging this union of the female with the male deity, his images of sublimity, of a transcendent world, are increasingly eroticised. There are also moments of great doubt, however, of despairing violence, of sexual loneliness, in which there echoes the need for ecstatic fulfilment.

PART I

Prolegomena to a
Yeatsian Metaphysics

2

MERCURY SUBLIMATE: GENDER, REVOLUTION AND THE BURKEAN SUBLIME

I never liked this continual talk of resistance and revolution, or the practice of making the extreme medicine of the constitution its daily bread. It renders the habit of society dangerously valetudinary: it is taking periodical doses of mercury sublimate, and swallowing down repeated provocatives of cantharides to our love of liberty.

. . . that subordination of the heart, which kept alive, even in servitude itself, the spirit of exalted freedom.

Burke, *Reflections on the Revolution in France*

The Burkean sublime is based in 'masculine' attributes of power, repulsion, severity. The exertion necessary in a confrontation with a sublime force leads to the 'delightful horror' of surviving what is not easily overcome. The beautiful, on the other hand, is based in the 'feminine' attributes of attraction, charm, submission, and tenderness. This gendering is of great significance to Yeats, though his application is somewhat different from Burke's. The political ramifications of these two categories are seemingly endless. For Burke, as for other aesthetic thinkers up to and including Yeats, there are true and false forms of sublimity and beauty. Before unfolding the construction of the feminine, of class and empire that underlie Burke's aesthetics and politics, it is necessary to examine the system of his aesthetic enquiry. The main aim throughout is to show how Burkean aesthetics are problematised by the relation between formalist and empiricist versions of the sublime and how, in turn, Burke's resistance to theory tightens the Gordian knot of his political philosophy, a knot whose strands consist of his various attitudes towards revolution in France, the American colonies, India and Ireland.

Burke wrote *A Philosophical Enquiry into the Origin of our Ideas of the Sublime and the Beautiful* (1757) some years before his political career began and his use of aesthetics (whether conscious or not) went through various transformations from the time of his early writing days. Under the influence of Locke, Burke insisted that aesthetics must be examined empirically. Though both Burke and Hume realised the impossibility of verifying a consensus, they made claims to a standard of taste. In order to verify the claims of a consensus of taste, Burke examined aesthetic judgements strictly as sensations. Imagination is only a collection of previously felt sensations (art is therefore mimetic rather than original, a product of imitation rather than genius – as it is for Kant). Burke is a forerunner of twentieth-century psychological studies in that taste, for him, is the result of behavioural conditioning. He overlooks final causes, epistemology, teleology. His later resistance to theory, to the metaphysical concept of 'the rights of man' as a mercurial prelude to demonic revolutionary practices (vis à vis the Revolution in France), is a coordinate of his early aesthetic stance. At the root of this movement in his philosophy is terror; he moves from the experience of sublime terror to the experience of a revolutionary one, that is, to the 'Reign of Terror'. In fact, Burke was probably most famous as an aesthetician for his insistence that the sublime is derived from terror and that this is what separates it from the beautiful. Terror, then, becomes the source of his political as well as his aesthetic judgement, moving from the personal to the public sphere.

POSITIVE AND NEGATIVE SUBLIME

Terror had been an aspect of the experience of the sublime even prior to Burke's treatise, although some critics such as Baillie had denied this.[1] There is an historical reason for the growth of terror as prerequisite of sublimity and that is the movement away from the religious sublime – a movement which Kant tries to correct in his insistence that we need not necessarily fear God and yet God remains sublime. When the final cause, or God, dropped away from the sublime – the noble, positive sublime, the heightened form of the beautiful, as the sublime was known in Longinus's rhetorical sublime, in Dennis's idea of the religious sublime, and Addison's idea of the 'great' – it became increasingly full of terror.[2] The dialectical nature of the sublime and the beautiful as characterised by terror and attraction respectively probably has its basis in the development of the natural sublime, when the Renaissance dread of mountains mingled with a Romanticised love of them.[3] Eventually, this mixture of revulsion and fascination with mountain landscapes came to characterise the sublime. Yet, whatever the background to the growth of aesthetics, for the Romantics, Burke's influence was rivalled only by Kant, and it is not difficult to see how the ubiquitous Gothic love of the spectacular, grotesque and awful is derived from Burke's famous emphasis on terror.[4]

Through his studies of terror, he challenges the morality of the aesthetic. He diplomatically rejects the whole doctrine of final causes.[5] This is not to say that he ignores morality, but, rather, he believes that in moments of terror we are confronted with the very real fascination of evil, of what, in 'The Tables Turned', Wordsworth calls 'moral evil' – a Romantic fascination of which the later Burke of the *Reflections* (1790) is much more suspicious. Like many other Romantics, Wordsworth is deeply influenced by Burke's treatise and its emphasis on sensation, on pain and pleasure; in *The Prelude*, he claims that 'beauty' and 'fear' had fostered his feeling for the beautiful and sublime respectively (Book I, lines 300–6) and called his moral understanding into question (the boat-stealing scene in Book I, the 'Simplon Pass' episode in Book VI and, of course, the French Revolution itself in the later books of *The Prelude*). The terror of the historical sublime is vital to Wordsworth, Burke and Yeats. Highlighting the moral ambiguity, Burke puts great emphasis on obscurity, on the unknown and unknowable quality of the sublime, even though he is not interested in its causes. Hence his famous dictum: 'A clear idea is therefore another name for a little idea.'[6] He believes that an experience of the sublime produces a sensation that may be ambiguously characterised as 'delightful horror' – horror because of fear, and delight upon self-preservation.[7]

Although Burke's philosophy lacks Kant's and Yeats's transcendental deductions, there is a strongly religious element, one not only traceable to his era and his own stated beliefs but to specific passages in the *Enquiry*. In addition to viewing obscurity and privation as causes of sublimity, he also states that pain can cause sublimity. Burke sees pain and pleasure as 'simple ideas, incapable of definition'.[8] An experience of pain and/or pleasure brings us towards the sublime unknown, or towards God. He speaks of both 'divine horror' and 'religious horror'.[9] In a famous instance, Burke uses Job as an example of the sublimity of power. His writing on this subject is one of the most extensive sections in the *Enquiry*. Suffering is necessary to the sublimity of power, 'the idea of suffering [as well as terror] must always be prevalent'.[10] Burke is quite Aristotelian as regards the terror, pity and theatricality of the sublime. Job is the chief spectacle of human suffering precisely because he is made to confront the purpose and meaning of his suffering; he is made to confront God. Although Burke does not formally separate them, because he does not allow for any ultimate meaning of suffering to be empirically understood, one can see both positive and negative elements to the sublime encounter – the positive sublime is when meaning or reason is given to the sublime confrontation, the negative is when it is not: 'If we rejoice, we rejoice with trembling; and even whilst we are receiving benefits, we cannot but shudder at a power which can confer benefits of such mighty importance'.[11]

The idea of 'benefits' has taken Burke away from his idea of terror and the negative sublime, and closer to his idea of the positive sublimity of tradition and sanctioned authority that is made so explicit in the *Reflections*. Such positive sublimity has less to do with origins, or the *a priori*, and more to do with custom, that apex of the *a posteriori*, which reconciles us to everything. Burke's false sublime was the French Revolution; his true one was that force (aristocratic or otherwise) which by its awe-inspiring power earns our communal respect. Burke realises that in his portrait of Job he has approached the questions of origins and universals that he had hoped to avoid, and so makes moves to disengage himself:

> I know some people are of opinion, that no awe, no degree of terror, accompanies the idea of power, and have hazarded to affirm, that we can contemplate the idea of God himself without any such emotion [here Burke is answering some early criticisms]. [. . .] I say then, that whilst we consider the Godhead merely as he is an object of the understanding, which forms a complex idea of power, wisdom, justice, goodness, all stretched to a degree far exceeding the bounds of our comprehension . . . the imagination and passions are little or nothing affected. But because we are bound by the condition of our nature to ascend to these pure and intellectual ideas, through the medium of sensible images, and to judge of these divine qualities by their evident acts and exertions, *it becomes extremely hard to disentangle our idea of the cause from the effect by which we are led to know it* [my emphasis].[12]

In the last clause, we come to the crux of the relationship between negative and positive sublimity, for we come to the sensible, empirical experience of a supersensible realm or faculty.

For critics such as Dennis and Addison who come before Burke, and for many of those who come after – from Kant to Bradley and Monk – this moment of confusion, of negative sublimity, is a prelude to positive sublimity. As an empiricist, Burke cannot follow them to such an ideal conclusion.[13] He presents an image of Old Testament numinousness. As a Christian, he needs to soften this image of God, even if it might make the nature of the Godhead seem less sublime as a result. He therefore concludes that 'false religions' are based only on 'fear'; that before Christianity 'humanised the idea of divinity, and brought it somewhat nearer to us', there was 'very little said of the love of God'.[14] The idea of love, as Burke has already told us, is an attribute of the beautiful as regards custom and society and of the sublime as regards origins – a combination, of course, that is at the base of positive sublimity, but one that is not explicitly a part of Burkean aesthetics as it is enunciated in the *Enquiry*. Burke concludes that love and devotion are 'not the first, the most natural, and the most striking effect which proceeds from that idea' – power is the most striking effect. Christian love is implicated in the result of such power; it is a realm protected by Jehovah just as the realm of the beautiful, which in the *Reflections* Marie Antoinette represents, was meant to be protected by the authority of the monarchy, or by any similar authority.

At this stage in the section, perhaps because he realises the difficulty of maintaining the idea that, while Christian love is the highest expression of religion, it may not be its most striking effect, Burke proceeds to emphasise the obscurity of his subject matter.[15] This is not to belittle Burke's ideas on this issue. In his contradiction, he has indeed highlighted the tension at the heart of religion between the fear one may feel towards God and the love He is supposed to represent. The double movement is also at the heart of the aesthetic question that he poses: what is the relationship of beauty to sublimity? It is a question whose resolution, in turn, is enacted in the relationship of negative to positive sublimity. To do all this, in any definitive manner, 'as far as we can possibly trace them', is to be where 'our imagination is finally lost'.[16] Here is surely a moment of negative theology – one which frightens Burke as it seems to lead to pure metaphysical speculation or, worse, to atheism. The movement from percept to concept, from custom to law, is one that is difficult enough to achieve in more empirical realms, not to mention the metaphysical; that is why Burke mistrusts the latter as much as he does. Just at that moment, however, one looks for some quality of the beautiful to reappear, for a universal standard of taste, a communal creed.

AESTHETICS OF HARMONY AND REBELLION

Instead of taste being the effect of any universal quality which any given object might innately contain, a taste for beauty, according to Burke, is biologically conditioned; it is the non-rational attraction we feel for one another in order to perpetuate the species ('that quality or those qualities in bodies by which they cause love, or some passion similar to it');[17] it is the result of good cultural conditioning, in that one is conditioned by pleasure. It is the result of the innate relationship to the feminine, at least for those who share Burke's male gaze. Besides the typical definitions of beauty as charm, delicacy, grace, love, smoothness and sweetness, Burke's definitions of the beautiful are notable because of their emphasis on gender. The sublime is masculine awe-inspiring power, the beautiful is feminine love-inspiring attraction. In Burke's view, society shifts on these two pivots. Yet care must be taken. As there are two types of sublimes, a false and a true one, so there are two types of beauty to Burke, false and true. In brief, the difficulties arise because, according to Isaac Kramnick, the sublime is activated by a masculine bourgeois principle, while the beautiful is activated by a feminine aristocratic principle; in Kramnick's view,

Burke's rage against the abuse of power stems from an unresolved Oedipal conflict. His discomfort with revolution stems from his unease with the masculine bourgeois principle of self-advancement and innovation, which he attached to his father. Tom Furniss, however, argues the opposite case: the feminine and female, and the world of leisure and sexuality associated with them, are often seen as disturbing the bourgeois principle of masculine hard-work and social order which Burke defended. Both readings interconnect in the Gordian knot of Burke's political and aesthetic attitudes. Burke defended the feminine when it stood for aristocratic privilege and culture, and attacked it when it presented sexual and political forms of subversion. He defended the capitalist masculine principle when it provided prosperity, but attacked it when it showed no respect for traditional sanctities. Kramnick is particularly telling when he states that Burke's conception of art and taste entails a balance between the sublime and the beautiful, the masculine and the feminine, the bourgeois and the aristocratic. Furniss, on the other hand, sees the sublime and the beautiful in Burke as incompatible, but, as we shall discover, this interpretation does not take Burke's sense of home and nation into account.[18] For it is in this balance that true sublimity is separated from false, and where we find a living conception of positive sublimity which is based in custom and the forms of the beautiful.

The false and true sublime are so interconnected with regard to revolution that by contrast they serve to introduce the beautiful, peaceful society. Burke's attitude towards revolution was not always as counter-revolutionary as it became known to be in the years surrounding the publication of *Reflections*. In early and in much later years, revolution had a place, however limited. In the late writing on 'Irish Affairs', Burke emphasises freedom, independence, equality if not outright revolution. He also has two instances of revolution in the *Enquiry*, which seem to contradict his later images of revolution in *Reflections*. One is his commentary on Milton's depiction of Satan, as not having lost all his 'original brightness', in an image of 'glory obscured'. Burke is using it for an example of how sublimity is derived from obscurity, but what is important here is that he admits the rebellious archangel is, in fact, sublime.[19] In another picture that presents positive ideas of rebellion, Burke refers to the mathematical sublimity of the multitude (as opposed to the murderousness of the mob).[20] In both instances, there are revolutionary implications to the image of sublimity. Their influence upon the mind is subversive. Burke's images of the infernal, mob-ruled, false sublime of the French Revolution seem to belie the above instances. These seeming contradictions illustrate the complexity and/or instability of Burke's argument, and indeed his attitude in general. Burke himself believes that revolution may be acceptable – the 'Glorious Revolution', or even more problematically for an Irishman of his Catholic associations, Cromwell's revolution[21] – as long as the 'mind' of the nation is not slain.[22] He then proceeds to explain what is wrong with the present violence.[23] Among the images of physical disease and moral decay he presents, one can sense that Burke's real reason for the social illness is traceable to the loss of tradition, hereditary rule, the loss of restraint that exists within a tested order.

For Burke, it is the loss of those very qualities that even Cromwell's insurrection did not uproot, at least in England. His reason becomes clear in the next sentence when he writes the refrain of the *Reflections*, that is, the Revolution will leave society at the mercy of opportunists, 'money-jobbers' and 'usurers'. Burke's perception of the mob and of Satanic revolution, like Yeats's, depends very much on whether such opportunistic elements will take control as a result of the upheaval. He might support a revolution that left the mind of the nation, the stabilising order, intact, that respected property and valued ceremony and the tradition of the Established Church in Ireland, and of the French aristocracy of Marie Antoinette, as does, for instance, the haute bourgeoisie of the American Revolution. Burke's judgements on such political matters, however, are inevitably as aesthetic as those he makes in the *Enquiry*; they become a matter of taste for which he vainly, though heroically, seeks universal consensus.

IRELAND, INDIA, AMERICA, FRANCE: COLONISATION, SEXUALITY AND MARRIAGE

An obvious basis for Burke's ideas of the false and true sublime can be found in his attitudes towards Ireland, America and India, as opposed to those towards France. Conor Cruise O'Brien makes this theme the point of his book on Burke entitled *The Great Melody*. The source of his title is Yeats's poem 'The Seven Sages': 'American colonies, Ireland, France and India/Harried, and Burke's great melody against it.' The 'it' that the 'great melody' is against is, as O'Brien notes, the 'abuse of power'.[24] Whereas the American Revolution was against the abuse of power, the French Revolution was the source of it. Burke's feelings on Ireland are probably the most complicated and the least available for comment. Child of a Catholic mother (and possibly of a convert father) and married to an Irish Catholic, Burke was necessarily very sensitive and quite elusive, indeed often secretive, on the subject of Ireland. The Burkean silence is one of the most sublime statements he could make.[25] For Burke, the predicament is truly uncanny. Home and not home, strange and familiar; the motherland he cannot bear to dwell upon. Ireland, in fact, is what Burke (transferring his passions on Ireland to India) most meant to protect from opportunists such as Warren Hastings, or even from the members of the French National Assembly, and which he does protect in the writings on Irish affairs, but with many telling ellipses, many silences over what he calls the 'melancholy subject' of Ireland.[26] Burke, in his letter to his son Richard, speaks of 'pedigrees of guilt' in regard to those Irish families that might have rebelled against the English (and by opposite implication those who had been too quick to convert to Protestantism for legal favour).[27] Seen in this light, the *Reflections* has the look of an *aisling* poem, as Declan Kiberd notes, with Marie Antoinette as a projection of the threatened motherland.[28]

This guilt is a web of Burke's feelings about his father's conversion, his personally ambiguous position in the British parliament, the effort to offer proof of his loyalty to the British constitution, and his wish to protect his wife and mother. The solution to this reticulation of problems is found in a familial figure, especially as regards Ireland; the family tree is just another aspect of the British Oak that Burke used as symbol of the state, a symbol which, in turn, Yeats cites approvingly for all its organic, racial (*vs* mechanical) associations in his poem, 'Blood and the Moon'. If natural relations are not respected, the subversiveness of sexuality is sure to be unleashed in its most anarchic forms. Burke's letter to Langrishe about Irish freedom and voting rights makes the importance of the family figure as guarantee of order quite clear.[29] As for the allegedly consummating acts of the Protestant ascendancy, if it had been a moral ascendancy it would indeed have worked, according to Burke, but it was not moral; rather, as he writes to his son, Burke believes that the word ascendancy 'signifies *pride and dominion* on the one part of the relation, and on the other *subserviency and contempt* – and it signifies nothing else'.[30] Using the figure of an unnatural marriage for the relationship of Protestant and Catholic under the Penal Laws, he also protests that 'they [the Protestants] produced a child of their old age, the shocking and unnatural act about marriage, which tended to finish the scheme for making the people not only two distinct parties for ever, but keeping them as two distinct species in the same land.[31] Burke believes that the Catholic Irish should be allowed the privileges of the British constitution. They need, as do the Established Church and Dissenters, the 'protection of a common father'.[32] In his opinion, the Act of Union (which did not happen in his lifetime) would not be 'for the mutual advantage of the two kingdoms' as the Catholics would not be accepted on equal grounds.[33] Like Kant, Burke sees the related marriage of sublime and beautiful as a way of taking the terror out of the sublime, only for Burke the terror is historical as much as philosophical, and the Act of Union is insufficient. Burke's greatest fear was that, as a result of inequality, the Catholics would be driven towards the more radical Jacobin example of the Dissenters, and would therefore attack their own traditional images. This would drive Ireland to the example and sexual licence of the Revolution in France, and the mind of the country would thenceforth be slain. In this light, we can see the *Enquiry* 'in its own terms as a legitimating and legislating theory' for Burke's political philosophy.[34]

Macpherson wonders why Burke, who was all for the virtues of labour and the middle class, and who was himself middle class, should be against the bourgeois Revolution in France, 'since in the view of most nineteenth-century historians, liberal as well as Marxist, it was essentially a bourgeois revolution, intent on clearing away feudal and absolutist impediments to the emergence of a capitalist order?' Macpherson concludes that it is because the National Assembly 'were not the *haute bourgeoisie* who in England, easily intermarrying with the aristocracy, dominated the House of Commons: they were a *petite bourgeoisie*, who could not be relied on to uphold established property'.[35] We shall see how Yeats also believed that Revolution should not leave the people at the mercy of the capitalist middle class. In order to begin to understand the significance of Burke's many mixed feelings, and how they pertain to the sublime and the beautiful, the gendering of the two aesthetic categories must be examined. For Burke, as for Yeats, Ireland is the sublime site of his repressed feelings which the beautiful means to unveil and to cure in the marriage of the qualities each represents.

THE BEAUTIFUL AND THE FEMININE

Again, one must remember that Burke has two ideas of the beautiful as well as of the sublime, the false and the true. Furniss writes that 'although Burke comes to champion beauty in the *Reflections*, it is clearly distrusted and repressed in the *Enquiry*'.[36] For all their qualities of charm, delicacy, grace, love, smoothness and sweetness, women also have a markedly subversive quality, one that is close to the sublime in its ability to undo the observer. Yeats has a similarly bifurcated view of the feminine, but he has a positive place – witnessed in the historical imperative of Helen's and Maud Gonne's beauty – for the subversive quality of the feminine which Burke did not. Burke has earlier remarked in the *Enquiry* that beauty does not only stimulate desire, but love as well, and in the *Reflections* he insists that rule must be based in a legitimate 'familial' relationship in order for it not to be merely fornication.[37] In a different part of the *Enquiry*, however, the feminine is subversive:

> Observe that part of a beautiful woman where she is perhaps the most
> beautiful, about the neck and breasts; the smoothness; the softness; the easy
> and insensible swell; the variety of the surface, which is never for the
> smallest space the same; the deceitful maze, through which the unsteady eye
> slides giddily, without knowing where to fix, or whither it is carried.[38]

The beginning of this passage seems quite appropriate from a male point
of view, sensitive and attentive, done with painterly detail. The last
phrases, from 'the deceitful maze' onwards, are tainted with fear of the
subversive potential of our sensible portion, even while Burke seems
strangely to glory in it. This subversive quality reappears exaggeratedly in
the 'vilest of women', 'the furies of hell' who help to lead the Revolution
in France.[39] Revolutionary society becomes a parody of the true society
that supports all of the sexual and political hegemonies in which Burke
believes. Burke makes clear in a passage of the *Reflections* that revolutionary women subvert society just as the female body loses the male gaze
in its 'deceitful maze'.[40] Women no longer stimulate love and desire, and
so are no longer 'beautiful' in Burke's definition of the term, because
they are no longer tender and submissive. Revolutionary France, Burke
writes elsewhere in the *Reflections*, has 'prostituted her virtue'; he sees
France throughout the extended metaphor of the entire passage as a
woman gone astray, bargaining away her birthright.[41]

Perhaps most dangerously of all for Burke, and remaining most hidden,
such an image of subversive sexuality and revolution threatens those in
Ireland whom he holds dear, especially, perhaps symbolically, his Catholic
wife and Catholic mother. Burke's sensitivity in this regard is made
evident when a friend, Richard Shackleton, unthinkingly gave evidence of
his wife's and mother's religion to the newspapers. Burke wrote in extreme
anger back to Shackleton that '. . . there is as natural and proper a
delicacy in the other Sex, which will not make it very pleasant to my wife
to be the daily subject of Grubstreet.'[42] His emphasis on order and
tradition is meant to protect what he felt was most vulnerable; Yeats
displays similar ideas of tradition and the feminine in 'A Prayer for my
Daughter'. Burke's emphasis bears all the hallmarks of the more conservative elements of his age. His idea of the necessary place of women in
the necessary order of things is, in his mind, meant to protect women and
any who may find themselves in a vulnerable or beleaguered position,
whether it be the Queen of France, his wife at home or Indian, American
and Irish colonial subjects. While he might unthinkingly subject one, he
would free the other. His aestheticisation of the feminine and the female
has, quite appropriately, two sides to it – the benevolent and the malevolent.
Yet, not all of Burke's constructions of the feminine are negative, fragile
or indeed masochistic, as Anne K. Mellor, one of his most vehement
recent critics, herself admits.[43]

We have seen evidence of Burke's idea of the female as animalistic subversion.[44] His famous description of the Queen of France, on the other hand, has all the characteristics of the maternal (in that she is Queen and must be loved and served) and of the erotic. These qualities are combined in an image of a woman on the verge of Burke's own speculated rape, one which he tries to forestall:

> Oh! What a revolution! and what an heart must I have, to contemplate without emotion that elevation and that fall! . . . I thought ten thousand swords must have leaped from their scabbards to avenge even a look that threatened her with insult. – But the age of chivalry is gone. – That of sophisters, oeconomists [sic], and calculators, has succeeded; and the glory of Europe is extinguished for ever.[45]

Surely the old threat to Ireland so much a part of the *aisling* tradition is a part of this description. That the Queen is taken half-naked from bed, according to Burke's description (though to no one else's) makes the phrase 'that chastity of honour, which felt a stain like a wound' resound with multiple significance of the uncanny, of female genitalia, of the blood of innocence and virginity, of Burke's response to the perceived slight to Ireland and to his wife. For like the poems in the *aisling* tradition, the image of the Queen suggests a forced union between vanquished old orders, whether Gaelic or French aristocracy and the new bourgeois Cromwellian or revolutionary order.

Both Seamus Deane and Kiberd write very tellingly of this connection to the *aisling*. Deane puts the *aisling* connection in general historical terms, and is acutely aware of Burke's sympathy for Ireland and the 'Irish Jacobite dream'.[46] Kiberd inscribes the sexual turbulence of the scene into his historical analogy and emphasises the sexual and the political threats involved in the colonial situation.[47] The contraints of civilisation are what Burke constantly refers to in the *Reflections* for the sake of France and implicitly of Ireland and India. In one of the earliest and most famous *aisling* poems by Aodhagán Ó Rathaille entitled 'Gile na Gile' or 'The Brightest of the Bright', we see a similar mixture of high idealisation of heavenly beauty and burning shame over the desecration of beauty.[48] With that image comes the loss of a civilisation in 'terror and alarm', as Ó Rathaille writes, a loss that threatens the potency and place of both Ó Rathaille and Burke and one whose post-colonial 'legacy/culminates inexorably', according to Seamus Heaney's violent poem 'Act of Union'.[49] Yet, for all of these writers of the deluge, something in the sense of loss is signally great. Ó Rathaille insists that it is 'a guide for safe and better keeping'; it is a defiant humanising gesture before the massacre begins. This is an aspect of the beautiful that is sustained throughout the sublime's disruption and which in some way redresses the violence of the negative sublime by returning to a preponderantly feminine image of positive sublimity.

THE POSITIVE SUBLIME: THE UNION
OF MASCULINE AND FEMININE

Besides the two aspects of the feminine already outlined, there is, in fact, a more positive one in Burke, a version of what is here delineated as the positive sublime. There is that element of beauty which chivalric love is meant to obey: 'Never, never more, shall we behold that generous loyalty to rank and sex, that proud submission, that dignified obedience', writes Burke, 'that subordination of the heart, which kept alive, even in servitude itself, the spirit of exalted freedom.'[50] This is a form of sublimity that is based in ideas of the beautiful; in fact, it is very reminiscent of Kant's sublime moral sacrifice, of the positive sublime. It is less explicit in Burke's *Enquiry* than in his political writings, but it exists in his idea of the Christian humanisation of the divine. Ironically, the above quotation partially agrees with Mary Wollstonecraft's response to Burke, in that she rejects 'a beauty [that] relaxes the solids of the soul as well as the body' and posits instead 'that there is a beauty in virtue, a charm in order, which necessarily implies exertion'.[51] By so doing, she imagines an authority that commands moral respect and which is likewise rooted in the female. 'Such a glorious change can only be produced by liberty', she insists.[52] Wollstonecraft is presenting an idea of beauty that transforms the hegemonic models on which Burke's treatise rests (however internalised the patriarchal law may be, however ascendant are reason and other 'masculine' virtues) in order to deploy them for an 'egalitarian politics whose very ground is the equality of the sexes and the reconciliation of the sublime and the beautiful'.[53]

Burke also presents an idea of authority, and of the feminine terms of the beautiful raised to the category of the sublime. It is an alternative to a system so heavily weighed in favour of the masculine, and is quite similar to Yeats's portrayal of Lady Gregory's authority:

> The authority of a father, so useful to our well-being, and so justly venerable upon all accounts, hinders us from having that entire love for him that we have for our mothers, where the parental authority is almost melted down into the mother's fondness and indulgence. But we generally have a great love for our grandfather, in whom this authority is removed a degree from us, and where the weakness of age mellows it into something of a feminine partiality.[54]

Despite the fact that ideas of power – placing masculine authority *vs* feminine submissiveness – dominate his political and aesthetic system, Burke does seem to have a very real place for a more maternal version of authority, one that is based in trust, and the social contract.

3

THE SMELL OF THE FIRE: KANT, AESTHETICS, MORALITY AND CULTURE

The light dove cleaving the air in her free flight, and feeling its resistance, might imagine that flight would be still easier in empty space.

Immanuel Kant, *Critique of Pure Reason*

Though Burke's empirical enquiry may have laid the groundwork for much recent aesthetic speculation, Kant's fiercely reasoned metaphysics continues to force us towards an ever-receding horizon of moral and aesthetic determinacy and metaphysical certainty. Many commentators on the sublime are therefore split between Burke and Kant, between empiricism and formal idealism. Coleridge considered Burke's *Enquiry* a 'poor thing',[1] even though he was influenced by it. In the first half of the twentieth century, formal idealist critics such as Samuel Monk could feel completely justified in quoting Coleridge's comment approvingly, but critical estimation of Burke's work has changed in more recent years. The change is owing, of course, to sceptical, materialist attitudes towards truth and 'the prison-house of language'. Burke's empirical psychological work is consequently in vogue, even though the vogue is always enjoyed in relation to Kant's Critiques. Frances Ferguson remarks:

> . . . to say that the debate over aesthetics and particularly over the sublime occurs between Burkean empiricism and Kantian formalist idealism in some sense states the obvious. This is a commonplace of the history of aesthetics, as is the usual expansion of it – that the discussion of art becomes less objective and more subjective, less oriented toward things and more oriented toward individual psychology.[2]

According to Ferguson, Paul de Man and Jacques Derrida believe that '[f]ormalism is always materialism in disguise, masquerading as something more than it can be'. She states that the 'achievement of deconstructive materialism is, thus, always to see Kantian aesthetics not so much as a contrast to Burkean empiricist aesthetics but as more of the same'.[3] Yet the present contention is that neither the old nor the deconstructionist attitude towards the relationship between Kant and Burke is so stable or so well verified as to stand monolithically, for as Ferguson herself skilfully concludes: '. . . aesthetic experience does not do away with the empirical infinite that dominates the empirical account but rather harnesses it by coordinating it with an artificial infinite. That is, . . . an empirical infinite can be connected with the artificial systems of representing infinity that have no empirical correlates'.[4] Kant's transcendental point of view can be quite instructively seen as a continuation of Burke's idea of self-preservation, as for example in Kristeva's idea of *jouissance*, of the sublime as cure. Likewise, in Jean-François Lyotard's examination of Kantian and Burkean aesthetics, Kant's continuation of Burke can be seen as an evocation of the postmodern condition – as the confrontation of indeterminate moral and aesthetic realms. On the other hand, in Marxist ideas of the sublime liberation of the sensible from the tyranny of reason, or in Gadamer's idea of the ontological significance of aesthetics as the bridge between the ideal and the real, Kant can also be usefully and dialectically seen in formal idealist contrast to Burke – as a way of emphasising the formal resistance of transcendental freedom, which sometimes is derided in the empiricist critique. The unstable relation between Kant and Burke is the crux whereon the negative and positive sublimes meet. It also represents the grounds of the Yeatsian lyric.

The metaphysical basis of the Yeatsian lyric moves on the distinction between the Burkean and Kantian sublimes. Though the Yeatsian sublime relies heavily on psychological, Burkean modes of experience, the 'something more' of the Kantian sublime, the transcendent possibilities on the immaterial edge of the material real, is also central to it, being as much a part of life's constellation of values as is one's sense of power. Yeats makes a transcendental deduction worthy of Kant. He too moves from the phenomenal to the noumenal; he too looks for *a priori* transcendental concepts in the field of experience. This chapter will trace Kant's flight in those domains in order to show how the crisis point of Kantian aesthetics (the relationship of art, morality and aesthetic judgement) provides a fertile prolegomenon to the Yeatsian metaphysic. For if aesthetic and moral experience are not as analogous as Kant had hoped, they also cannot be satisfactorily severed from one another. The hope for resolution, it is here argued, is in some reconciliation of the sublime and the beautiful, and of the principles attached to them. The feminine, sensible, objective and natural realm of the beautiful must be united to the masculine, supersensible, subjective and free realm of the sublime. How this is to be done is a subject of controversy. For teleological reasons, Kant himself avoided art as object and looked instead to taste and culture to provide a figure for unifying the 'charm' of the beautiful and the 'morality' of the sublime; later Kantians, from Schiller to Yeats, see art as the most creative, erotic grounds for possible resolution of the aesthetic crisis.

BETWEEN BURKEAN AND KANTIAN SUBLIMITY

In his seminal study entitled *The Romantic Sublime*, Thomas Weiskel elaborates a version of the positive psychoanalytical sublime that wavers between the Burkean and Kantian sublimes. He describes the Kantian sublime as organised into three phases. The first is that in which the relation between the subject (mind) and object (or textual image) is balanced and 'harmonious'. In the second phase 'the habitual relation of mind and object suddenly breaks down'; there is a sudden crisis triggered by 'a natural phenomenon [that] catches us unprepared and unable to grasp its scale' or a text 'which exceeds comprehension'. Experienced on its own, this phase is the negative sublime. The third phase is when the sublime becomes positive: '. . . the mind recovers its balance of outer and inner by constituting a fresh relation between itself and the object such that the very indeterminacy which erupted in phase two is taken as symbolising the mind's relation to a transcendent order. This relation has a "meta" character'.[5] The essentialist idea of this 'meta' character is precisely what Weiskel calls into question, saying that the sublime moment is one of aphasia and that, quite correctly, the restorative aspect of the sublime is often ironic in Modernism because of this aphasia. It is correct with the exception of Yeats, however, as Weiskel himself states:

> . . . there is another logic of response to fictionality, equally central to Romanticism as a whole. The egotistical sublime strips fictions of their ontological significance – their power, as symbol or epiphany, to crash through the phenomenal and articulate essence of eternity. The poet, like Yeats, who invests fictions with ontological meaning inevitably resurrects the question of belief. His answer to Stevens's question, What am I to believe? is going to take a quasi-religious form.[6]

Weiskel thereby signifies the need to maintain the distinction between the Burkean and Kantian sublimes and the relationship of aesthetic questions to epistemological and ontological ones when discussing the Yeatsian sublime, or when discussing writers whose perspectives are similar to Yeats's.

Behind all these ideas of transcendence and the metaphysical is the notion essential to Kant that, in the third phase of the positive sublime, human reason apprehends what it cannot comprehend. In this phase we are able to imagine the incomprehensible whole through the apprehension of its constituent parts. What is essentially metaphysical about the sublime is that it is proof of both pure reason and a higher, supersensible morality of which we are shown to share a sense with others. Kant's inner sense is a moral sense. Postmodernists such as Paul Crowther and Lyotard have difficulty with the connection Kant makes between morality and aesthetics. Crowther believes that the Kantian sublime is too much like moral feeling to be an aesthetic reflection, that it is, in fact, a moral determination.[7] Crowther's point is that rather than realising morality's or reason's power through the simulacrum of aesthetic feeling, reason and morality dominate the imagination in the sublime moment – just as, through the categorical imperative, reason dominates the sensible world. Lyotard has a similar conclusion as regards the split between Kantian aesthetics and Kantian morality and ethics. He writes of the necessity of the synthesis between terror and exaltation in the Kantian sublime: 'Thus sensation must be double, or split into two heterogeneous yet indissociable sensations. We are of course referring to terror, which has to do with the presentable, and to exaltation, which refers to the unpresentable.'[8] If terror does not synthesise with a transcendent exaltation (in contrast to the limited exaltation of self-preservation in the Burkean sublime), the subject experiences negative sublimity. The transcendental illusion is necessary to the Kantian sublime, but this does not mean that reason and morality are unproblematically awakened. What the sublime actually awakens, according to Lyotard, is the sense of the division between morality and aesthetics. Kant's much vaunted idea of freedom in aesthetic judgement is severely compromised in such a scenario.

A.C. Bradley's idealist consideration of the sublime reveals the essential paradox of the movement from the negative to the positive sublime, as well as the volatile relation between morality and aesthetics. He admits that the two stages are not in any fixed order, that negative sublimity might well follow the positive, a succession which, of course, is unusual in most cases, and which has the potential to disrupt the very idea of the transcendental deduction. It is interesting to remember that Wordsworth places the sublime in this order, positive and then negative, in the 'Simplon Pass' episode, but he does it, it seems, to mitigate the negative effect from the privilege of hindsight.[9] The uncertain ordering is a sign of uncertainty as regards the true priority between the two sublimes. Bradley also realises the disruptive potential of the Burkean, negative sublime within the Kantian positive sublime: 'These [positive] feelings, even when the sublime thing might be called forbidding, menacing, or terrible, are always positive . . . and, when its nature permits of this, they may amount to rapture or adoration. But the mark of the negation from which they have issued, the "smell of the fire," usually remains on them.'[10] Considering the power of the negative in his rendering, it seems strange that later in the same passage Bradley would regard 'negative' as 'too strong a name'. Throughout the description, and remembering that the order is not fixed, negativity seems the dominant mood, in spite of all his insistence on the transcendental union. The sublime is a disruptive force and its negative dimension is what is most disruptive about it. Nevertheless, if we are to make sense of the sublime experience, it seems necessary to insist on its rational and positive character. The Old Testament God, the source of sublimity, has two sides: Yahweh, the aspect who reeks destruction, and Elohim, the aspect who makes the covenants, and who is the rational aspect. One without the other leaves Job without hope of restoration.[11]

KANT'S TRANSCENDENTAL DEDUCTION

The most suggestive phrase in Bradley's description is that of the 'smell of the fire' – the smell of the negative that remains during the positive stage. This description resembles Kant's idea of 'negative pleasure', Burke's of 'delightful horror', and Yeats's idea of 'terrible beauty', 'tragic ecstasy', and 'tragic joy'. They all suggest the coincidence of the negative and the positive in any experience of the sublime. The combination is also suggestive of Derrida's conception of the paradoxical trace, whose existence is proved by a Kantian transcendental deduction, 'by means of which', as Kant writes, 'the ground for this mode of judging must be traced to the *a priori* sources of knowledge'.[12] The invisibility and existence of the 'trace' is assured by the occurrence of that of which it is a necessary condition, just as the negativity or positivity of the sublime is assured by the necessary existence, or precondition, of the other. According to Derrida, the trace 'carries its other within itself'. These are the fields of discourse on which play blindness and insight, presence and absence, and, most importantly for a discussion of the sublime, death and life. The paradox of the trace is not only ungraspable but also unsolvable, with the consequence that there always remains what cannot be comprehended.[13] The paradox of the necessary but unverifiable source of knowledge is crucial to Kant's philosophy for, even though the *a priori* is the unifying grounds of all thought, he nevertheless '. . . dismissed as insubstantial any pretence to an absolute form of knowledge, which seeks to soar above the resistant medium of experience . . . The idea is posited only as a point of view'.[14] Sensing the weight of the empirical world, Kant nevertheless writes of an impossible yearning for the absolute: 'The light dove cleaving the air in her free flight, and feeling its resistance, might imagine that flight would be still easier in empty space.'[15]

In order to understand how Kant came to this poetic determination in the *Critique of Pure Reason* (1781), we must examine in greater detail the aesthetic philosophy of the *Critique of Judgement* (1790), as its transcendental point of view is meant to form the bridge between practical and theoretical reason. Kant tries to answer the sceptics and the empiricists with this simple question: how does the mind know it has limits unless it can transcend them? To answer them more thoroughly he must first ground both the subject and the object in innate principles and final causes – those Ideas which had been rejected by Burke, Hume and Locke. His theory of the sublime and the beautiful is separated into three sections: the subject in whom the sublime is based, the object in which, or whom, the beautiful is perceived, and the aesthetic experience in which the variable conflict of the sublime and the beautiful moves towards difficult reconciliation. Kant's obsession with threes (i.e. the three Critiques) aims to resolve the essential mystery of the subject–object relationship by seeking the elusive link in the medium of aesthetic feeling.

In terms of the debate over the place of the subject, Kant answers Locke's point on the instability of the self (the subject) with a complicated theory of apperception, or self-consciousness, which may be simplified thus: What I think I feel is mine *a priori*; who else could feel it? To doubt this unity of consciousness is to cease to be self-conscious.[16] Apperception is transcendental. It is sensible proof of a supersensible world. The argument leads to a glorification of sensation as proof of unity, to a valorisation of suffering as proof of morality, to Kant's concept of the sublime sacrifice, in which, against the rule of self-preservation, one sacrifices oneself for the larger good; here, Kant is like Hutcheson and Shaftesbury. The sublime experience being entirely subjective is the closest we can come to proving the existence of a transcendental, stable and unified individual. In order to prove the stability of the subject, one must examine its relationship to the external world.

There are two basic categories used to define the object: the phenomenal, or the empirical world of appearance and the noumenal transcendental object, which is the thing-in-itself (the Platonic circle which lies behind the object, a shadow whose beauty we experience when viewing the object). The thing-in-itself is the eternal quality of an object, something which must exist outside our perception of it. All we know of the truth of the object (its final end, why God put it here) is what we can perceive of it, but nonetheless it exists in its finality (the appearance it has). In other words, we know the finality of an object, its colour, form, but we can sense only its final end. Kant writes of Plato's circle: 'The finality of the object is the symbol of perfection. The final end we know not, but [we know] that the finality is beautiful in that we connect it with natural laws and causes'.[17] The beautiful comes as close to aesthetic objective universality (to a *sensus communis*, to proving a sense which is common to us all) as any experience may, and, in so doing, (almost) proves that there is objective truth.[18] The presumed universality of the object is the reason why the beautiful, being based in the object, is the only aesthetic used in the second part of Kant's *Critique of Judgement*, namely the 'Critique of Teleological Judgement', where he discusses the divine in light of the purposiveness of the object-world. As regards our subjective aesthetic response to the power of form, which is the province of the sublime and not of the beautiful ('sublimity is discoverable in the mind'), Kant is in opposition to Platonism, by seeing aesthetic experience as compatible with moral good, and as 'mutually inclusive if not identical'.[19]

ART, MORALITY AND THE PURITY OF AESTHETIC JUDGEMENT

The purity of aesthetic judgement is of tremendous significance in the contemporary debate over the ethical and political place of the sublime. One must remember that the sublime is inscribed in the terms of the beautiful, but its purity rests on being separate from it. A general, comparative review of ideas makes this clear: beauty is in form, sublimity in formlessness; beauty is in nature, sublimity is within; beauty can be dependent or free, sublimity must be free, for the freedom of the imagination is what it sacrifices to reason; beauty is in the harmony of understanding and reason, sublimity in the harmony of imagination and reason; beauty is a product of the sensible world (even its ideal form is visible in the sensible), sublimity is a product of the supersensible world – Kant makes the latter point clear when he writes: 'The sublime is that, the mere capacity of thinking which evidences a faculty of mind transcending every standard of sense'.[20] Yet therein lies the difficulty in terms of the relationship between beauty and sublimity. As Kant writes on the same page as the previous quotation, it is the 'disposition of the soul evoked by a particular representation engaging the attention of the reflective judgement, and not the Object [which is the realm of the beautiful], that is to be called sublime'. The explanation is confusingly difficult, however; as Byron remarked of Coleridge's *Biographia*, one wishes that Kant would explain his explanation.

According to Kant, the soul is an item in the world, while the transcendental unity of apperception (that 'I' which one is sure is the same 'I' of yesterday and the day before) is a point of view, and yet the consubstantiality of the soul with the self is the conclusion of the unity of apperception that underlies the stable subject. The soul is sublime but the object is not. Does the soul play an intermediary role? And how? Pure reason cannot validly move from self to soul. Yeats's 'A Dialogue of Self

and Soul' illustrates many of the same difficulties in the relation of the self
and the soul, as of subject to object, and so presents a confrontation of
empiricist Burkean aesthetics and formalist Kantian ones. A gulf lies
between subjective and objective reality as unbridgeable as that between
theoretical (pure) reason and practical reason. Aesthetic judgement, the
sublime, is there as the ghost, or trace, of a bridge, between receiving and
bestowing the blessings of their unity. It is significant that for Kant the
soul is found through practical reason, through interaction with the
world of objects of sense, which is, of course, the world of the beautiful.
Again, the empirical world is the basis of all transcendental ideas.

   This interaction recalls Adorno's idea of the 'primacy of the object'.
The way to the subject is through the object. Yet Kant insists that 'the
unity of consciousness which underlies the categories . . . is mistaken for
an intuition of subject as object, and the category of substance is then
applied to it'.[21] His insistence on the subjectivity of the sublime is one of
the main reasons for which objects of art are not seen as the highest
example of sublimity. Any such intuition of subject as object comes close
to presenting *a priori* truths that are objectively verifiable, which is an
idea Kant denies. We cannot think without the existence of such truths,
but we also cannot prove they exist. Adorno's ideas on the 'primacy of
the object' nevertheless have a clear basis in aesthetic feeling; the sensible
world – the mountain, the ocean – is the way to the supersensible, even if,
for Kant, it is only to be later suppressed.[22] The reasons for the suppres-
sion of the sensible in the subjective rendering of the sublime are
manifold, but one of the most important is Kant's idea that morality is
what differentiates the sublime from the beautiful: 'Hence it follows that
the intellectual and intrinsically final (moral) good, estimated aesthetically,
instead of being represented as beautiful, must rather be represented as
sublime . . . by virtue of the dominion which reason exercises over
sensibility'.[23] One wonders where it is possible to draw the line at which
beauty acquires a final, moral good. What are the various stages during
which beauty moves from finality (nature's purposiveness) to final ends
(God's purposiveness), from the phenomenal to the noumenal. How do
we move from a moment of reason being moved by the sensible world
(however disinterested) to its domination of it. Here, any enquiry will
show, the boundaries overlap. Perhaps as a result of this transgression
between beauty and sublimity and out of the belief that 'human nature'
does not accord with the good out of its own 'motion', Kant at times
insists that the dominion of reason over a susceptible sensibility is the
source of the sublime.[24] It must be remembered, however, that Kant's
definition of the sublime also comprehends the harmony of imagination
and reason and not always the dominion of reason. It is this confusion

that prompts Crowther and Donald Crawford to see Kant's sublime as just another version of moral rather than aesthetic feeling.[25]

In the case of moral feeling we have the pain of reason striking down desire, followed by the pleasure of having the will more easily determinable to the categorical imperative.[26] Crowther insists that the disinterestedness of the sublime is suspect, that reason has a very real interest in securing its dominion.[27] Patricia M. Matthews, on the other hand, describes what she believes is the difference between purely moral and aesthetic feeling: the morality of the aesthetic is not an imperative but rather an awakening, a revelation which results from the analogy between the two supersensible experiences.[28] She proceeds to discuss a passage from Kant that supports her point (though she admits that there are many contradictory statements). In her examples such words as 'attunement' and 'harmonise' are used rather than words such as 'dominate'.[29] The third critique is full of contradictions and complexities. It is important to emphasise that, in any scenario, there is a moment of violence inflicted on the imagination, one that must be healed. In the subsequent healing, harmony is established between reason and imagination, but it is a harmony which is known only by 'virtue of their [reason's and imagination's] contrast',[30] that is, by the extent of the violence inflicted. We are at the point where negative and positive sublimity (and by implication beauty, the basis of the positive) intermingle. The philosophical issue at stake is the purity of the aesthetic reflection versus the perceived intrusion of the moral into the aesthetic realm. If the reflection is not pure (its purity makes it a vital *analogy* to moral feeling), then it suggests that morality and aesthetics cannot be reconciled, that Keats's cry of 'Beauty is Truth and Truth Beauty' is most powerful in its impossibility.

In his *Lessons on the Analytic of the Sublime*, Lyotard explains how the sublime negotiates the relationship between aesthetics and morality through the violent contrast between a subverted imagination and an incomprehensible reason – Kant's harmony that is analogously present by its absence is at best peripheral in this explanation. The sublime is suggestive of what is unpresentable in any historical moment of monstrous suffering, or of revolutionary change, such as Yeats presents in 'Leda and the Swan' and 'The Second Coming'. Lyotard insists that 'the sublime feeling is neither moral universality nor aesthetic universalisation, but is, rather, the destruction of one by the other in the violence of their differend. This differend cannot demand, even subjectively, to be communicated to all thought'.[31] The sublime reveals the conflict of interests between moral and aesthetic understanding. The harmony that is implicit in the contrast between a violated imagination and an incomprehensible reason may be interminably deferred, but it is nevertheless highly meaningful; for the idea of solving the 'differend', or of assuaging the conflict of interest, is what makes the moment sublime, regardless of how unpresentable it is. The analogy to the harmony between reason and imagination is made through the moral and aesthetic crisis at hand. One is aware of something better, but also aware that it may be incommunicable and unrealisable.

Whatever compensation may exist in such a crisis is found in the synthesis of the sublime and the beautiful, the supersensible and sensible, in the harmony between Nature and the transcendental freedom of the subject, which morality potentially provides. As though too aware of the very real division between them, Kant's aesthetics are, as Bernstein calls them, 'memorial aesthetics'[32] – a memorial for the days when truth and beauty were not divided, when the aesthetic of the sublime was not needed as proof of the *a priori* (miracle was sufficient). Like the Yeatsian aesthetic, Kant's is an autumn beauty. Quite fittingly Kant allows for a union of the sublime and beautiful in which tragic, didactic and sacred elements are central: 'Even the presentation of the sublime, so far as it belongs to fine art, may be brought into union with beauty in a *tragedy in verse*, a *didactic poem* or an *oratorio*, and in this combination fine art is even more artistic'.[33] Kant proceeds to suggest that any resulting diminution of beauty is worth the sacred and tragic meanings which are imparted by the union of the sublime and beautiful. The influence on the soul, 'dispose[d] to ideas [and] susceptible of such pleasure and entertainment in greater abundance'[34] is considerable. Being that aspect of the self which is an item in the world, the soul combines subjectivity and objectivity (as the soul is consubstantial with the self), and is therefore appropriately moved by the mingling of the sublime and the beautiful. The tragic element seems to highlight how such a combination, although clearly a vital bridge between morality and aesthetics, is doomed to fall short of its goal. Yeats's conceptions of 'tragic ecstasy' and 'tragic joy', his idea of supersensible sexuality, are also directed towards this imperfect union of the sensible and supersensible, of physical and metaphysical worlds. Kant, however, is not very expressive on this subject, nor, for that matter, on the subject of sublimity and art. The sublime in art is not to be sought if judgements are to be pure and untainted by '*any teleological judgement*'.[35] Sublimity is more aligned than beauty to pure reason, morality and religion whose *a priori* purposes and forms are not determined by human or natural ends.

Hans-Georg Gadamer's comments on the absence of the discussion of art in Kant's *Critique of Judgement* touch on the possibility that the sensible world of art forms (art, like beauty, is based in the sensible) may be seen as sublime, and that art may approach *a priori* purposes and forms although it is determined by human ends. He argues that

. . . when the product of genius 'elevates' us, it is always connected with 'transcendental freedom', as Kant would say. That the work of art not only pleases but 'elevates' us, clearly includes the fact that it excites not only pleasure but also displeasure. This is not just occasionally so, as with the explicit presentation of the sublime in art, in great tragedy for instance. No, the true work of art does not blend neatly into the context of life as mere decoration, but stands out in its own right, and hence always presents itself as something of a provocation.[36]

Gadamer tries to answer any question that Kant might have raised about the relationship between the two aesthetic categories. His points are well taken. The ability of art and the beautiful to please may assuredly elevate us to a feeling which, at its pitch, borders on sublime displeasure. We see how the experience of a form, although it is determined by human ends, may be connected to *a priori* or 'transcendental' freedom through the genius of its creator and the mind of the perceiver. We also have a picture of how the elevation of a provocative 'moral', represented aesthetically, can unite the beautiful and the sublime. As regards tragedy, he and Kant are closer in spirit. The objective performance, of which beauty is the symbol, and the supersensible subjective faculty of the audience's moral sense meet in a catharsis of terror and pity; and that doubled emotion of catharsis is itself a union of positive and negative sublimity. The tragedy, however, is not only that there is a divide between beauty and sublimity, but that there is one between aesthetics and morality as well. The task of aesthetic feeling is to imagine a reason for the division that will somehow help to resolve it.

CULTURE, GENDER AND AESTHETIC UNITY

Although art does not provide much of a context for aesthetic unity in Kant's work, his writing does allow for the importance of taste and culture, however, and in this it leaves room for those later Kantians who returned to art for their synthesis. According to Kant, culture and taste, 'by conveying a pleasure that admits of universal communication, and by introducing polish and refinement into society, make [us] civilised'.[37] Stuart Hampshire notes: 'Culture is the bridge that leads from nature to freedom and rationality', that is, it is the bridge between the realm of the beautiful and the sublime, and so consequently bridges the qualities they represent. 'So culture, as Kant interprets it here, as binding humanity together,' Hamphire concludes, 'is neither a naturally occurring pheno-menon, like happiness, nor a supernatural ideal, like the rational will, but is something intermediate between them'.[38] Kant, when discussing culture, tries to marry many of the qualities of sublimity and beauty, especially as regards gender, in order to present a coherent idea of social and moral perfection.

A clearer indication of the social constituents and sexual figures of Kant's aesthetic theory is in his earlier work, *Observations on the Feeling of the Beautiful and the Sublime* (1764). The gendering of *Observations* is explicit and prepares one for his later analogy between gender and morality. The second section, 'Of the Attributes of the Beautiful and Sublime in Man in General', contains an encoded sexual politics. In it, Kant notes that 'Friendship is sublime', so are 'truthfulness', 'self-will', 'dignity', 'justice', 'stoicism', and 'self-sacrificing courage' – all traditionally masculine characteristics that Burke too associated with sublimity and by which he separated the sexes.[39] Kant is readying us for the discussion of gender in the third section, 'Of the Distinction of the Beautiful and Sublime in the Interrelations of the Two Sexes', which is more specifically gendered. Woman is associated with the beautiful, and the beautiful consists of the 'elegant', 'decorated', 'pleasant', 'trivial', 'sympathetic', 'goodhearted', 'compassionate', and 'delicate'[40] – in short, all those qualities that Burke also associates with the beautiful and the feminine. In Kant's turn of phrase, 'Her philosophy is not to reason, but to sense'.[41] Her virtues are seductive and even her faults as such are *'beautiful faults'*.[42] He does allow women to have some sublimity, however; and he does so in a way that calls to mind his later insistence on beauty's symbolic relationship to moral objectivity.[43] Yet, even here her morality is to be perceived in a reification of her beauty and agreeable disposition rather than in any depth of character.

All this leads to the most important passage of the third section, when Kant contemplates the marriage of the sublime and the beautiful. He has admitted that individual men and women should contain elements of both the beautiful and sublime within them.[44] The element of androgyny is analogous to Yeats's idea of the Trinity in 'Supernatural Songs'. Kant is nearing a synthesis of the sensible and supersensible, feminine and masculine, those dialectics that underlie the relationship between the beautiful and the sublime. He proceeds to consider the relationship of power and, even though he endeavours to avoid this notion by stating that 'a dispute over precedence is trifling and . . . coarse', the hierarchy, the dominion of Reason over the sensible, is made clear:

> In matrimonial life the united pair should, as it were, constitute a single moral person, which is animated and governed by the understanding of the man and the taste of the wife. For not only can one credit more insight founded on experience to the former, and more freedom and accuracy in sensation to the latter; but also, the more sublime a disposition is, the more inclined it is to place the greatest purpose of its exertions in the

contentment of a beloved object, and likewise the more beautiful it is, the more it seeks to requite these exertions by complaisance.[45]

Regardless of the hierarchy, the idea of such a marriage emphasises the intimate relationship between subject and object, self and other, and moves them towards the sexual figures, the *jouissance,* and the erotics of the text, which lie beneath the relationship between the object of beauty and the gaze of the viewer.

To conclude, for Yeats, art and culture are most definitely provocations and in no way are based in any disinterestedness on our part, except, perhaps, as regards our disinterest in the object's utility. Art as beautiful object becomes sublime because it proves the imagination inadequate to the subjective ideas of reason, as well as to the purposiveness of what is being dramatised. In his subjugation of the sensible, Kant has gone in the worst direction of the Enlightenment and has forgotten the possibilities which the birth of aesthetics suggested. The repression of the senses can be catastrophic. This is not to valorise natural law over moral law, however, for that would be just another form of tyranny. The idea is to find a balance. Art may be the place to begin the task, even if it cannot contain all the ends. In order to achieve that level of satisfaction, the feminine figure of the beautiful and the masculine figure of the sublime should be viewed in a manner that results in consummation rather than dominance. This end is predicated on the idea that the sensible world of the beautiful can somehow find moral expression in the supersensible sphere of the sublime. Yeats, for example, seeks such a balance when he converts Kant's idea of Reason into the 'Celestial Body' as sensible, sexual expression of divinity, and as a transcendent form of the objects of mind.[46]

4
NIGHT OR JOY: YEATS, THE NEGATIVE AND POSITIVE SUBLIME

Heaven and hell are built always anew and in hell or heaven all do what they please and all are surrounded by scenes and circumstances which are the expression of their natures and the creation of their thought. Swedenborg, because he belongs to an eighteenth century not yet touched by the romantic revival, feels horror amid rocky uninhabited places, and so believes that the evil are in such places while the good are amid smooth grass and garden walks and the clear sunlight of Claude Lorraine.

Yeats, 'Swedenborg, Mediums, Desolate Places'

In Kant and Burke, the aesthetic is seen to be the solution to the various crises of modernity, such as the philosophical quandary over questions of knowledge, the place of revolution, the nature of society, but most especially, and at the heart of all the questions, the subject–object relationship. Consequently, their gendering of the aesthetic lays the basis for that erotic figure which Yeats (like the poet Schiller and the philosopher Nietzsche before him) views as the answer to these crises.

POSITIVE AND NEGATIVE BEAUTY

The gendering of the sublime and the beautiful has been discussed at length with regard to Burke and, to a lesser extent, to Kant. An examination of Yeats's poetry discovers that his version of what is here called the sublime is a variation on a theme. His ideas of the false and true sublime, the false and true forms of beauty, are different from them both, although it is not difficult to find poems that represent each category. If Burke's formative idea of the false form of beauty, for example, is when the libertine French women inverted the order of society during the Revolution and led the others to infamy, it finds little resemblance in Yeats's thought. Female sexual wantonness, or active power, is rarely a negative form. He is too timid a man for that attitude to do him much good. From Niamh to

Crazy Jane, we see, instead, that sexual candour in women is almost always positive; even the negative effects of Helen of Troy are impressive enough to become a type of destiny. Nevertheless, his point of view does have two sides to it: he definitely believes that women have a potentially negative effect as well as a positive one. Rather than separate his views of beauty into true and false beauty, it is better to name them terrible beauty and beauty. The only false form of beauty, for Yeats, is the sacrifice of its aesthetic and social expression to an abstract ideal; it is this falsity that threatens to undo both types of beauty.

In the phrase 'a terrible beauty' from 'Easter, 1916', Yeats conflates the terms of the sublime and the beautiful in order to hint at the power of the 1916 rebellion, suggesting that it had a God-like power to determine the fate of a nation for both good and ill. The phrase has wider and earlier application, however; if the negative sublime presents the cataclysmic proportions of last things such as death and God, then negative, or terrible beauty presents the terror of social transformation in general. Since late Romanticism, in fact, the conflation of beauty and sublimity, of social and religious ills, 'this beauty into which the soul with all its maladies has passed', as Pater writes of the Mona Lisa, has become 'a symbol of the modern idea.'[1] The most typical examples of terrible beauty in Yeats's poetry before 'Easter, 1916', are the closely aligned ones of Maud Gonne and Helen of Troy. In 'No Second Troy', Yeats does not paint a picture of the 'vilest women' or of 'women lost to shame'[2] as does Burke in his portrait of the French Revolution; rather, he portrays a personal beauty and nobility misapplied, of someone who 'taught to ignorant men most violent ways . . . [and] . . . hurled the little streets upon the great'. The deleterious effect of such beauty is the result of what the age itself lacks. A beauty like Gonne's could never have succumbed to the peaceful characteristics of the age, for she is a terrible beauty. In 'No Second Troy', Yeats concludes that, given the right historical circumstances, Gonne herself could have been part of the defining moment of an antithetical age, as Helen was when she began the Trojan War. Zeus has not yet arrived in the guise of the swan, however; as the title reminds us, there will be no second Troy for some time to come.

The noble or positive form of beauty, on the other hand, is best seen in poems such as 'Adam's Curse'; here beauty has the ability to overcome the curse of the Fall. The beauty of art and that of women are explicitly connected in order to allow the being which women labour to represent and the action which ends and/or fulfils all artistic contemplation to achieve some aesthetic unity. The Yeatsian aesthetic also stands in contrast to the world of getting and spending, just as the beauty of the Queen of France in Burke's famous passage contrasts with the ugliness of the rising class of opportunists. The word 'beautiful' appears five times in the poem as a signature of paradise before the Fall, which occurred when Locke was born and the 'Garden died' ('Fragments'), and before 'bankers, school-masters, and clergymen' took control of 'the world' ('Adam's Curse'). As part of Yeats's interpenetration of opposites, it must be remembered that Gonne contains positive and negative aspects of beauty; she is central both to 'Adam's Curse' and 'No Second Troy'. Interconnected forms of positive and negative beauty also appear later in 'A Prayer for my Daughter'. There, we have the terrible beauty of Helen and Venus, then Maud Gonne, treated analogously, and lastly the positive type Yeats wants for his daughter, Anne. In the instance of Helen's beauty, we see the various negative female sexual powers that seem destined both to represent Nature's bounty and to undo it because their representation is so complete that it makes life 'flat and dull'.

The threat to male powers is obvious in the undoing of the 'Horn of Plenty', although the threat to those powers is not posed by sexual sub-version, as in Burke, but rather by neglect, as in Aristophanes' Lysistrata. In the penultimate stanza of 'A Prayer for my Daughter', we have a picture of the autonomous soul, one that is similar to that which springs from life's own self-delight in 'Meditations in Time of Civil War'. The union of his daughter's will and God's will is the objectification of the moral and supersensual life that Yeats so desires. Yet this is not enough. Consummation is the final need; Yeats ends on notes of sexual ceremony and custom in order to strike the conciliatory chord. It is interesting to note that Yeats ends 'Coole and Ballylee, 1931' similarly; we see every 'bride's ambition satisfied'. The cornucopia is full and the laurel tree, image of Daphne, no longer twists in the denial of threatened violence, but, as Yeats writes in the last stanza of 'A Prayer for my Daughter', it spreads '[w]here all's accustomed, ceremonious'.

Perhaps, in some final transcendent fashion, the positive form of beauty is truer than the negative form because it accommodates both qualities. In this regard it is a short step, perhaps no step at all, from negative and positive beauty to the negative and positive sublime. As beauty approaches moral reconciliation, or even as it threatens catastrophe, it approaches sublimity. Blurring the lines does not erase them, however. One might easily discuss 'No Second Troy' in terms of the negative sublime; only, it is important to remember in the discussion that the feminine aesthetic principle comes out of the realm of the beautiful as it is defined in eighteenth-century terms. If one were to discuss 'No Second Troy' in terms of the sublime rather than the beautiful, the references to society, culture, human relations would be less important than those to destiny, morality, the transcendent.

THE REVOLUTIONARY SUBLIME

Any idea of maintaining the falseness or trueness of revolution in Yeats, in comparison to Burke, is difficult. To state too blankly that the conflict in 'Meditations in Time of Civil War' is a false sublime while that in 'Easter, 1916' is true would simplify Yeats's interrogation of violence in either poem. His position has some fundamental ambiguities that run along the lines of transcendence and engagement. It grows more difficult still, however, to apply the same terms to 'The Rose Tree', and to late poems like 'Under Ben Bulben' and 'Three Marching Songs', which in many ways extol violence. 'The Second Coming' is the most problematic. For though it comes out of Yeats's admiration for Burke's reading of the French Revolution and the latter's passage on the Dauphiness who became Queen of France, and though Yeats is most certainly applying Burke's critique of the French to the Russian Revolution (as well as to socialist revolutions in Germany and Italy), the violence of the poetry is not definitively false. Like Nietzsche, Yeats identifies with the drive on a very personal level and believes that there are creative forms of destruction as well as the more brutal lower expressions of the will to power. He sees such violence as necessary for transformation of self and society alike. Unlike Burke, Yeats believes that the unleashed negative energy shall have formative influence. His description of the conception of the poem places a very different source besides Burke's famous passage. Yeats writes: '. . . I began to imagine, as always at my left side just out of range of the sight, a brazen winged beast that I associated with laughing ecstatic destruction [His own note reads: 'Afterwards described in my poem "The Second Coming"'].'[3] The resonance of the title 'The Second Coming' is further emphasised, if we observe that this quotation is from his introduction to the play *The Resurrection* (1931). He closes the introduction with an explanation of the play that also explains our poem and its relationship to the sequence 'Two Songs from a Play', set as its opposite: 'It has seemed to me of late that the sense of spiritual reality comes whether to the individual or to crowds from some violent shock, and that idea has the support of tradition.'[4] Yeats is writing of the return of the irrational. The shock will come not from a Christ-like figure at the start of a primary age, giving the irrational transcendent expression, but rather from a God, an anti-Christ who, in the monstrousness of its advent, its reification or objectification of the subject, leaves the hollowed-out subject a vessel for the rising of turbulent sexual instinct. All subjectivity will thenceforth move towards multiplicity, evil, fiction. It will move towards an antithetical culture that, rather than being based on love and wisdom, is based on knowledge and power.

For all of the differences in attitude between Yeats and Burke, especially as regards violent revolution, the Burkean echoes of 'The Second Coming' are nevertheless quite real. This is because their opinions of the situation in Ireland, which are complex and perhaps closer, make them appreciative of the place of rebellion in the cultural desire for a harmonious aesthetic order. In early drafts of the poem, Yeats actually names Burke and Marie Antoinette:

> Ever more wide sweeps the gyre
> Ever further hawk flies outward
> From the falconer's hand. Scarcely
> is armed tyranny fallen when
> when [an] this mob bred anarchy
> takes its place. For this
> Marie Antoinette has
> more brutally died & no
> Burke [has shook his] has an[swered]
> with his voice. No Pit[t]
> arraigns revolution. Surely the second
> birth comes near.[5]

Obviously, Yeats feels that it is a barbaric revolution. The 'revelation' of the finished poem was 'revolution' in the early drafts. What Burke saw as useless revolution, Yeats saw as necessary for revelation. The Queen is implicitly raped; she is unable to spare herself the last insult through suicide as Burke had projected. In this she becomes the prototype for Leda, and importantly so. Leda, in fact, incurs 'the violent shock' of 'spiritual reality'. Though Yeats may differ from Burke in his point of view, he certainly has inherited his preoccupation with the abuse of power and the suffering of the vulnerable from dispassionate radical change. The second stanza from a later poem, 'The Gyres', explores this knotty relationship. The riding of the nightmare has obvious sexual significance; the 'blood and mire' that 'stain' the 'sensitive body' are examples of Kristevan abjection, of estranging suffering, of the violence of desire that draws us to a defining moment of *jouissance*; it is an example of Yeatsian ecstasy and self-knowledge as regards the conceptualisation of what is at best an impermanently realised ideal. Leda is also like the shy woman of the *aisling* tradition that shadows Burke. Yeats does not see this abject situation as ideal; on the contrary, the ideal is where 'body is not bruised to pleasure soul' ('Among School Children'), where there is no conflict. He is accepting the violence of revolution in order to allow for the return of the ideal age of chivalry, which Burke had said was extinguished.

What may finally be false about the violence of 'The Second Coming' are its temporal uses (as opposed to its spiritual value). In other words, the 'passionate intensity' is in the heads, hearts and hands of the worst people. This aspect separates it from the violence of the positive sublime, in which violence is inflicted in a just war. The latter is a type of bloodshed that can make 'a right Rose Tree' ('The Rose Tree') or can change a culture from 'motley' to 'terrible beauty'. It is how the dialectic between negative and positive sublimity can achieve transcendental synthesis.

AESTHETICS AND MORALITY

The problematic nature of these relationships reflects the problematic nature of the relationship between aesthetics and morality. The certainty for which Kant is striving in his Critiques has become increasingly difficult until, by Yeats's period, it is a quasi-mystical assertion to state that the aesthetic and the moral, or better still for Yeats's usage, the religious sense were united. This partly results from the amoral reaction of the Late Victorian movements (Aestheticism, Symbolism and Decadence) to the overtly moralised sense of art and literature of the mid-Victorian age. Ironically enough, the best of Victorian writing is often concerned with the difficulty in achieving any union between the aesthetic, or sensual life, and the religious one. The Late Victorians and early Modernists resurrect the Romantic interest in discovering morality through the investigation of evil, supernatural emotion, and broken taboos. Yeats is very much part of the Late Victorian and the Modernist return to the Romantic search for moral evil. He makes a famous and indicative criticism of George Eliot along these lines: '. . . she has morals but no religion. If she had more religion she would have less morals. The moral impulse and the religious destroy each other in most cases.'[6] For Yeats, the freedom that distinguishes the aesthetic impulse must also characterise the religious impulse, or else religion will lose what throughout his work Yeats calls a 'Vision of Evil', and which is necessary for sublimity. He therefore rewrites Dante's line '. . . la sua volontade è nostra pace' (*Paradiso*, III, l. 85) as 'Thy Will is our freedom'.[7]

During his early to middle years, Yeats moves from the above-mentioned amorality to the strongly aestheticised politics that has become a hallmark of the Modernists. The Romantic avatar of Modernism unites with the conservative Victorian love of cultured objectivity and tradition to produce a heady form of reactionary politics. We see an example of this quite clearly when, in the volume *Responsibilities* (1914), Yeats separates right from wrong along the lines of good and bad taste as it is exhibited among the classes. The sometimes harsh simplification of this mood reappears at various times in Yeats's oeuvre ('To a Young Beauty', 'Why should not Old Men be Mad?', 'A Bronze Head'), but what taste means has much broader significance throughout most of his work. His eye for

the particular and his love of self-contradiction are the best aids against
the effect of his most sweeping judgements. Though he is always wary of
any explicit connection between politics and poetry, he does move in his
career towards a conjunction of culture and society, of aesthetic and political rule, which is quite clearly a rendition of harmony between morality
and aesthetics. Through Unity of Being and Unity of Culture, his favoured
civilisations of Greece, Byzantium and Renaissance Italy give aesthetic
shape and value to moral questions. For though Yeats so often and
publicly tried to separate his political and poetic life (from 'On being asked
for a War Poem' to 'Politics'), they do merge in his vision of Byzantium.
The 'delicate skill' of the Byzantine worker, vents the 'murderous madness
of the mob'.[8] Sacred art has the ability to fuse the competing antithetical
and primary dispensations. The division between aesthetics and morality
is thereby healed. In the end, Yeatsian aesthetics are effectively politicised.
They are politicised in such a way as to take what he believes are the best
ideas of the left and right and to hammer them into unity.

By the The Wild Swans at Coole (1919) Yeats is already beginning to
imagine a society of the beautiful, an Irish Urbino that stands in
confrontation to his contemporary society, and which can synthesise the
moral questions of state, the intellectual concerns of scholarship, and
the emotional affairs of poetry. One of Yeats's chief figures for this
connection is that of bride and bridegroom, which he discovers in
Castiglione's Il Libro Del Cortegiano.[9] It is Yeats's figure for the marriage
of sublime protective strength of character and the cultivated delicacy of
the beautiful. In this, Yeats also follows Kant's idea of the two sexes joining
to form the complete moral and aesthetic individual. It is an image that
ends the last poem of the next volume, 'A Prayer for my Daughter' from
Michael Robartes and the Dancer (1921). In The Wild Swans at Coole
(1919), this erotic figure is ever present in Yeats's poems to Iseult, where
he admonishes her to marry well. Unity of Being and Culture are best
exemplified in a consummating marriage, but the terms are elusive and so
the autumnal quality of the volume colours all of Yeats's images of the
beautiful. As soon as he is able to imagine a balanced society in some
convincing detail, its terms are written out of existence. The civilisation of
the aristocracy and the folklore of the peasantry are increasingly diminished
by the advent of mass culture. In the two subsequent volumes, Michael
Robartes and the Dancer (1921) and The Tower (1928), Yeats meditates
on the reasons for the growth and decadence of culture, the need for
creative, if violent change, and the lamentable destructiveness of that
change. Throughout the volumes The Wild Swans at Coole (1919) and
The Winding Stair and Other Poems (1933), the most moral and creative
form of violence is found in individual experience, especially in one's

intimate relationship to transcendent reality, whether within oneself or with a lover. The implication is that society so greatly complicates the relationship between violent change and its transcendent aim that it ineluctably negates that aim and leaves self-perpetuating violence in its place.

Yeats must come to terms with the whole Kantian question of the dominance of morality and reason versus the power and needs of the sensible world. He realises that the fastest way to paradise is through renunciation of the world, but he is also aware that art's power is derived from the sensible world. This reckoning chiefly takes place in the volume *The Winding Stair and Other Poems* (1933). His poems of the positive sublime, 'Veronica's Napkin', 'Oil and Blood', 'At Algeciras – A Meditation upon Death', 'The Mother of God', 'Stream and Sun at Glendalough', all acknowledge the rights of morality and conscience, of reason and the primary God over the antithetical sensible world. They all also show (contra Kant) how interdependent the sensible world and the transcendent one are, how eroticised is the relationship between the subjective and objective realities that they explore, and how eroticised is the religious unity which his poetics seeks. The two realities are weighed against each other in such major poems as 'A Dialogue of Self and Soul' and 'Vacillation' where Yeats views the balance tipping in favour of the sensible world. In the end, the strife and tumult of the sensible world, the aesthetic pleasures and the individual love of freedom, although necessary to artistic creation, must combine with the moral world of reason if they are to achieve any profound type of purposiveness, or any true, lasting form of religion; and yet they must not be unduly suppressed by the moral or the reasonable. The dialogue and the vacillation are concerned with the difficult balance of this relationship. With reference to Kant, Yeats specifically mentions the relationship in the language of his system of antithetical and primary movements:

> I found myself upon the third antinomy of Immanuel Kant, thesis: freedom, antithesis: necessity; but I restate it. Every action of man declares the soul's ultimate, particular freedom, and the soul's disappearance in God; declares that reality is a congeries of beings and a single being.[10]

The antithetical evil that may be necessary to assert the particular freedom of the soul must end in the primary submission of the soul as it disappears into God. Yeats's investigation of the theme illustrates Kant's idea that harmony is finally established through the contrast of reason and imagination, that absence implies presence, and that this is how the second negative stage of the sublime moves to the third positive stage of sublimity – where sweetness is drawn from strength. To believe this, however, is indeed a leap of faith. Yeats is willing to take such a leap on the evidence that his ecstatic experience gives him. As Kant in his *Observations* presents an image of the complete moral person exhibited through the marriage of sublime reason and beautiful taste, Yeats sees that it is through the meeting of opposites, the synthesis of Kant's antinomies, that we are able to reach the sphere of the positive sublime.

The Neo-Platonic Yeats, like the later Kant, has a tendency to think that the sensible world must in the end be sacrificed to reason and, by analogy, to morality. The chief difference between Kant and Yeats is that there is another more powerful side to the latter that rejects reason's domination. Both sides of Yeats are graphically drawn in the title poem of the volume *The Tower* (1928). He later insists that heaven has just as sensible a portion as does earth, that human sexuality has a correspondence in supernatural sexuality which only a sublimely erotic religious vision reveals. He had said as much in 'The Magi'. Ecstasy is his word for such vision because it has erotic and religious connotations. It is something that he fully admits when writing the volume *The Winding Stair and Other Poems* (1933); but by the time he reaches 'Supernatural Songs', he has systematised this belief. The Celestial Body, which in *A Vision* is equal to Kant's idea of Reason, finds its explication in this sequence. It is put into sweeping historical context so that the body may be freed of our own fearful tendency to suppress it. Consequently, our suffering Body of Fate (the known) may merge with the Celestial Body ('the Divine Ideas in their unity').[11] Yeats is spatialising reason, just as in *A Vision* he hoped to spatialise Kant's idea of time as an inner sense (time, in Kant, is opposed to the external sense of space).[12]

By placing history into geometrical patterns, Yeats has combined both space and time and the objective and the subjective in those defining moments of sublimity. He is thereby able to equate his own ecstatic experience with divine examples of ecstasy and to place it in direct contrast to the common light of day, as he makes clear in part III, 'Ribh in Ecstasy' of 'Supernatural Songs'. Through our Blakean emanation, we momentarily transcend our world to view the divine energy, only to be brought back to earth having forgotten half of what we had seen; we 'wake', as Yeats writes in part VII of the same sequence, '[i]gnorant of what Dramatis Personae spake'. That transcendent place is the soul's realm; it is a 'quarter where all thought is done' ('A Dialogue of Self and Soul'). We may glimpse it in a moment of positive sublimity, in which the subject and object, reality and the idea, the sensible and moral, are reconciled. Such fusion implies death, however, and so Yeats recoils to the realm of the self, the realm of the negative as the stuff of the antithetical world of art. We return again to the uncertain ordering of positive and negative sublimity – perhaps the negative may come after one's return from the state of ecstasy. The dark night of the soul is the sense that any union with God is illusory.

THE NEGATIVE AND POSITIVE SUBLIME

The aporia between the positive and negative sublime becomes more thunderous and stormy when Yeats nears the end of his life. He is not sure if God will 'burn Nature with a kiss' ('The Man who Dreamed of Faeryland') or if 'the last kiss is given to the void', as in old age he writes to T. Sturge Moore.[13] His poetic visions either alternate between the negative, terrible sublime of 'The Black Tower' and 'Man and the Echo' and the positive moral sublime of 'Cuchulain Comforted' and 'Lapis Lazuli', or they dwell in some volatile highly eroticised combination of the two versions of the sublime ('News for the Delphic Oracle', 'Long-legged Fly'). All these meditations have been born of the great purgatorial poem on the subject, 'Byzantium'. Their contrasting visions number among Yeats's greatest achievements. They make him important to an age that is itself oscillating between metaphysical extremes of militant faith and nihilism. The five concluding poems in the volume *Last Poems* (1939) are studies in contrasting visions; they explain the way in which Yeats hoped to move from the negative to the positive sublime, and how he was not certain he could do so.

Though Yeats's visions are desublimated in such poems as 'Man and the Echo' and 'The Circus Animals' Desertion', the erotic force of his whole system continues to drive him towards positive sexual and religious affirmations that may, for all they affirm, still acknowledge his driving sexual and religious torments. From 'Supernatural Songs' on, Yeats has explicitly accepted that there must be a female aspect to the deity. The beautiful and its harmonious social structure begin to take eternal, objective and indeed moral, sublime form. As though presaging the union of the female with the male deity, Yeats's late images of sublimity, of a transcendent world, are profanely eroticised (for example 'The Statues' and even more so 'News for the Delphic Oracle' and 'A Stick of Incense'). There are also moments of despairing violence, of angry sexual loneliness, which echo the need for ecstatic fulfilment ('John Kinsella's Lament for Mrs Mary Moore', 'The Wild Old Wicked Man' and especially 'The Spur'). The sexual despondency takes on metaphysical proportions in the close of both 'The Apparitions' and 'A Nativity'. The poem entitled 'In Tara's Halls' stiltedly endeavours to assuage the pain, when the 101-year-old speaker tells the women on his knee to 'lie still' and then proceeds to prepare his own funeral in which he (rather too much in control) 'lay in the coffin, stopped his breath and died'. The final stanza of 'The

Apparitions', on the other hand, ends more insightfully, making the power of the female aspect more threatening, much less domesticated:

> When a man grows old his joy
> Grows more deep day after day,
> His empty heart is full at length
> But he has need of all that strength
> Because of the increasing Night
> That opens her mystery and fright.
> *Fifteen apparitions have I seen;*
> *The worst a coat upon a coat-hanger.*

The emphasis of the refrain, the idea that the garment of the empirical world once cast off leaves nothing, haunts Yeats so much that death itself appears to make the womb behind desire a darkening tomb. The last kiss is given to the void in an effort to make the 'dark grow luminous' and 'the void fruitful', as Yeats writes in *Per Amica Silentia Lunae*, when 'the ringers in the tower have appointed for the hymen of the soul a passing bell'.[14] The negative sublime, by comparison, offers one only impotence before the terror of death. The vaunted potency of Burkean self-preservation is exposed as being based on a sense of safety as well as on survival that would otherwise wither into horror. The supersensible significance of the Yeatsian sublime, however, possesses the latent ability to maintain desire at much more intimate quarters with death. At the close of 'A Nativity', Yeats wonders at a religious scene whose combination of mystery, fear and hope is of consistent relevance to him: 'Why is the woman terror-struck?/Can there be mercy in that look?' Yeats is looking to the redemptive force of the primary world that, blent with the antithetical needs of selfhood, made Byzantium and Greece havens for the imagination, and which made Coole Park under Lady Gregory such a haven for him. He must examine whether the aesthetic power of the antithetical dispensation can be reconciled to the redemptive force of the primary in order to affirm the erotics of the sublime. If the prophetic face of the Virgin Mary is not merciful, death is annihilation or worse, it is damnation.

In 'Man and the Echo', Yeats wonders if aesthetics and morality are irreconcilable ('Did that play of mine send out/Certain men the English shot?'), and wonders if there is no positive form of the sublime; if the hope he placed in the erotic figure was, in fact, misplaced, are we left with only the frustrations of desire? Lost in 'the labyrinth of another's being' ('The Tower'), are we mere food for the Minotaur – the tyranny of the natural law incarnate – because there is no Ariadne, no golden thread to guide us out? Yeats writes in 'Man and the Echo' that 'all seems evil until I/Sleepless would lie down die'. He also realises that death or suicide is no answer: 'There is no release/In a bodkin or disease'. The 'spiritual intellect's great work' is to clean 'man's dirty slate', that is, to moralise the evil before one 'sinks at last into the night'. The strain of the age, and the rift between morality and aesthetics, is variously evident. Yeats must call the intellect 'spiritual' because he lives in an era that has separated intellect from spirit – up to the nineteenth century such a split, the idea of intellect functioning independently from spirit, that is, scientifically, was relatively unknown outside the scope of experimental science. This division is one of many. In this poem, Echo does not fall in love with Narcissus nor woo him to his death, as she does in the Greek myth; rather, she flatly and undesiringly repeats his words in order to parody his intent. There is a split between words and meaning, intellect and spirit, aesthetics and morality; nothing reflects our own desires as does the mythological Echo. The close of the poem brings Yeats's questions to the fore:

> O rocky voice
> Shall we in that great night rejoice?
> What do we know but that we face
> One another in this place?
> But hush, for I have lost the theme,
> Its joy or night seem but a dream;
> Up there some hawk or owl has struck
> Dropping out of sky or rock,
> A stricken rabbit is crying out
> And its cry distracts my thought.

In these lines, we have the confrontation of the night of the negative sublime and the joy of the positive sublime. Is the empirical world all we have? Shall we face another's terror-stricken face over a dying fire like those characters at the end of Byron's poetic vision of universal 'Darkness'? If that is so, and if aesthetics can have no moral value, then we are left with the aesthetics of terror and suffering, the rabbit's cry, rather than the aesthetics of meaning.

Burke's view of the meaningfulness of the 'cries of animals' is very similar to Yeats's idea that profound philosophy is derived from terror:[15]

> Such sounds as imitate the natural inarticulate voices of men, or any animals in pain or danger, are capable of conveying great ideas [. . .] It might seem that these modulations of sound carry some connection with the nature of the things they represent, and are not merely arbitrary; because the natural cries of all animals, even of those animals with whom we have not been acquainted, never fail to make themselves sufficiently understood; this cannot be said of language.[16]

Deprived of its moral spiritual force, the intellect is left distracted, undone by terror, as the rabbit is undone. The great idea that goes beyond language is the terrible unknown. The great work of the spiritual intellect is reduced to animal terror; the hearer recognises it to be fundamental to all existence. The desublimating close of this poem leads directly to the 'The Circus Animals' Desertion', the desublimating summary of Yeats's corpus.

As in *King Lear*, the rhetorical questions of eloquence versus truth underlie the poem and threaten to expose the moral-aesthetic divide as unbridgeable. What is realised, however, is that the relationship between subjective empirical reality ('the mound of refuse') and the objective ideal ('the pure mind') is a dialectic whose synthesis is never complete or permanent, though it can be momentarily imagined. Were Yeats's *Collected Poems* to finish here, the open-ended questions of 'Man and the Echo' and 'The Circus Animals' Desertion' would close the Yeatsian aesthetic in negative sublimity; the weight of the argument between the negative, terrible Burkean sublime and the positive, moral Kantian sublime would make the former preponderant, but that would not be consistent with Yeats's balanced system of thought. Like Schiller, Yeats moves to resolve the controversy between rationalist, empiricist and idealist theories of beauty. Though he is never certain, he is always aware of the possibility of the positive sublime, and that possibility, like Dante's vision of divine love, or Ptolemy's *Primum Mobile*, sets his visionary system in motion. For though the sublime is a mixed feeling of delightful horror, or negative pleasure, it is nevertheless a pleasure, a heightened aesthetic. Somewhere within that pleasure is the presence of a transcendent or supersensible sphere. Kant writes of the moral significance of the sublime: 'The pleasure in the sublime in nature, as one of rationalising contemplation, lays claim also to universal participation, but still it presupposes another feeling, that, namely of our supersensible sphere, which feeling, however obscure it may be, has a moral foundation.'[17] This obscure feeling is what may make the void fruitful. The interpenetrating gyres must be regenerated. The best figure for such a pull of opposites, for such a synthesis of dialectical changes, for the suffering of the empirical world and the redemption of the formal ideal, for subjective power and knowledge and objective wisdom and love, is a religious version of Eros, a fusion of the sacred and profane.

From the erotics of conception to the erotics of death, the political terms of destiny are sexual in nature, and should move towards that Unity of Being and Unity of Culture which satisfies both an 'old man upon a winter's night' and 'a young girl in the indolence of her youth' ('On being asked for a War Poem'). If people in those positions are contented, so is the country. According to the first generation of Romantics (and their withdrawal from the public to the private world), Unity of Being ensures Unity of Culture. In order to achieve that level of satisfaction, the aesthetic figure of the beautiful, with its construction in the feminine, and the figure of the sublime, with its masculine construction, must be reconciled in a manner that leads to consummation rather than to dominance. The reconciliation is predicated on the idea that the absolute freedom of the sensible world of the beautiful can somehow find moral expression in the supersensible sphere of the sublime. Before Yeats (or Marcuse, Eagleton and Gadamer), Schiller also had wanted to free the sensible from the domination of reason that exists in Kant's system; he did not see too much aesthetic play in our sensible portion as potentially subversive, but rather as an avenue towards the union of the sensible and supersensible.[18] He writes:

> Without Beauty there would be lasting strife between our natural and our purely rational destiny. We should neglect our *humanity* in the endeavour to satisfy our *spirituality*, and, every moment prepared for a disruption from the world of sense, should constantly remain aliens in the sphere of action. [. . .] Only if Sublimity is wedded to Beauty, and our susceptibility for both equally developed, are we finished citizens of nature, without consequently being her slaves, and without forfeiting our citizenship in the world of intelligence.[19]

In his own winter's night, Yeats recognises that this wedding must be sought, although it continue to elude realisation; for it is a realisation whose fruitful void and luminous darkness he yearns for more than ever, as he endeavours to move from night to joy:

> . . . maybe what they say is true
> Of war and war's alarms,
> But O that I were young again
> And held her in my arms.

PART II

Ascending Breathless Starlit Air: The Beautiful and the Positive Sublime

5

ETERNAL BEAUTY: EARLY TRANSCENDENTAL AESTHETICS

Come near, that no more blinded by man's fate,
I find under the boughs of love and hate,
In all poor foolish things that live a day,
Eternal beauty wandering on her way.

Yeats, 'To the Rose upon the Rood of Time'

The ontological function of the beautiful is to bridge the chasm between the ideal and the real.

Hans-Georg Gadamer, *The Relevance of the Beautiful*

Yeats's first two volumes, *Crossways* (1889) and *The Rose* (1893), are hazy images of a transcendental realm that catches fire in the last two volumes of his poetry, as he approaches death. The first volumes hesitate before a world that is full of conflict. There is little faith in any possibility of the beautiful here on earth, although the poems are full of promise as to the hereafter. The closest they come to paradisal beauty is in the hope they hold of intimacy and love, as in 'The White Birds', or in the idealised solitude of the pastoral, as in 'The Lake Isle of Innisfree'. The best historical and/or personal reason for this inability is given in 'The Dedication to a Book of Stories selected from the Irish Novelists', a poem which presents the troubled history of Ireland and the rival claims of pagan and Christian forces as background to Yeats's and earlier writers' often thwarted attempts to describe these complexities in a unified artistic form. Most other poems in the early volumes, which will be dealt with in this chapter, give more mystical evidence for the unsettling of the Irish sense of the beautiful. In 'The Countess Cathleen in Paradise', for example, Yeats presents a transcendental, Kantian sacrifice as solution to the Irish Famine.[1] Yeats's mysticism is not merely an escape from the political, social and personal problems which beset him and the era in which he wrote. It is as much a part of the solution as are more material, political movements because it is a definition of what he believed should be Ireland's cultural idealism. The real challenge is to understand how early subjective, mystical ideas of eternal beauty formed the basis for later, more practical, objective and temporal ideas of the beautiful.

The mystical influence on Irish or Celtic sensibility and poetry has long been an established stereotype drawn on as far back as James Macpherson, used throughout the nineteenth century by Thomas Moore, James Clarence Mangan, William Allingham and Samuel Ferguson, and critiqued by Ernest Renan, Matthew Arnold and others. The use reached its height in the Irish literary revival when writers such as Yeats, Gregory, Shaw, and Wilde pitted Irish mysticism against English empiricism. There have been various recent political readings of Yeats's mysticism. Edward Said views Yeats's esoteric system as a 'super-terrestrial idea of revolution'.[2] In many respects he is justified in so doing; it is a very self-conscious flight from what Yeats felt were the necessary limitations of collectivised experience, of colonisation, from those limits which he aimed to transcend. Roy Foster has written with historical weightiness that the Anglo-Irish withdrew into mystical ideas not for revolutionary purposes but because they could accept neither the historical demise of their class nor the social responsibility the Ascendancy entailed.[3] Although his overall reading makes Yeats more incoherent and wilfully mystical than is here maintained, Seamus Deane writes insightfully of Yeats: '. . . his demand was always that Ireland should retain its culture by keeping awake its consciousness of metaphysical questions. By doing so it kept its own identity and its links with ancient European culture alive. As always with Yeats to be traditionalist in the modern world was to be revolutionary'.[4] Each of these readings undoubtedly reveals different aspects of Yeats's complicated, sometimes contradictory, attitudes to his personal and political dilemmas, but the nature of the formal resistance of his metaphysics must be explored if one is to understand Yeats, the revolutionary nationalist and Protestant apologist.

Mysticism in Ireland is a product of the effort to escape the harsh political realities of the day. Although mysticism can be retrogressively apolitical in its uncertainty and unpresentability, it nevertheless is an effort to bring both the unspeakable in history (and the Utopian hopes that sustained the populace throughout that history) to bear on the political future. Irish mysticism is an effort to confront those realities in a way which is perhaps no more mystical than Nietzsche's vitalism or Marx's emancipation of the senses. Irish mysticism could be seen as a response to the historical unavailability of the harmony (and *sensus communis*) of the beautiful. There are significant connections between mysticism and the dream of a unified culture that cannot be labelled mere escapism. The mystery of the beautiful unites the real to the ideal. Its ontological significance lies in its perhaps mostly unrealisable potential. In Adorno's words, 'Art's Utopia, the counterfactual yet-to-come is draped in black. It goes on being a recollection of the possible with a critical edge against the real . . . it is freedom which did not come to pass under the spell of necessity and which may well not come to pass ever at all'.[5] In the mysticism of the Irish Literary Renaissance, the subjective beginnings of the transcendence of historical necessity would at least nominally achieve objective value both in the 'Easter Rising' of 1916 and, inversely, in Yeats's rebellious apologia for liberal Protestantism many years later.

THE SUBJECTIVE AND OBJECTIVE VALUES OF TRANSCENDENCE

The mystical element of the Irish sense of the beautiful is what aligns it so closely (and so confusedly) to the sublime, especially to eighteenth-century ideas of the sublime as a highly elevated form of the beautiful. It is the restitution of harmony and order at the base of 'Art's Utopia'. This positive sublime is a vision of eternal beauty, a condition in which the moral, harmonising final ends of the beautiful are revealed in such a way as to unite a society in objective consensus. It is also the resolution of the struggle between subject and object. Denis Donoghue makes the point in *William Butler Yeats* that Yeats consistently refers to such a struggle, but he allows Yeats less respect for the object than is allowed here.[6] Earlier in the book, Donoghue follows Blackmur in naming Yeats an 'erotic' poet rather than a 'sacramental' one because he would possess the object rather than worship it in its separateness (or what is now called its 'otherness').[7] One might say that the early Yeats is sacramental while the elder Yeats is erotic, as Donoghue implies, but such oppositions always tend to interpenetrate. The sacred and profane are interconnected. In reality, Yeats is most sacramental and respectful of otherness when referring to the beautiful and positive sublime, as in 'The Wild Swans at Coole', and most erotic and possessive when referring to the negative sublime or terrible beauty, as in 'A Thought from Propertius'. His early work is very much a case of the former. As we near Yeats's later verse, we move towards a conflation of terms. Yeats never completely abandons his early aesthetic, but he does realise that the intrusion of negative forms of the sublime leads to a 'terrible beauty'. He also insists that the subjugation of this terror can lead to a more fertile form of the beautiful.

While the terrible, negative sublime discussed below (see chapter 9) often takes place when the terms of finality are planted into the unwilling subject's breast, whomever is the object, the positive sublime, on the other hand, is the peaceful accommodation of disparate categories of objective and subjective realities. It implies similar reconciliations in social and political fields. These two sublimities are ever in the process of conflict and resolution. Ironically enough, in Yeats's early work, so famously subjective, there is quite a strong strain of obedience to the primary, to what might be termed 'objective' reality in the religio-philosophical sense of the word. This is because, in his early work, he found morality and meaning in subjectivity transcending Nature. In his later work, he found amorality and meaning in acting according to Nature. We must be careful, for, inversely, his early emphasis on the amorality and indifference of the faeryworld is very Nietzschean, while his later conception of the soul in judgement, of the afterworld in which Cuchulain is comforted and feels duty-bound is very Kantian. The worlds of the sensible and supersensible are always mirror images – even in his own thought. This constant interpenetration is due to the fact that both 'object' and 'subject' worlds consist of some combination of God and Nature. Like Blake, the early Yeats assiduously eschewed Nature precisely because it is antithetical to God. The webs of such a construction are unnatural for they are not made in the external world. The obedience towards the 'object' world in Yeats's early work is therefore often, though not always, rather undefined. Its beauty is the impossibility of his own early project of immaculate self-transcendence.

The most obvious, maudlin example is 'The Ballad of Father Gilligan'. It is maudlin because there is no antithesis. A just man is justly rewarded when God takes 'pity on the least of things/Asleep upon a chair', by substituting for him at the bed of a dying man, by contravening Nature. The real tears of Magdalene (the root of the word maudlin), on the other hand, are the product of sin, and her reward is that given to penitence, as Yeats later realised when he wrote that all antithetical cruelty and deceit must end in primary surrender. Father Gilligan's failure would have been the true test of God's presence, had it been allowed to take place. In better early poems the quality of the deity's objective presence is questioned. In 'The Song of the Happy Shepherd', Yeats considers that subjective temporal reality is reduced to a word in the mind of God. The Biblical echoes of the 'flaming word' increase the revelatory objective quality of this statement and so highlight the doubt. The Indian poems ('Anashuya and Vijaya', 'The Indian upon God' and 'The Indian to His Love') of the volume Crossways (1889) further illustrate the idea that Yeats's early verse is highly primary, but they are rather hazy examples of mysticism. Yeats is a better poet when he attacks the competing form of objectivity, that is science or 'Grey Truth'. Instead of ignoring Nature for the love of the supersensible, or seeing Nature as evidence of a higher reality, science ignores the unseen for the purpose of studying how the natural world functions. It does so at the expense of more emotional and mysterious questions of why things function as they do, and thereby makes Nature a 'painted toy'. It robs the objective temporal world of its sacredness, and shows no concern for the thing-in-itself, the final end of the object, which is what connects the natural to the divine. There is an eventual change in his attitude. As Yeats later corrected the former early tendency away from Nature, and some of science's best means, he later judiciously used quasi-scientific methods (from seance to experiences of ecstasy) in order to prove the reality in Nature of a transcendent world – methods which alienated less questioning believers of the Theosophical Society who then asked him to resign.[8]

A large part of Yeats's early subjective dreaming is of a hypothetical sacred world, an elsewhere, the land of the imagination, of an objective final truth which transforms the order of the known and validates symbolic judgements of the beautiful. This movement reaches its height in the symbolism of *The Wind Among the Reeds* (1899). The symbol reconfers the sacredness of the object world. That the magic of the object relies heavily on subjective understanding in order to exist is not the contradiction it would seem to be. Yeats insists that understanding a symbol demands the right instinct. Yet there must be a balance between subject and object. For transformative power to reside in the subject and not in the object is a contradiction as potentially destructive as is Locke's emphasis on the objective world. The power of Yeats's middle and later poetry depends upon the balance he is able to strike between object and subject. In this, he is part of a larger tendency in Victorianism and Modernism to correct Romantic subjectivity. The balance is also seen in that interpenetration between life and poetry which he effected when he moved beyond symbolism. The symbolism of *The Wind Among the Reeds* (1899) reflects the loss of Yeats's virginally subjective dreaming, as well as the entrance into Nature which attended the loss of his virginity. From then onward, he understood that his previous ideas of the objective world were often too escapist, that knowledge of insight into God, or into the primary, came through antagonism, and was with antithetical knowledge of Nature. The chief exception to the early escapist mood was in his conception of the faeryworld, for that is where he projected his frustrated sexuality, as the relationship between Oisin and Niamh in *The Wanderings of Oisin* (1889) makes clear. His comment in 'The Circus Animals' Desertion' is telling: 'what cared I that set him on to ride/I, starved for the bosom of his faery bride?' The early Yeats establishes a fruitful tension in his conception of the imagination as the erotic zone between the mortal and immortal world, one that blossoms in his middle and later poetry.

Rather than being in accord with the Will, as Donoghue believes (apropos of Yeats's connection with Nietzsche), Yeats's conception of imagination is in the oppositional relationship between Will and Mask, between what is and what should be. The imagination takes its life from the Mask as much as from the Will. Donoghue feels that imagination for Yeats takes place in the struggle towards a goal and not in the goal itself; imagination must therefore be equated with the Will, as being unimaginable the Mask and God are the limit or defeat of the imagination.[9] Yeats, however, poeticises in 'A Dialogue of Self and Soul' that the limits of the imagination are the beginning of eternal beauty, of positive sublimity. Without the Mask's image of such beauty, the Will is purely mechanical and scientific.[10] Donoghue admits this relationship between the morality of Mask and the desire of Will when he writes that 'the distinction [between Will and the Mask, which is "at home in trance, reverie, and its attendant rhythms", as he writes on the same page] persists in Yeats's later poetry, but it is greatly modified'.[11] He does not directly explain what the modification entails. The defeat of the imagination is one of the victories in defeat beloved by Yeats; as such, defeat is the final vindication of the imagination. It is imagination's *raison d'être*. The positive sublime is the end of subjective imagination and the beginning of objective, final beauty. Donoghue is certainly right when he states that God to Yeats is Death. Yeats describes God in 'A Dialogue of Self and Soul' as that 'quarter where all thought is done'; however, if the 15th phase (the most completely subjective or antithetical phase, characterised by pulchritude), and the 1st phase (the completely primary objective phase, characterised by sapience) are both supernatural, that is life-negating, impossible for mortal existence, and if all historical progression is moved by their gyring interrelationship, then any sublime moment of insight not only unites beauty and wisdom but must defy death, even if only momentarily, returning to the conflict half-forgetful. Death then becomes a defeat of imagination that nevertheless realises the latent potential of the imagination's insights. Death is imagination's figure for the finality of the objective world, a finality that plays at the margins of consciousness and without which the Will would be a mere collator. It is not coincidental that Yeats, the Symbolist poet of the mysterious object, writes poems full of death-longing, as if the erotic death-dealing spell of the object were all-powerful.

In his earlier works, Yeats is torn between the subjective and the objective world. Many poems are explorations of the pull of these dual realities. 'The Stolen Child' ends with a eulogy to the temporal world which the child leaves behind on his way to the land of the faeries. In this poem, the mortal danger and sublime freedom of the faery world (connecting Death, God and eternal beauty) blends extraordinarily with the security and serenity of the pastoral setting (of the beautiful) left behind by the child. Even though Yeats sees freedom as superior to security, he knows that their needs must be balanced. The potential for sublimity and beauty is in both worlds: the world of Death and God and that of Life and Nature. The poem is ambiguous; it hesitates between the antithetical and primary, the subjective and objective, moving in the hazy truth of the belief that dreams are as close as we get to reality.[12]

The famous ambivalence of the later Yeats has its early precedents. In 'To the Rose upon the Rood of Time', for instance, Yeats wavers between longing to be subsumed in eternal beauty and deep appreciation for the world of frustrated desires, for the frustration of the beautiful, for the lack of harmony, and the struggle towards peace. The poem contains a realisation that we desire the rose that would destroy us, just as the imagination imagines its own defeat. Such an end, however, is the verification of desire and imagination. Our desire for the rose helps us find, in mortal things that pass, 'Eternal beauty wandering on her way'. A vision of immortal beauty is predicated on the danger of destruction, although it finds sublimity and fulfilment not in destruction, but in the resulting revelation of its eternal, teleological form – the reason for which it came into being and the reason for which it had to die. Shakespeare had already meditated on the idea: 'The summer's flower is to the summer sweet,/Though to itself it only live and die' (Sonnet 94). In short, the rose is not sublime; it is beautiful. The eternal beauty that it quite literally represents to summer, however, is sublime in the highest sense, the noble, the magnificent, the splendid, and the lofty.

The idea of the rose, the rose-breath, sends the poet into transport; nonetheless, as is made clear in 'To Ireland in the Coming Times', the vision of beauty must remain partial, for complete ecstasis, or disorientation from the self, means the death of consciousness itself. Yeats was beginning to comprehend that art must remain this side of the unseen before it can make any meaningful reference to a transcendental signifier. The partial wisdom of a moment of illumination is a way of establishing such a balance, for it tragically hovers, with Kierkegaardian irony, between the 'is' of the temporal world and the 'ought' of the eternal. It can offer no ultimate form of solace; hence the term: 'tragic ecstasy'. In this regard, the coming times present a quandary:

> And we, our singing and our love,
> What measurer Time has lit above,
> And all benighted things that go
> About my table to and fro,
> Are passing on to where may be,
> In truth's consuming ecstasy,
> No place for love and dream at all;
> For God goes by with white footfall.

This fear of annihilation in union with God runs through Yeats's corpus. Physical death is the death of poetry and imagination, even if paradoxically the idea of death is their basis for being. At some point the wish for transcendence has to be resisted; for what is the spiritual life without some form of sensual embodiment? Yeats's later philosophy of religion would endeavour to reconcile these contrary movements. Moments of vision are essential to his perception of being, as in these moments the spirit finds its most physical manifestation. These epiphanies link to form the basis for our eternal self. In *A Vision*, Yeats writes that our Mask, our eternal self is our 'object of desire or idea of the good' and it is shaped out of our 'memory of exaltation',[13] of those passionate moments in our life in which we establish our deepest convictions, in which we have seen '[e]ternal beauty wandering on her way' ('To the Rose upon the Rood of Time').

As he grows older, Yeats sees that the ability to see eternal beauty is the result of engagement and not merely of gestures towards the world of forms. This is the result of an effort to invest the objective world with a significance that is more than symbolic. Images of human, animal or of the landscape begin to be discussed both in terms of their operations, of their interactions, of the way in which they work, and in the terms of any essential quality they might connote. Yeats's imagination is introducing the world of the Mask to that of the Will, introducing the ideal to the real. Yeats defines the Mask as our 'object of desire or idea of the good' and the Will as that faculty which 'knows how things are done, how windows are open and shut, how roads are crossed, everything that we call utility'.[14] The introduction of Mask to Will is most manifest in the volume entitled *Responsibilities* (1914). Yet, as always, the process towards a working construction of the beautiful is more gradual than at first it seems. It does not just suddenly appear in *Responsibilities* (1914).

One need only look at its most potent manifestation in 'The Secret Rose' in order to see how the mystical quality of the earliest verse prepares the way for the concept of the beautiful in 'Adam's Curse', which is from the volume *In the Seven Woods* (1904). 'The Secret Rose' is an imagined union of object and subject – a rose that is both far-off and secret. It exists in the Holy Sepulchre beyond the ends of knowledge and existence. It has that objective finality which is 'an elimination of the individual intellect and a discovery of the moral life',[15] as Yeats describes the completely objective phase 1 in *A Vision*; yet, the rose is mysterious. Yeats recites a litany of heroes and heroines of his early poems: the Magi, Conchobar, Cuchulain and Fand, Caoilte and Fergus. All of them have liminal experiences that make them worshippers of the Rose, and worshippers of conflicting values. Though they are all ultimately frustrated, they have the 'nobility of defeated things' which Yeats so deeply admired.

Cuchulain, the man of action, loses 'Emer for a kiss', and Fergus, the man of contemplation, surrenders his crown so that he can find peace and wisdom in dreaming. Fergus finds no ultimate wisdom or peace and Cuchulain finds no satisfaction, but the gestures they have made are illuminating in themselves. Through such illumination, they see the Rose in its Holy Sepulchre. They are like the nameless man at the end of the poem who gives up all he has earned for the sake of a woman so beautiful that 'men threshed corn at midnight by a tress/A little stolen tress.' Whether they seek it through action or contemplation, the light of the world nevertheless fades as they reach their bright ideal.

Yeats understands that neither action nor contemplation can reach fulfilment. Their gestures, however, become worthy of a place on the petals of the Rose. They become like one of the immortal moods; successful only in the attempt and not in the completion. Yeats discovers such immortal moods in 'mortal desires, an undecaying hope in our trivial ambitions, a divine love in sexual passion'.[16] At the time of composition of the poem, he believes that any attempt to create such beauty is doomed to failure; nevertheless, the closing image of the men working by the light of the tress, by the light of the ideal, reveals a kinship with later, more developed images of the relationship between the beautiful and the harmonious in society. The men find a purpose in their midnight work. This image of work resembles Yeats's later one of the Byzantine artisan whose craft possessed Unity of Being and Culture; the former is as strangely emblematic of the beautiful as anything in Yeats's writing. The very purposiveness of the labour is unusual in Yeats's early verse, however. Most early images of beauty are closer to the apocalyptic ending of 'The Secret Rose'.

Yeats never entirely relinquishes the idea of apocalypse, but he does greatly alter it by finding a specific place in his historical cosmology: the catastrophic movement of the historical sublime. The alteration is strongly connected to his idea of reincarnation. Once Yeats has established a visionary system which in some way interconnected life and death (a reconciliation not without periods of enormous conflict), his sense of apocalypse together with his idea of beauty – the 'rough beast' of 'The Second Coming', the 'terrible beauty' of 'Easter, 1916' – becomes a part of history as it unfolds, rather than just the end of history as we know it. Death is no longer the end of life's failure and the achievement of our dreams and desires; it is now a place from which dreams of beauty could effect historical movement and the lives of individuals in a systematic way. A quotation from *Per Amica Silentia Lunae* bears this out:[17] 'The dead living in their memories are, I am persuaded, the source of all that we call instinct, and it is their love and their desire, all unknowing, that make us drive beyond our reason, or in defiance of our interest it may be'.[18] Instinct connects us to the unseen world in a way that no one can fathom. In the same passage, Yeats uses a bird's nest to prove God's existence by design, an idea he elaborates in *A Vision*.[19] The nest in question is placed on a church in order to emphasise the connection.

Similarly, the world of 'The Soul in Judgment' in *A Vision* is the *modus operandi* of existence, and its Alpha and Omega. Our lives are but a series of exaltations, of passions whose source in the spirit world and whose temporal and eternal meanings shall be revealed when the soul is judged. History can also be understood in a similar fashion. This spiralling of time and space through various crises to an ultimate meaning is the architectonic of Yeats's vast design. The first lines of 'The Secret Rose' contain this design in embryonic form:

> Far-off, most secret, and inviolate Rose,
> Enfold me in my hour of hours; where those
> Who sought thee in the Holy Sepulchre,
> Or in the wine-vat, dwell beyond the stir
> And tumult of defeated dreams; and deep
> Among pale eyelids, heavy with the sleep
> Men have named beauty.

In the story 'Rosa Alchemica', Yeats writes of a 'Death which is Beauty herself'.[20] Here, we also see an image of beauty among supersensible, potential moral truths (giving moral sanction to defeated dreams) that Kant normally associates with sublimity. This image is found within both Romantic and mystical traditions. Eternal beauty is the focus of profane workaday desire and of poetic or sacred desire. It is one of the shaping forces of society.

It is often noted of Yeats's poetic development that the forms of beauty or society (they are contingent terms) are not cogently established until after the volume *The Wind Among the Reeds* (1899). They do not take definite shape until the watershed of the Maud Gonne crises – her refusals of his proposals of marriage and her marriage to MacBride – and the end of the 1890s and the death of its writers. Beauty, which had been sought among disembodied eternal forms, is now sought in distinctly embodied (and therefore temporal) forms. 'Adam's Curse' is a poem that shows Yeats's keen awareness of this poetic fall into time and of the pivotal quality of this period in his life. It presents an image of beauty in both its temporal and eternal conditions.

The volume *In the Seven Woods* (1904), which contains 'Adam's Curse', is a meditation on the relationship between these two types of beauty. Eternal beauty descends into its temporal form to be the ever-present supplement. Beauty now is 'kinder', as Yeats writes in 'The

Arrow', but he laments that the old is 'out of season'. The beauty of faeryland has now begun its transformation into the Yeatsian conception of the beautiful which is best manifested at Coole Park. With these transformations beauty becomes more substantial, more quotidian; it is increasingly defined in outward form. Yeats has learned to accommodate history and society in his quest for permanence and the ideal, but he never ceases to put forth the early transcendental, eternal and disembodied type of beauty as spirit of the new temporal embodied form. Beside Coole Park and houses like it, and alongside the conversations about poetry in 'Adam's Curse', there still is the eternal beauty that is found in death, the 'grave ecstasy' of the long narrative poem *The Shadowy Waters* (1906) – begun in 1894 and originally included in the volume *In the Seven Woods* (1904) – where he writes:

> Now the secret's out;
> For it is love that I am seeking for,
> But of a beautiful, unheard-of kind
> That is not in the world. (lines 140–3)

Eternal beauty also exists in the happy townland of the eponymous poem. It is a place whose edenic image of a beautiful society stands in contrast to our own.

It is now a cliché to point out that as Yeats begins to see the necessity and to experience the pleasure of a more substantial type of beauty (both on an artistic and sexual plane), he also reinterpreted the Platonic relationship between ideal forms and their reflections. In terms of the recognition of the temporal forms of beauty, he begins to direct his attention to the reasons for the discrepancy between the ideal and the real. The transformation begins in the 'Seven Woods' of Lady Gregory's Coole Park estate. The terrible exacting beauty of faeryland, where queens have eyes 'blue as ice' ('The Happy Townland') now makes its presence felt in Lady Gregory's aristocratic ideal of both selfless service and commanding authority. In this realm, Yeats sees that art can finally become a vision of beauty which for all its corporeality still competes with the most transcendental type. Have not his immortals always longed for the powerful emotions of the temporal world? He sees that his vision of beauty can move beyond the 1890s vision of impossible beauty, which had only wakened 'dissipation and despair' (as Yeats later writes of Johnson and Dowson in 'Ego Dominus Tuus'). Walking through the 'Seven Woods', he turns to the reasons for which any given society is not an image of the beautiful, and those reasons for which he himself is so unhappy in order to find a solution. The image of a society without leadership, with no feeling for tradition, whether it be the commonness on the throne of England or the excavation of Tara, the seat of the high

kings of Ireland, is contrasted implicitly with the authority of Coole Park.
It also finds a personal reflection in Yeats's Coleridgean attempt to master
himself, to put away the 'unavailing cries . . . That empty the heart'.
Instead of endeavouring merely to be happy, for happiness in the fallen
world means no more than hanging 'paper flowers from post to post',
Yeats must find a way to heal his divided self. He must learn to labour 'in
ecstasy' ('Friends') for in the fallen world all 'must labour to be beautiful'.

MAUD GONNE AND THE BEAUTIFUL

'Adam's Curse' is a meditation on why society is hostile or at least ambivalent to the beauties of poetry. Intimately connected to his idea of the
beautiful, Maud Gonne is now put in temporal as well as mythological
terms. Like Yeats, she is ageing. There is an intricate connection in this
volume between the eternal beauty which Gonne in her youth embodies
and that temporal one which, upon growing old, she comes to represent.
Her youthful beauty is of a terrible aspect that might 'call up a new age',
as Yeats writes in 'Old Memory'. It is that beauty of 'No Second Troy'
which had changed the formation of the classical world, that is, Helen and
the Trojan War, and could do so again in the person of Gonne. This beauty
is connected to violence, to the negative sublime, from the very moment
when Yeats first met her and she praised the excitement of violence.[21] The
later type is generally kinder, and yet, her beauty had always possessed both
qualities: the quality that stirs a crowd to violent, revolutionary change and
that quality that moves one towards peace and unity. Being the unrequited
lover that he was, Yeats at first could only see the violence of her beauty.
Her falling into time, her growing old, made her subject to time's changes
as well. Though Yeats later writes more extensively about her dual relationship to the people – in 'The People' and 'His Phoenix' from *The Wild Swans
at Coole* (1919) – even his early verse shows an understanding of how
defining her public and private roles had helped him to define his own.
He writes in 'The Folly of Being Comforted' that, though she is getting
old, 'The fire that stirs about her, when she stirs,/Burns but more clearly.'
Her beauty has the power of the empyrean to purge as well as to burn.
Gonne's beauty then can unite (in positive sublimity) as well as divide (in
negative sublimity); for she is 'lofty, fierce and kind' ('Old Memory') – three
terms which combine positive (lofty) and negative (fierce) sublimity and the
beautiful (kind). The beauty of 'Adam's Curse', so connected to Gonne, is
meant to harmonise society, to repair the divisiveness of the Fall.

The poem begins with the fall into time which is so characteristic of
this volume. It then proceeds to discuss the difficulties of composition in
terms of feminine and/or domestic chores, whose completion is the basis

of any working social fulfilment of the beautiful. In 'Meditations in Time of Civil War' from the volume *The Tower* (1928), the symbolic fountain seems to function without labour, as though it flowed from paradise to symbolise the soul. This present poem is the poem of the curse, however. The confluence of domestic labour and the beautiful is not only reminiscent of the Fall and Adam's curse but of the division of labour between body and soul and that between the classes. A union of these is the paradise of poetry, although the society of 'bankers, schoolmasters and clergymen' does not appreciate the ability of poetry to effect it through a combination of tedious labour and aesthetic richness. The five appearances of the word beautiful are a signature of Paradise, a signature, however, which bears the strain of labour's expiation. Beauty's redemptive power is purely mimetic. It mirrors a prelapsarian world, but its achievement requires all the cost of the Fall. It bears great promise and exacts great cost.

The positive side of Gonne's beauty is central to the poem, as it is the basis of the beautiful in society. It is the beauty that commands her audience, that allies the listeners to some public good. Her ability to escape abstraction when speaking is what made her image of the beautiful so powerful to Yeats. She helped the audience escape the mechanical philosophy of the eighteenth century. Her beauty suggested the escape of 'joy and freedom'.[22] Oratory was still of enormous importance in Ireland, whose culture readily identified with voice and presence. To Yeats, Maud Gonne's 'body thought' to borrow a phrase from Donne.[23]

The physical expression of the beautiful in an age of abstraction is found in exile, in an 'outlawed solitude' that the later Yeats associates with the Anglo-Irish, and which has additional applications.[24] The figure of Gonne that Yeats gives us is little different from that which he gives of the poet in the late poem entitled 'The Choice'. The poet of the beautiful in a culture which is hostile to beauty rages in the dark. The artist in a more amenable culture such as Byzantium, on the other hand, finds that the culture complements his artistry. The violence of beauty's separation and of all satanic self-creation finds unifying primary expression in the Byzantine motif of worship. In Whitaker's phrase, the latter tends towards 'a subjective yet transcendental and corporate ideal',[25] thereby fusing the primary (the corporate) and the antithetical (the subjective) and all their attendant and opposing qualities of love and violence, submission and rebellion, compassion and power. It has always been Yeats's aim to find one action that vents both the primary and antithetical needs. There is no choice between a heavenly mansion and raging in the dark; the heavenly mansion has its semblance in the earthly mansion which the artist inhabits and makes beautiful. The end of 'Adam's Curse' is full of nostalgia for its home in such a mansion, for the culture of the beautiful.

As has often been remarked, the style of the last two stanzas is a return to his former style, one which is full of transcendent beauty and which eschews the quotidian; it is a return to the belief that all knowledge and discipline are secret and, in order to be discovered, require a vision which is a kind of death. This makes perfect sense within the context of the poem, however; the last two stanzas are nostalgic for the time in which the beautiful old books were more than just an idle trade. The style is decorated with the high courtesy of that age. The borders of reality are shifting in a way that Yeats the magician thought they must; the sky is the colour of the sea, blue-green. The moon, rising out of Renaissance Neo-Platonic lore, as so much of Yeats's poetry does, is a picture of the line between the immutable and the mutable, both above time and affected by its changes.[26] It is a ruin, a shell of the sea whose tides it controls, and like a shell it contains the sounds and secrets of the sea. It is an image of the beautiful which Yeats the burgeoning poet of modernity can no longer present. Its purple tone is like Burke's paean to the Queen of France in *Reflections on the Revolution in France*, although for Yeats the glory of Europe is not extinguished forever; it is only out of phase, awaiting the next dispensation which Gonne in her terrible Helen-like beauty represents as powerfully as the Dauphiness represents the Age of Chivalry. The purpose of terrible beauty, like Delacroix's female personification of liberty climbing over the front lines, is to recreate the society in which lovers sigh and quote with learned looks, whose image the beautiful mild woman has conjured. Therein lies an obvious political complexity which, like his paradoxical love of both individual freedom and aristocratic sovereignty, will become a source of poetic meditation for Yeats.

'Adam's Curse' bids farewell to the early verse in a way that seems aware both of what the future will bring and of what the past has brought. The old high beautiful way of love will give way to the negative sublimity of 'No Second Troy' in the next volume *The Green Helmet and Other Poems* (1910). Increasingly, Yeats hopes for a new type of beauty, one to re-establish an aesthetic of the beautiful. He places his hope in some violent shift of the gyres, in the terrible sublime of historical change that is discussed in the next section (a gentle turn, such as the birth of Christ, no longer being possible). The positive sublime, the entry of the beautiful into the supersensible, must come after terror. To some degree, Yeats's middle and later poetry can be delineated along these lines. First comes the beautiful of *The Wild Swans at Coole* (1919), then the negative sublime of *Michael Robartes and the Dancer* (1921) and *The Tower* (1928), and finally, the third stage, the positive sublime of *The Winding Stair* (1933). The last volumes combine the two categories in a way that accords well with Yeats's old age and his sense of approaching death. Yet, before he separates his volumes along the lines suggested above, and must confront death's sublimity, Yeats is forced to reckon how the relationship between eternal and temporal beauty, God, the individual and society, actually works.

6

THE LABOUR TO BE BEAUTIFUL: CONSTRUCTING AN AESTHETIC

> . . . strength that could unbind
> What none can understand,
> What none can have and thrive,
> Youth's dreamy load, till she
> So changed me that I live
> Labouring in ecstasy.
>
> Yeats, 'Friends'

The *cultivation* of the fives senses is the work of all previous history. *Sense* which is a prisoner of crude practical need has only a *restricted* sense [. . .]. A society that is *fully developed* produces man in all the richness of his being, the *rich* man who is *profoundly and abundantly endowed with all the senses*, as its constant reality.

Karl Marx, *Economic and Philosophical Manuscripts*

In *The Green Helmet and Other Poems* (1910) and *Responsibilities* (1914), which are the intermediary volumes between *In the Seven Woods* (1904) and *The Wild Swans at Coole* (1919), Yeats formulates the relationship between eternal and temporal beauty, the individual and society, in more explicitly empirical detail. He turns on society, its classes, and himself in order to ascertain how both have failed in their responsibilities to God and to eternal beauty, to 'the Divine Ideas in their unity'.[1] *The Green Helmet* (1910) is an extension of the pivotal *In the Seven Woods* (1904). Death has still its former apocalyptic splendour, but now the poetry is beginning to lose some of its mystical quality. Most importantly, in this volume, the poem 'No Second Troy' is the first presentation of how acts of violence transform society, which is an idea that is not fully developed until *Michael Robartes and the Dancer* (1921) and *The Tower* (1928). More germane to this discussion of the beautiful and positive sublime are the poems concerning society's inability to find Unity of Culture. Yeats is turning to satires, as some of the poems and the play of the volume's title, *The Green Helmet* (1910), illustrate. Without the heroic, there is only the mock-heroic. He nevertheless continues to delineate what he believes is the heroic and the marvellous in poetry. He looks to the feminine for his construction of a living aesthetic, for some reflection of the transcendent, and examines how this reflection is distorted. Eternal beauty comes to us in a dream, from the 'flowing changing world that the heart longs for', as he writes in *The Shadowy Waters* (1906), a long nearly contemporaneous dramatic poem. Our task in life is to find a suitable form of existence to reflect that world. Yeats's theory of our relationship with the Mask, here in embryonic form, consists of our striving towards an often self-made image of what we should be. It is based on the premise that we enact this relationship between what is and what should be in order to escape the infinite pain of self-realisation. Yet it also is a source of that pain, as poems in this volume illustrate.

One must not overemphasise Yeats's commitment to transcendental Kantian values to the exclusion of all others. For within his work is a constantly increasing recognition of the value of the temporal and empirical: they are the basis for literature and perhaps the mundane sum of existence, as resounds in 'King and No King':

> . . . how shall I know
> That in the blinding light beyond the grave
> We'll find so good a thing as that we have lost?
> The hourly kindness, the day's common speech,
> The habitual content of each with each
> When neither soul nor body has been crossed.

It is a vein running through his work and is investigated thoroughly in the next volume entitled *Responsibilities* (1914) and throughout the rest of *The Green Helmet* (1910) volume. Yeats believes habitual content and hourly kindness are what a society and a relationship should seek, regardless of the eternal significance. The journey there, however, requires the discipline of beauty. This difficulty makes most people avoid beauty's discipline. The haughty text of Gonne's beauty, which moves Yeats, earns only 'slander' and 'ingratitude' ('Against Unworthy Praise'). This slander and ingratitude are dealt with on two levels in Yeats's work. There is the contrasting culture that fosters fine aesthetics (the 'high laughter, loveliness and ease' of the beautiful in 'Upon a House Shaken by the Land Agitation'), and another closely allied endeavour to discover the realm of the positive sublime, to look into the majesty of the sun that 'shuts the burning eye' ('These are the Clouds'). It is with this ideal in mind that Yeats develops his aesthetics of class.

THE AESTHETICS OF CLASS

Yeats believes that society must act as a conduit to the experience of the beautiful and the sublime and that its failure to achieve this is due to the attitude of the three classes. The upper class has failed to set an example, the middle class has failed its cultural role because it insists on creating a society that is founded on economics alone, while, for the poor, the exigencies of poverty impede aesthetic experience. These, of course, are the negative qualities, and if the middle class only rarely acts positively in Yeats's rendering, the poor and the rich, being above and below caring about economics, sometimes do. As for many who have come before him, at the base of Yeats's aesthetic is a disregard for utilitarian values. This is not to say that there is a lack of desire. The aesthetic is always balanced by the right desire, the right passion. Economically, this means not trying to be popular and not worrying about getting on. Transcendence can appear as a false claim to individual distinction, in that only the rich can appreciate sublime scenery when, in truth, it is merely a result of circumstance – only they can afford to cultivate it. It can be an assertion of property rights in collective, socially induced experience. Only few can experience beauty and sublimity, so it is their economic prerogative to take those costly journeys through sublime and beautiful scenery, while others like Wordsworth's solitary reaper stay at home and tend the fields. It is as if the aesthetics of the sublime and the beautiful were restricted to those beings who are at or near the top of The Great Chain of Being. To an extent this is true of Yeats, and leads him to such windy Great-Chain-of-Being rhetoric as 'sweet laughing eagle thoughts' and such class disdain as the metonymy of 'mean roof-trees' for poor cottages. For Yeats, the aristocratic emphasis is nevertheless as much on being as it is on inheritance. People can achieve nobility regardless of their birth or class standing.

Experience of the sublime and the beautiful is open to all. Yeats's belief is that 'There cannot be, confusion of our sound forgot,/A single soul that lacks a sweet crystalline cry' ('Paudeen'). Even though he often takes a sharply aristocratic stance, he does conclude that economics is the problem because it creates a false hierarchy. People are prevented from experiencing that 'sweet crystalline cry' which is their birthright. If economics is the problem, the aesthetic experience is the answer, for a society founded on economics increases the division between Will and Mask, between what is and what ought to be, and this in turn makes the aesthetic experience more difficult to achieve, as that which the aesthetic seeks to harmonise is in further disarray. The sublime experience should liberate the oppressed senses and reveal to them the universality of the soul. The difficulty that the senses encounter in a sublime experience becomes empirical testimony to a nonsensory world which, although denied, is continuous with it. The sensible becomes living witness to the supersensible.

Yeats's poems 'Upon a House Shaken by the Land Agitation', 'These are the Clouds' and 'At Galway Races' illustrate how the relationship between the sensible and the supersensible functions in his social theory of the sublime. In the first poem, the phrase which follows the overly rhetorical 'sweet laughing eagle thoughts' demonstrates how the non-sensory world exists next to the empirical, for 'wings have memory of wings'. The point of the poem is that if we completely destroy the 'gifts that govern men', the image of the beautiful and of written speech, which is wrought of 'high laughter, loveliness and ease' merely because they have been badly employed, then we spite only ourselves. In this point he follows Burke, although this idea is also at the heart of attempts to aestheticise politics, and reveals that the beauty which attended aristocracy, or the sublimity attendant upon fascism, has had very valuable stakes in the consciousness of the nineteenth- and twentieth-century world. To be able to maintain aesthetic qualities while divorcing oneself from the worst attitudes of hierarchical government, or government by force, is to strike a most difficult but highly desirable balance; for however imperial the activity of the imagination might be its highest goal remains Utopian. 'At the Abbey Theatre' is an instance of such balance. Yeats writes with some envy (as he would later of Maud Gonne in 'Her People' and 'His Phoenix') of Douglas Hyde's ability to speak of lofty and common things without becoming disdainful, vulgar or mocking, although perhaps he does so with some condescension at his easy populism. The relationship between aesthetics and class in 'Upon a House Shaken by Land Agitation' and 'At the Abbey Theatre' is repeated in the following poems.

The lidless eye that loves the sun, that appreciates the sublime, in 'Upon a House Shaken by the Land Agitation', experiences the sun's sublimity in 'These are the Clouds', but it is threatened by class discord. Yeats again attacks what he sees as the vindictive violence of those who do not value the spirit of grandeur: '[t]he weak lay hand on what the strong has done'. They too have the capacity for aesthetic appreciation, although they have not been enabled by social circumstances to explore it, and so destroy the very beauty of which they feel they have been cheated. Ironically enough, the vindictive destructiveness is itself of a sublime character, of terrible sublimity (in many ways as 'false' a sublime for Yeats as was mob violence for Burke), because it attacks the transcendent quality of the aesthetic experience, and reminds one of its vulnerable human basis. In spite of the ill effect mob rule might have, Yeats insists that the sublime view remains untouched, even though the future and one's progeny are affected: 'Although it be for children that you sigh'. Everyone possesses the capacity for aesthetic experience. The pitiless determining factor, regardless of class, is whether one can achieve and appreciate greatness, and here even one's offspring are in question. The image of the sun's sublimity is essential not only for its regal connotations but also because its power is symbolic on a psychological level. Burke argues that 'Mere light is too common a thing to make a strong impression on the mind, and without a strong impression nothing can be sublime. But such a light as that of the sun, immediately exerted on the eye, as it overpowers the sense, is a very great idea'.[2] In a passage of great relevance to Yeats's political philosophy, Burke had concluded that 'extremes operate equally in favour of the sublime, which in all things abhors mediocrity'. This abhorrence of mediocrity is the reason Yeats determines that social equality and intellectual freedom are incompatible: to him the doctrine does not register the hierarchy of skills – and yet his own idea of the beautiful shows that this cannot be so simply put.

The beautiful is associated with the painless labouring of the prelapsarian world of Coole Park: 'Before the merchant and the clerk/Breathed on the world with timid breath'. Lady Gregory is the one who taught Yeats to labour in ecstasy, to feel blessed rather than cursed in the process of creation. The ability to think as though it were an action is an edenic notion for Yeats. It also crosses class barriers. 'At Galway Races' illustrates that the greatest enemy to such passionate enjoyment is the timid, corporate mentality. Here, the rider becomes the embodiment of beauty and passion that unifies the crowd: 'There where the course is/Delight makes all of the one mind'. This ability existed before the fall of Newton's apple, of Lockean epistemology, when overemphasis of the external world made the will overly self-effacing (here of course Yeats, like the Romantics, somewhat simplistically ignores the active side of Locke's philosophy).[3] Still, Yeats has hope that this embodiment of beauty will not become passive, even when confronted with a relentlessly mechanical economic system:

> Sing on: somewhere at some new moon,
> We'll learn that sleeping is not death,
> Hearing the whole earth change its tune,
> Its flesh being wild, and it again
> Crying aloud as the racecourse is,
> And we find hearteners among men
> That ride upon horses.

Yeats weighs mortal existence against immortality and sees that for all its solidity, extension, and volume the balance between the subject and object world swings under the greater weight of the soul and the pressure of the unseen, proving 'that sleeping is not death.' He does this wildly, however, always aware that it might not be true.

In *Responsibilities* (1914) and other writings of the time, all these themes are examined in even greater clarity and detail. The relationship between the eternal and the temporal world, the supersensible and the sensible, is examined at its most painful pressure point: the value of earthly love in the face of its fated subsumption (and possible anonymity and unimportance) by the omnipotent Godhead, or worse in absolute annihilation. Yeats also examines the failures of the classes to live up to the goal of aesthetic experience. The relationship between eternal and temporal experience again provides the frame; the sensibility of each class is constructed on the idea of the supersensible. One epigraph to the volume which reads 'in dreams begin responsibilities' sets the tone for the volume's discussion of the relationship between the eternal and the temporal, the general and the particular, the *a priori* and the *a posteriori,* the ideal and the real.

The introductory lines present all of these central ideas. Yeats stakes his being in the *Lebenswelt* or life-world of his forebears. It is a temporal display of the many qualities his ancestors embody. To find his responsibilities, Yeats looks towards the metanarrative dream which his ancestral life has become, and for the continuance of which he feels inadequate. He has 'fallen from himself' as did Khoung-fou-tseu in the second epigraph to the volume. The Chinese philosopher feels inadequate because he cannot see the Prince of Chang in his dreams. Yeats feels that 'for a barren passion's sake' (his love for Maud Gonne) he has nothing to prove himself worthy of his ancestry of courage and action, of whom he haughtily states there have never been any shopkeepers. Yeats's sublime finds this disdainful, almost anti-social expression in order to protect his aesthetic of the beautiful and its vulnerable social expression of paradisal harmony.

The aesthetics of the eighteenth and early nineteenth century, especially for the Romantics, is an attempt to counteract the mechanising influence, the commodification, of the industrial revolution. Yeats's special awareness of his ancestry is an attempt to come down on the aesthetic side of the contest between the orderliness and sterility of bourgeois commodification and any potentially disruptive, Romantic aesthetic experience. He writes as a family credo: 'Only the wasteful virtues earn the sun'. The idea of a 'wasteful virtue' underlies Yeats's conception of society throughout the volume and it is one of the many connections between the eternal and temporal realities. The endeavour to be frugal is a hopeless and even enervating attempt to cheat death; wastefulness is the natural temper of the immortals as they have no need to conserve, and it strengthens any who can achieve it. To be a wasteful mortal then is to transcend mortality and thereby to earn the healing illusion of Nietzsche's immortal Apollonian world. It is also a quality that is notably aristocratic in character, like the lidless eye which looks upon the sun. This ability, akin to the 'disinterestedness' of many definitions of 'true' aesthetic appreciation, particularly Kant's, is at the heart of Yeats's idea of aristocracy.

In 'To a Wealthy Man who promised a Second Subscription to the Dublin Municipal Gallery if it were proved the People wanted Pictures', Yeats criticises a ruling member of society for losing this 'disinterestedness', for displaying a frugality and populism that cares more for what others think than for setting a standard of culture and behaviour which others should follow. He remarks how the aristocracy of Urbino were '[i]ndifferent how the rancour ran'. Sublime behaviour in the aristocracy (the standard-setting recklessness and yet specific discipline of Castiglione's idea of *sprezzatura*) redefines the aesthetic of beauty in the culture as a whole. Yeats rebukes the wealthy man for not earning the sun, for not living up to his sublime role as God-like maker of aesthetics, for letting an unstructured and untutored class decide what would suit the feminine domain of culture when such a decision must be dictated by beauty. Yeats, however, shows in the poem 'Paudeen' that the problem with this notion of *noblesse oblige* is that we (Yeats included) are the mob of Paudeens, and yet we, the middle class, also have epiphanies or sublime moments which are not necessarily dependent on others. He does allow some small room for this individual complexity in 'To a Wealthy Man'. The morality attendant on the experience of the sublime is dealt with directly. Goodness is found in any heart's exultance; however, he nearly makes this reading impossible when he speaks of the breed of eagles in the last line. His obsession with countering Locke's dismissal of any innate value forces him, in this instance, nearly to contradict himself. For surely he would have the Duke set an outward standard of culture to be learned, or what is the point of his example? His concept of breeding, however, spans the divide between Nature and nurture and therefore makes for some confusion.

Sublime indifference or aristocratic hauteur in Yeats's system is very similar to Burke's sublime masculine force that protects the feminine domain of beauty. Nevertheless, it must draw its taste for beauty from the type of maternal authority that Yeats associates with Lady Gregory, and Burke with the Dauphiness of France. If Coole Park is an image of Renaissance Urbino, then Lady Gregory, for Yeats, is an image of Elisabetta Gonzaga, Duchess of Urbino. The ferocity of the ruling class finds its delight in beauty within that feminine domain not through its potential violence, but platonically, as does a child, through what Burke called a 'proud submission':[4]

> Whence turbulent Italy should draw
> Delight in Art whose end is peace,
> In logic and in natural law
> By sucking at the dugs of Greece.

The central idea in Yeats's aesthetic is that, in spite of apparent contradictions, the physical experience of nurturing the feminine idea of beauty produces the physical proof of moral good. This is the 'moral sense' at work in him. It is also proof that any wasteful virtue which makes the heart exultant is good. Of course, one is caught within the moral rough, for, as Kant insists, the good is always beautiful but the beautiful is not always good.[5] The heart's exultancy is sometimes satanic. We are not yet discussing the idea of a 'terrible beauty', however, we are dealing with a concept of goodness that ideally is beautiful. Yeats's idea, then, is that sublime aristocratic disinterest will inculcate an appreciation for the beautiful into the masses until they too 'may breed the best'; enough nurturing of the beautiful makes it a natural quality. When found in the heart's exultance, goodness and beauty are visionary, are an evocation of a new order, are that positive brand of sublimity which is exalting. Not only the aristocracy understands this, because the poor, having naught to lose and the impossible to gain, know implicitly that 'wasteful virtues earn the sun'.

The object of Yeats's attack is the refusal of the middle class to dream, and its obsession with material prosperity. Yeats's hatred of them, as Symons noted of antagonism towards the petite bourgeoisie in general, is itself middle class.[6] George Moore famously satirises this very quality in Yeats.[7] Nevertheless, it is in some ways done consciously, for Yeats knows that he possessed many personal characteristics, chief among them gregariousness and timidity, which he attacks in the middle class. In 'September 1913', the poem following 'To a Wealthy Man', Yeats makes his most infamous attack:

> What need you, being come to sense,
> But fumble in a greasy till
> And add the halfpence to the pence
> And prayer to shivering prayer, until
> You have dried the marrow from the bone;
> For men were born to pray and save:
> Romantic Ireland's dead and gone,
> It's with O'Leary in the grave.

His positioning of the phrase 'being come to sense' right after 'what the exultant heart calls good' in the previous poem is significant, as they are two ways of dealing with desire. The former is the commodification of desire, the latter is its aesthetic emancipation or completion. Commodification and aestheticisation address the same senses. Their historical origins are coincident.

Aesthetics is an attempt to counteract society's purely commercial appeal to the senses. One of the qualities Yeats admires most about the old Fenian John O'Leary is his belief that art should never be sacrificed to the Nationalist cause. The Romantic Ireland of O'Leary is aesthetic Ireland. In 'September 1913', the art that should have given direction to the cause has been made of secondary importance, while more propa-gandistic writing, such as Thomas Davis's (whose poetry had moved the early Yeats, although eventually he was seen by him as a minor poet), was prized regardless of its quality, simply because it was highly nationalistic. Ideally, being come to sense in any aesthetic way, middle-class people should understand that wasteful virtues earn the sun, that only the exultant heart has sense enough to find what is truly good. They must let the aestheticising passions reign as they should, and not let a raw national passion, represented by Davis, be what moves them. The aesthetic of the early Irish rebels (Fitzgerald, Wolfe Tone and the Wild Geese before) is a type that 'stilled' the 'childish play' of the Irish nation. In other words, their bravery gave shape, meaning and commitment to Irish Nationalism, gave it aesthetic value.

To be a wasteful mortal is to transcend mortality. The rebels achieved the heart's exultance, the 'delirium of the brave', during those passionate rebellious moments in which, striving towards their Mask – the ought of Irish nationhood – they glimpsed a transcendent eternal form of beauty. They achieved a visionary aesthetics of a consensual world beyond the world's strife. They achieved a visionary aesthetics of a supersensible society. The world of heroes, like that of saints and angels, always works as a Mask of what individuals and society should be like; it is a fictive world of final emancipation. Yeats feels that bourgeois timidity, religiosity and materialism fail the test. He wonders whether, with the years turned back, members of the middle class could have seen anything ideal in the desire of Irish heroes, or, rather than having seen it in its ideal aesthetic sense, would they have written it down to a sensual cause in the basest definition of that phrase 'being come to sense'. Would the middle class deduce from the 'delirium of the brave' that 'Some woman's yellow hair/ Has maddened every mother's son'? Love in its highest sense awakens all the noblest human passions, and yet they would reduce it to lust because they fear both the 'loneliness and pain' of being an idealist, and the poverty and death which often ensues. By so doing, they lose the unifying power of the sacrifice. The loneliness and pain of their ideals drove the heroes to their early deaths, and their deaths, because faced courageously, unified all classes in a final form of beauty.

Fortunately, Yeats's feeling for the Celtic idea of victory in defeat saves him from the worst excesses of false heroics and class hatred, from believing only the strong are heroes and only the rich are aesthetic. This is evident in the poems 'To a Friend whose Work has come to Nothing' and

'Paudeen'. In the first he advises Lady Gregory to be 'Bred to a harder thing/Than Triumph', to be 'secret and exult/Because of all things known/That is most difficult'. The volatile word 'bred' leads us back to the notion that the body possesses meaning and has the impress of God. The secret instinctual life is the source of the sublime because it is the often subconscious root of subjective experience, especially the uncanny experience of the sublime. To be able to experience the heart's exultance, to be secret and exult, to keep the object of desire and morality in view, is the secret of life, and of the indifference which makes for great, tragic figures. Yeats is very specific about this in *A Vision*, where he uses words very similar to the last lines of this poem: 'Only by pursuit or acceptance of its [the Will's] direct opposite [the Mask], that object of desire or moral idea which is of all possible things most difficult, and by forcing that form upon the *Body of Fate*, can it attain self-knowledge and expression'.[8] He is certain that his idea of the *Übermensch* or superman is hardly a conventional one; strength is not defined solely by physical victory, but by being able to experience the highest quality of the aesthetic, regardless of what others think, regardless of success or failure in the world's terms. The form that it forces upon the Body of Fate is not necessarily an alteration of that fate, but a transcendental point of view.

The aesthetic experience finally surpasses concerns of class in the moral perspective of 'Paudeen'. Yeats begins the poem with reference to the 'obscure spite' of the middle class which he attacks in 'September 1913'. He grasps that such a crudely class-structured aesthetic severely limits his poetic vision, and endeavours to complete it in a primary moment of visionary sublimity. The exultant heart in its blind loneliness and pain finds something in the 'luminous wind' that is sublime because he can call it good in the teleological sense, because he sees it 'on the lonely height where all are in God's eye.' In his heart's exultance, Yeats has seen the soul take crystalline, or definite and permanent form: 'There cannot be, confusion of our sound forgot,/A single soul that lacks a sweet crystalline cry'. This is positive sublimity in its highest and most moral sense. Indignant at the division in society and the insufficiency of its cultural outlook, Yeats has a moment of clarity in which, disoriented from himself, he experiences ecstatic union with the object of his peevish contemplation, in this case the life of the shopkeeper. He surpasses himself, and in some ways the faults of his aesthetic system, in order to see how others too become worthy.

Responsibilities may begin in dreams and that is certainly when they end (the 'Soul in Judgment', the dream of the afterlife), but dreams are not where they are tested. In 'To a Shade', Yeats imagines Parnell at the margins of the known world, ready to come to terms with the verities. He admonishes him to wait, however, as those who cripple exultant hearts and look away from the sun, are 'at their old tricks yet.' The juxtaposition of this poem with that before it in the volume, 'Paudeen', makes Yeats (and Parnell) seem like Moses returning from the mountain top only to see the people worshipping the fatted calf. Yeats has seen that no soul lacks the sweet crystalline cry, and yet he returns from his 'vision' only to see the people acting as though they lacked it. The eternal truths are ever present but ever on the periphery, unable to gain sway. Schiller writes incisively concerning the dangers that attend idealism like Parnell's and Yeats's, as compared to the easy life that attends materialism:

> No one will deny that the physical man is better provided for in the meadows of Batavia than beneath the treacherous crater of Vesuvius, and that a comprehensive and methodical intellect finds its account in a regular kitchen garden, far more than in a wild natural landscape, but man has a want beyond his life and welfare and better destiny than to comprehend the phenomena that surround him.[9]

Yeats, however, does not possess such completely undimmed Romantic assurance. In the next poem 'When Helen Lived', he wonders if he too would have only had a 'word and a jest' for the beauty of Helen, if he too would have been unappreciative of beauty that has been 'won/From bitterest hours' like the bravery of Irish rebels, won from loneliness and pain. Yeats's poems on poverty, materialism and ecstasy are balanced on either the fulfilment or the withering of expectation. The poor too, like the rich, must 'not seem to care' ('The Three Beggars'); they too must have heroic indifference, sublime disinterestedness, only theirs is a parody, a sublimity in the heart of the ridiculous. Yeats writes in 'The Three Beggars' of the violent envy which is often the lot of the poor, and knows that it is this negative passion which can thwart all hopes of transcendence. Not having the environment to support the aristocratic nonchalance of its wasteful virtues, the poor must avail of other types of severity (for surely disinterestedness is a type of severity) and/or excess. They have only asceticism, wanderlust or drinking.

The working class is caught between the negative formless sublime of their own poverty, and that more positive one figured in the image of their emancipation. What the transcendent signifier of emancipation means is vital to Yeats's idea of how beauty and positive sublimity negotiate the strife of a troubled society. The envy and rancour of the beggars in the above poem is symptomatic of the ills of a larger field of social intercourse. The materialistic ethos (in the economic rather than in the philosophical sense) of society shows itself most strongly in the bickering of those who have the least, whose problems are material ones. In 'Beggar to Beggar Cried' Yeats writes that the rich are driven by wealth 'as beggars by the itch.' The materialistic ethos is attacked most adeptly in this volume by the portrayal of the poor. The rich must unite their material inheritance with a transcendent consciousness. The poor, on the other hand, must seek such consciousness without any hope of finding a material example of it. In other words, they must look for the garden without a hope of living 'amid a rich man's flowering lawns' ('Meditations in Time of Civil War'). The lack is not entirely negative; they are not distracted from the ideal by any inferior material representation. They are not victims of the abstraction of money. Money, like vanity, is a distortion of the happiness it represents; both vanity and money can subvert our natural longings, for 'there's a devil in the looking glass.'

The paradise which the beggars run to, or dream of, being 'frenzy-struck', is one which transforms the notion of power by expressing the natural qualities of the soul. In this preface to paradise where 'king is but as the beggar' no one knows more of human plenitude than those with nothing. This is a truism, but in Yeats's beggar poems it is given specific force. Take the last stanza of 'Beggar to Beggar Cried':

> 'And there I'll grow respected at my ease,
> And hear amid the garden's nightly peace,'
> *Beggar to beggar cried, being frenzy-struck,*
> 'The wind-blown clamour of the barnacle-geese.'

In the image of paradise, when the beggar has made his soul, the heterogeneity or deformity of experience ('The wind-blown clamour of the barnacle-geese.') finds formal paradisal value ('amid the garden's nightly peace'). For the wind-blown clamour resembles the arguing of the beggars in the poem 'The Three Beggars', although here a beggar can understand the quarrelsome nature of desire and can understand how, lacking the formal gardens of the aristocracy, beggars are reduced to the deformity of economic materialism and possessiveness, to a type of ridiculous or parodic sublime. The 'garden's nightly peace', which the beggar experiences, is ambiguously positioned; it would seem to be at least a spiritual representation of the paradise to which he is running amid such clamour. If that is so, then it is the final end, the real Eden of those gardens which the rich have built. The ancestral gardens of the rich are fallen copies of Eden. In 'Meditations in Time of Civil War', Yeats contemplates the antithetical violence that was needed to build the house and gardens. For the beggar, the garden is the perfect expression of desire because it is completely imagined. Paradise is best found in the very elusiveness of the object of desire; it is a receding horizon towards which we journey. For Yeats the subject is not always the centre of the transcendent experience, as it is in Kant. The violence wreaked on the beggars forces all aspirations to be in the object, or imaginary world. The wish of subjectivity sometimes finds its expression in the object, even if the object is 'like the wind/That nobody can buy or bind ('Running to Paradise').

In 'The Witch', Yeats explores the reason for the impossibility of paradise: perpetually frustrated desire. We look in the wrong room for the wrong object of desire, the wrong Mask, the wrong lover. In its rich configuration of various sublimities, the poem is paradoxically pregnant with meaning (political, religious, and psychoanalytical) about the fundamental sterility of trying to be rich, of neglecting the spiritual for the sake of the material:

> Toil and grow rich,
> What's that but to lie
> With a foul witch
> And after, drained dry,
> To be brought
> To the chamber where
> Lies one long sought
> With despair?

Here we have a reference to the Marxist sublime of labour finding transcendental signifier in sexuality, of the potential emancipation of Art's Utopia.[10] The negative sublime is the figure of intercourse with a 'foul witch', while the positive sublime is the figure of union with her whom we have sought with despair. We have religious notions of the wasteland 'drained dry' as well as the Freudian idea of true meaning in the intimate, idealised body of the mother whom the male in lovemaking seeks in despair. This body represents a good form of materiality. It is the positive sublimity for which the beggarman runs, the spiritualised body of the resurrection, the positive sublime of beauty witnessed in the ecstasy of sexual union. It is also in the realm of *a priori* truths and may therefore be an impossible sublime, being incommensurable, a body which is only seen at the risk of Oedipal blindness, for no one 'can distinguish darkness from the soul ('A Dialogue of Self and Soul'). That is why the competing witch is so enticing: though she offers none of the sublimity of the unspecified ideal, she offers none of the dangers. The most sustained figure is how the spiritual emancipation of the beautiful has been corrupted by capitalism.[11]

CORRUPTIONS OF THE BEAUTIFUL

Unsatisfied, Yeats spends the rest of the volume discussing his feelings towards his poetry, towards women and how their representations of the beautiful and positive sublime have been malformed. In the two poems to Iseult Gonne, 'To a Child Dancing in the Wind' and 'Two Years Later', female beauty is pivotal in the relationship between the harmony of the beautiful (in art and society), the loftiness of the positive sublime (though only implicitly), and the 'monstrousness' of the negative sublime. Essentially, the young girl's beauty has all the latent possibilities of Unity of Being and Culture. It expresses a healthy harmonious society, an art that glorifies both humanity and God, simply because her beauty represents these possibilities as regards her own personal happiness. That image of personal happiness, the dancing in the wind, has not been influenced by the 'fool's triumph' or 'Love lost as soon as won'. She has not personally known the divisiveness that Yeats believed contributed to Synge's death and to the loss of all that Ireland needed him to write: 'the best labourer dead/And all the sheaves to bind'. The grief that she will experience is that which her mother, Maud Gonne, has known. They must suffer because their beauty is 'unnatural in an age like this'. In fact, it is because their beauty offers hope of unity and harmony that they inevitably suffer.

Placed within the span of the male gaze, beauty's female incarnation has an especially pertinent role in the making of patriarchal society, the female body being the vehicle of meaning, the seductiveness of the physical world, the play of interpretation, the transcendental cultural signifier. The failure of Maud Gonne's beauty to unify, to be the vehicle of meaning, of interpretation, and to provide the violent transcendental signifier that transforms society, bodes the failure of all. This deficiency makes the younger Gonne's beauty like a moth shrivelling in a fruitless fire. Yeats takes Tennyson's symbol of religious desire and the ultimate religious meaning of suffering (*In Memoriam*, 54) as a figure for the place of beauty in a world that lends less meaning to the perception and embodiment of beauty than to its acquisition – something he later connects to the idea of modern education and women (cf. 'Michael Robartes and the Dancer'). In the end, this figure has all the religious implications of Tennyson's, for in its discussion of suffering it approaches a conception of the religious (positive) sublime. In order to survive in this world, beauty must be protected by knowledge, although knowledge can prove as dangerous to Yeats's idea of beauty as it did to Tennyson's idea of faith. It can be a 'blear-eyed' strain upon beauty in both male and female beauty, considering Yeats's attitudes to Sargent's painting of Woodrow Wilson and to the political aspirations of the handsome T.W. Rolleston.[12] The separation between beauty and intellect, in Yeats's conception, will lead to Iseult's disappointment and Rolleston's failure. The inability to unite beauty and intellect holds profound moral significance.

As the intractable abstractions of most philosophical discussions of aesthetics crave an appropriate form, be it parable or poetry, so too the deeply intellectual, subjective sense of sublimity, and its analogy in morality, craves elusive objective proof, a form of the beautiful. In the first stanza of 'A Memory of Youth', Yeats experiences the Unity of Being that is associated with the maternal aspects of the Godhead ('the wisdom love brings forth', the 'mother-wit'), and which, of course, is found in most conceptions of the beautiful. It is experienced until there is an interruption, a moment of negative sublimity when all *a priori* final ends of understanding are removed by a 'cloud blown from the cut-throat north' that 'Suddenly hid Love's moon away'. The eclipse of the eternal world, the forgetting of its spiritual values, leads Yeats in the next stanza to use the illicit language of *amour courtois*; that language of courtly love which Milton has the Serpent use when wooing Eve in *Paradise Lost* (Book IX, lines 532–48). Physical beauty is praised ('I praised her body and her mind') without any reference to spiritual ideals, without any reference to the moral goodness that must inform beauty. The appeal to 'vanity' and 'pride' conjures the devil in the looking-glass. We sense the fracture exposed in Kant's comment that goodness is beautiful, even though the beautiful is not always good. There is 'Nothing but darkness overhead'. Yeats has been led astray because the reflection of the spiritual has been hidden from him and his love, as it was from Adam and Eve. Pride becomes the focus of this fallen ceremony. The pleasure is of an embarrassed rather than innocent type. Vanity and not Grace makes the woman's footfall light; we therefore have a corrupt form of the graceful as well as of the beautiful.

Reading this stanza through Milton's 'darkness visible', the language becomes satanic and the praise that of the worst egocentric kind. It is not surprising that the praise is unregenerate. It is given without any sense of the ideal and solely to exalt the temporal aspects of beauty. As the third stanza shows, the temporal aspects of beauty are in themselves nothing – neither ultimately ennobling nor transcendent. The tension between these two realities exists even in Yeats's late verse, in which 'all true love must die'. If neither love nor beauty lead to an eternal reality, they 'alter at the best/Into some lesser thing' ('Her Anxiety'). Yeats's poetic is meant to prove that this is a lie, that in spite of its inevitable and seemingly faithless growth and decay, love has its transcendent signification:

> We sat as silent as a stone,
> We knew, though she'd not said a word,
> That even the best of love must die,
> And had been savagely undone
> Were it not that Love upon the cry
> Of a most ridiculous little bird
> Tore from the clouds his marvellous moon.

The ending of the poem is proof of Yeats's complicated aesthetic. Sublimity is again neither completely in the subject nor in the object, but it is in their union. The cry that reveals the moon, the reflection of eternal spiritual beauty and love, is of a ridiculous little bird, and not from within. Such simple creatures are always most apt to be open to the supersensible world, to let the objective world speak through them, because they have not intellect enough to establish an antithesis. Primitivism always carries a message of a golden world with all its creatures, human, animal, vegetable representing the natural undivided expression of the will of God. Being demoniac (as is a similar 'stupid happy creature' in 'Demon and Beast'), the bird allows Kant's supersensible and Yeats's Principles to work directly through it. Being far removed from the supersensible world, being so antithetical, the speaker and lover must contemplate a reflection of the supersensible in order to feel some spiritual correspondence. That is why they are so moved when the moon's glory is revealed.

Divided from such a reflection, our love becomes satanic; it becomes a parody of eternal love, rather than its incarnation. The lovers become inanimate, soul-less, and 'silent as a stone'. The moon, the line between the immutable and the mutable, had to have been shining brightly for them to have any faith. If the moon had been dark (the unilluminated side of the third stanza's positive sublimity) they would have remained in the negative sublime of the second stanza, lacking the force of imagination to redeem them. It is no coincidence that the next poem in the volume is called 'Fallen Majesty', for in it, Yeats records how Gonne's beauty is disappearing. The very spiritual essence that the transcendent signifier of her beauty made real is cast into doubt, though once she 'seemed a burning cloud'. If Yeats in his remembered youth had praised that transcendent quality as well as the earthly one, if he had praised the metaphysical as well as the physical, he would not have been so deeply struck by both the disappearance of the moon and the loss of beauty's metaphysical lineaments. In 'Fallen Majesty', he is left to record 'what's gone'.

What this sense of fallen majesty meant to Yeats is that he has seen that image of beauty, and of the beautiful, which could bring Unity of Being and Unity of Culture, now beginning to grow old, to become mutable, to cast the dark side of its reflection. He sees the process of ageing both in the person of Gonne and in society at large. The image of beauty is now a fragment of the 'ancient ceremony' of Greece or Byzantium, in which a spontaneous knowledge of the whole of society was available in the parts. Such an artifact of beauty is now one of those 'priceless things' which 'passing dogs defile'. A divided society has made the positive terms of fame become the negative ones of notoriety. Whereas the famous were once unusual standard bearers, they have now become definable, generalised, as fallible as everyone else. For Yeats, the terms of beauty and its implications of some limited *sensus communis* are still very real. The limitations which he felt were being imposed by the levelling forces of democracy and communism would lead to some of his worst, and most defensive, autocratic posturing. The sense of cultural ending about this time in Yeats's poetry accounts for much of the autumnal quality, the decadence of beauty in the next volume, *The Wild Swans at Coole* (1919). There is nevertheless something positive in his poem 'Friends', near the end of *Responsibilities* (1914), that will prove a lasting antidote. It contains a convincing idea of what the redeeming values of the beautiful are in both love and society.

TOWARDS REDEEMING BEAUTY

'Friends' is full of the balance between subject and object and of the emotional power of their mysterious relationship. It is very Wordsworthean in that women are the source and soul of the beautiful. In this poem, Yeats recounts the various influences of his friendships with Olivia Shakespear, Lady Gregory and Maud Gonne. As regards the first, he places equal emphasis on subject–object, on 'Mind and delighted mind'; the line between the external and the internal is eclipsed in the relationship, and so nothing seems to come between them. This smooth harmonious mood is indicative of how the beautiful works in the realm of human intercourse. If boundaries exist, they are only there to express the joy of the relationship, as a part of the *felix culpa* which Olivia Shakespear provided for Yeats when he was a shy and virginal idealist, and one whose beneficence was sustained throughout the various types of relationships they had.

Lady Gregory's role is also quite complicated. In the gendering of authority, she plays a very interesting role, especially when considered within Burke's conception of feminine and masculine authority in the aesthetics of the beautiful and the sublime.[13] She offers a strong possibility to resolve the quandary that we do not respect what we love nor love what we respect, for she is both loved and respected. She later becomes 'a laurelled head' who could 'keep a swallow to its first intent' ('Coole Park, 1929'), when giving guiding shape to the Irish Literary Renaissance. In 'Friends', she is the perfect embodiment of the beautiful and positive sublime, having both the power of the sublime and the tenderness of beauty. Even Elizabeth Butler Cullingford in *Gender and History in Yeats's Love Poetry*, so complete in many respects, omits any mention of her in this regard. Gregory allows Yeats the rare privilege to labour in 'ecstasy', as opposed to labouring by 'the sweat of his brow'. The idea of labour returns us to 'Adam's Curse', the labour to be beautiful being like the labour to create the beautiful. In a perfect society, labour should express the unified prelapsarian ideal of the beautiful.

For Yeats, it is ecstasy in the mystical sense: a vision of eternal beauty to which he endeavours to give temporal form – this is why he labours in ecstasy. Lady Gregory and Coole Park provide a Unity of Culture because her strength unbinds youth's dreamy load, because she helps Yeats relinquish the overly subjective, transcendental dreaming of his early poetry. While Olivia Shakespear's presence provides the harmony of the beautiful, Gregory's presence has the world-shaping and conscious-changing authority to make her estate at Coole Park and her own personal influence on Yeats considerable to the literary movement in Ireland. She thus becomes one of the laurelled heads of Yeats's Pantheon, an 'Olympian' ('Beautiful Lofty Things'). Maud Gonne also becomes a member of the Pantheon, for a different, almost opposite reason. Her beauty and persona are symbols of terrible sublimity, of pain and division, of Athena the predatory huntress, of the desire for the beautiful which, instead of harmonising society, becomes frustrated and leads to war, or to the crisis of discovering forms for a new type of beauty. Yeats wonders how he can praise her influence. From the safe position of positive sublimity, of Gregory's influence, Yeats is able to come to terms with the terror of Gonne's beauty. This coming to terms is his Vision of Evil.

Maud Gonne represents that violence which is at the heart of all desire, and divisiveness which desire seeks to heal. From the aesthetic distance that his labour in ecstasy affords him, Yeats is able to reflect on the power of Maud Gonne's beauty, and, like Adam listening to Raphael on the consequence of the Fall and the return to a Paradise within him 'happier far', he is able to see its place in the scheme of things, whether of history or of his own life. He is able to see that his disappointed love for Gonne was a happy fall, a terrible sublimity that would redefine the realm of the beautiful. Yeats, as Decadent–Symbolist, departs from the more conventional gendering of the sublime's role in history as solely masculine; he presents the femme fatale as his angel of history:

> When day begins to break
> I count my good and bad,
> Being wakeful for her sake,
> Remembering what she had,
> What eagle look still shows,
> While up from my heart's root
> So great a sweetness flows
> I shake from head to foot.

The sweetness of Yeats's ecstasy is the recognition of the meaning of his mainly unrequited love for Gonne. Once he is able to derive this sweetness, to see Maud Gonne as friend, along with Lady Gregory and Olivia Shakespear, he can present his idea of the beautiful in an ever more clearly delineated form.

7

LIVING BEAUTY: AESTHETIC ACCOMMODATION OF HISTORY AND SOCIETY

The autumn of beautiful persons is beautiful. Beauty is as summer fruits, which are easy to corrupt, and cannot last; and, for the most part, it makes a dissolute youth, and age a little out of countenance; but yet certainly again, if it light well, it maketh virtues shine, and vices blush.

Francis Bacon, 'On Beauty'

. . . O heart we are old;
The living beauty is for younger men:
We cannot pay its tribute of wild tears.

Yeats, 'The Living Beauty'

What is exceptional in *The Wild Swans at Coole* (1919) is how Yeats deftly captures the sense of perfection that augurs decline in such a way as to display both its personal and social implications. He was ageing and yet achieving mastery of his art; he was finally married but still struggled against old obsessions. His sense of growing old, his sense that the class and beauty of Coole Park are doomed just at the moment in which it has reached the height of its perfection; his languishing hopes for the rising Catholic peasantry;[1] his tentativeness about his own marriage and, lastly, Maud Gonne's position in this autumnal scene are all elements which make the volume the cornerstone of Yeats's aesthetic of the beautiful and positive sublime. Coole Park not only created a stable beautiful environment for a literary Renaissance but it gave birth to Robert Gregory, the perfect Renaissance man, a kind growing ever rarer since Sidney's death and the end of the Renaissance. The implicit cultural promise of Gregory, which even put Yeats into competition with him, was enormous;[2] yet, it seemed to die with him in World War I. With the living symbol of beauty that Robert and Lady Gregory, Maud Gonne and others provide, Yeats comes to an aesthetic accommodation of history and society that fruitfully marries conventionally masculine qualities of courage, violence, and authority, with feminine qualities of passivity, tenderness, and self-sacrifice. This erotically charged perfection of the beautiful is increasingly made in preparation for death. By the end of the volume, after fashioning his own aesthetic, Yeats speculates in *A Vision* and in poetry stemming most directly from it on the Principles, the eternal forces which set history and society in motion.

AUTUMN BEAUTY

The autumnal note of beauty is struck in the title poem of the volume:

> The trees are in their autumn beauty,
> The woodland paths are dry,
> Under the October twilight the water
> Mirrors a still sky;
> Upon the brimming water among the stones
> Are nine-and-fifty swans.

The water that had fallen in spring mirrors the still sky. Nature reaches its most clear-aired and balanced harmony just as it begins to decay. Though it is autumn and the woodland paths have not been brought to life by the rains, nor yet been kept warm by winter, Coole Lake mirrors the sky's equanimity above the melancholy scene. Such autumnal imagery, such tragic calm, coupled with the beauty of the swans (sometime image of the soul), reminds Yeats of his own age, of his own autumn and imminent winter, and of the tragic calm with which he must learn to build his soul in preparation for death. The 'broken rings' of the ascending birds are symbolic of the loss of harmony, of that most musical moment of their ascent towards perfection – Plato's perfect circle – which being temporal must in time disperse. Beauty's highest pitch borders on discordant 'clamouring wings'. The Romantic, dissonant clamour illustrates how the Renaissance and Baroque melodies of earlier ascents are now impossible to reproduce:

> I have looked upon those brilliant creatures,
> And now my heart is sore.
> All's changed since I, hearing at twilight,
> The first time on this shore,
> The bell-beat of their wings above my head,
> Trod with a lighter tread.

In Yeats's increasing age, beauty makes him 'out of countenance', to use Bacon's phrase.[3] It possesses the sexual power that Yeats knows he is losing, and which in turn drives him to marry. In this regard, the word 'tread' may take on the subtextual significance of copulation (which is one of the secondary definitions of 'tread', used of birds),[4] and 'bell-beat' may signify the birds' efforts to maintain balance while copulating. This reading is supported by the poem's sense of sexual impotence, as Yeats is heartsore at the image of their pleasure. It may also be the tintinnabulation that announces the coming beatitude of the soul as it meets Christ. As Yeats writes in *Per Amica Silentia Lunae*, 'the ringers in the tower have appointed for the hymen of the soul a passing bell'.[5]

The spirituality of the swans is almost too pure. It reminds him of what he has lost, of what only memory can restore. It is a reference to a spiritual essence, the shadow of the thing-in-itself, the natural object of which has disappeared with time, the essence of which forever eludes him. The swans are not necessarily the same swans, but the returning species carry on the essence of the experience; they are the general type that breaks down each year into more temporal particularities. Yeats implicitly mourns the loss of the company of his friends who 'troop with those the world's forgot' ('The Grey Rock'), and wonders how much he has changed since they died, while looking at the swans' unageing image of passion, conquest, fidelity and harmony. His heart has grown old, as he tells us later in the volume ('A Song'), and because he is old, he cannot give to 'The Living Beauty' its 'tribute of wild tears'. He has lost the heart so passionate it seemed 't'would burn [his] body/Laid on the death-bed' ('A Song'), a heart that seemed to be able to conquer death. The paradox of this latter poem is that, though Yeats has lost much passion and power, and has withered into truth, he can yet bear even greater witness to the power of the beautiful from his present distance than can many younger eyes. In the last stanza, the eternal quality of the swans' beauty moves into the eternal mysterious realm of the *a priori*. Their beauty thus becomes a positive form of sublimity, one which moves beyond Yeats's own death – for the sleep from which he awakens at the end of the poem is analogous to death. He knows that when he ceases to be able to enjoy the swans' beauty other eyes will:

> But now they drift on the still water,
> Mysterious, beautiful;
> Among what rushes will they build,
> By what lakes' edge or pool
> Delight men's eyes when I awake some day
> To find they have flown away?

The ability to appreciate the beauty of the swans will last as long as the beauty of the swans, only the individual types will change. The mysteriousness of the beautiful is that it lives beyond the pale of individual existence or cultural borders. The melancholy delight of temporal beauty is the glimpse one gains of the eternal forms in all their indeterminacy.

The autumnal quality of temporal beauty has its root in what, in *The Fate of Art*, Bernstein calls 'memorial aesthetics'. To him, Kant's third

Critique implicitly mourns the separation of truth from beauty, of ethics from aesthetics. This division is a result of the separation between scientific truth and ethical, or moral truth. Commenting on Kant's idea of the beautiful, Bernstein identifies a pattern that also applies to Yeats: 'What issues from the experience of beauty is not the recognition of morality and nature in a transcendent beyond, but rather a recognition of their present intractable but contingent separation'. The aesthetic experience of the supersensible, for Yeats and Kant, is meant to bridge the great gulf between Freedom and Nature. It would then answer the final question of beauty's relationship to truth, which remaining unanswerable leaves the sublime 'a sepulchre to stand over their lost unity'.[6]

The autumnal quality of the swans' beauty has cultural as well as personal significance in this volume. The faith that the swans shall delight other men's eyes, combined with the grief over loss of the object of one's own delight, underlies the eulogy to Robert Gregory that follows 'The Wild Swans at Coole'. In 'In Memory of Robert Gregory', Yeats reviews the qualities, the strengths and weaknesses of those he has known, and who like Gregory have died. The sum of all these qualities of good and ill, and the dramatic roles the people played in Yeats's life, converge in the composition of a great tragedy, whose culmination is reached in the death of the person nearest to perfection.

IN SEARCH OF UNITY OF BEING

The elegy is a composite picture of those qualities that Yeats valued most in individuals and society alike, and of which Gregory is presented as the highest example. Yeats begins the poem by establishing that the basis for the soul's ascension to positive sublimity is in communion with the dead. He then climbs the narrow 'winding stair', symbol of the soul's ascension, to his bed, which is locus for the eternal figures of sexuality and dreams. As the movement is towards harmony, Maud Gonne and all the discord she represents to his marriage with Georgie Hyde-Lees must be absent. Having assured himself of the delicate harmony of the elegy, he discusses his relationship to Lionel Johnson. Johnson was one of those who fall, as both Yeats in this poem and Johnson himself remarked – fall from religious grace and fall drunkenly to the ground.[7] Johnson could not balance his severe religion and his profligate and homosexual lifestyle. Unable to maintain a steady footing, he staged the setting for each of his descents. His life and beliefs illustrate that he could have done little else except to have abandoned his way of life, which was evidently impossible, or to have modified his faith, which was unacceptable. Given his desires, each question his religion answered offered a graver one. After he converted to

Catholicism, Johnson believed that he had to avoid damnation no matter what the cost to personal expression. Although it is difficult to know for certain, it seems that Johnson discontinued the practice of homosexuality, if not of excessive drinking, upon admittance to the Catholic Church.[8]

Such an individual was bound to lead a life that mixed Platonic idealism, satanic torment and Christian self-denial. It is the stoical self-denial and idealism, gazing into the abyss of torment, that struck Yeats as essential to a just and moral society, on the one hand, and as potentially repressive, on the other. Johnson might have overcome the division had he been able to combine his asceticism, his stoicism and his love of the ecstatic, for even Synge confided to Yeats: 'We should unite stoicism, asceticism and ecstasy. Two of them have often come together, but the three never.'[9] The union would be religious expression perfected. Each person in the poem is the epitome of only one facet of society, and each except Gregory is unable to sustain that Unity of Being at the root of Unity of Culture. Johnson is the world-renouncing intellectual, while George Pollexfen is the muscular horse-rider who in old age becomes a hypochondriac. Each represents those qualities of mind and body that the other lacks. In Yeats's rendering, Synge – the death-defying, sickly artist who seeks the company of heroes – comes closest to Gregory's Unity of Being because, unlike the others, he seeks his Mask or his opposite. His weak body seeks symbols of physical strength to match the power of his mind and spirit. Combining all these qualities, the asceticism of Johnson, the strength and potential heroism of young Pollexfen, the tragic ecstasy of Synge, Robert Gregory is 'Our Sidney and our perfect man'. Gregory's Unity of Being hearkens back to an age before 'the seventeenth century when man became passive before a mechanised nature'.[10]

Throughout the volume, Yeats is searching for a subject worthy of the beautiful, an individual that can represent Irish society in the way that Odysseus represents the Greeks. Although he never reaches Joyce's conclusion that the modern sense of exiled subjectivity is best represented by an eternal exile, such as the wandering Jew, he does use the tramp and fisherman as symbols of those who have been uprooted, or outcast, by the Industrial Age. The Gregory of 'An Irish Airman Foresees his Death' also shows a distaste for society's demands. The culture he leaves behind is not unified. Robert Gregory, the archetypal universal man, is gone in the moment of his heralding. The volume then turns to that more solitary subject of poetry, 'The Fisherman'. As professional producers, men and constructions of the masculine have become overly specialised. Men have had to ignore their genius and its connection with instinct. Yeats would give this imaginary fisherman a poem as 'cold/And passionate as the dawn'. He has taken a line from one of his father's letters to him, which his father meant as an artistic credo, and he has imagined the suitable subject. If not necessarily a Christ-like fisher of souls, the fisherman is an image of a type of beatitude and redemption that deserves a poem still warm from Aurora's embrace. The seeming paradox of cold and passionate is one of Yeats's attempts to establish a link between mortal vulnerabilities and immortal indifference. He saw Parnell as living proof of such a link and imagined literature as another. 'The Fisherman' becomes the muse of Yeats's solitude. Fishing is the only 'hunt' in which he would engage. The fisherman stands in contrast to the feminine principle that pervades the volume. He bolsters Yeats's fears of his own timidity and gregariousness. Perhaps it is for this reason that Yeats increasingly relies on a construction of the feminine for his conception of the beautiful in society, one not necessarily based only on softness, submissiveness, love, tenderness and affection, as is Burke's, but also on aspects such as strength, courage, sexual appetite and wisdom, which are normally associated with the masculine. He could thereby strengthen himself in a less threatening manner. In his later work, a more self-assured Yeats includes those aspects of the feminine that have traditionally made it the dark continent of philosophical inquiry: the uncanny, the abject, the ambiguous, the sexually subversive.[11] These are aspects he encourages women to protect and which he would awaken in himself and in other men.

On a biographical front, Yeats's own movement towards coherent subjectivity and a more fulfilled lifestyle may have progressed through his recent marriage, but it is still split between Gonne and his wife, Georgie Hyde-Lees. In poems such as 'On Woman' (Maud Gonne), 'To a Young Beauty', 'The Living Beauty' (Iseult Gonne), 'Solomon to Sheba' and 'Under the Round Tower' (Georgie Hyde-Lees), he meditates on the important role that the construction of the feminine plays in any aesthetic conception of society. One may perhaps less controversially say of Yeats what has been said of Twain, that he was 'so dependent upon female interaction and influence that without it, the sublimity of his [work] would have been lost'.[12] In his various poems to women, Yeats continues the quest romance of Shelley's 'Alastor' and Keats's 'Endymion'; women are seen as ideal and highly erotic, potentially subversive forces. His construction of the feminine also matches Wordsworth's in that both see it as a recuperating force, as a cure for alienation. *The Wild Swans at Coole* (1919) is an effort to write the sublimely Romantic poem. It even has that staple of Romanticism: 'Lines Written in Dejection'. Like all good Romantic poets, Yeats seeks an otherness in the sexuality of the feminine that may revivify a failing sense of self, an otherness that might provide a sacred image to help society coalesce.

In 'Solomon and Sheba', Yeats also echoes Donne's exaltation of the power of love in 'The Sun Rising'. At the centre of Donne's world is the bed. Similarly, for Yeats, there's 'not a thing but love can make/The world a narrow pound'. The Yeatsian synthesis between love and wisdom, power and knowledge, is here envisioned. He knows that in his fifty odd years he is late to the wisdom and potential harmony of love (though grown used to much divisiveness). Youthful passion is also out of reach. The next two poems in the volume, 'The Living Beauty' and 'A Song', lament this aspect of ageing. The refrain of the second, 'O who could have foretold/That the heart grows old?', strikes the central note. This theme echoes the autumnal quality of the title poem and reaffirms the larger issues at stake throughout the volume. Beauty as it was defined in Yeats's generation (the Aesthetic and the Decadent) is no longer appreciated. The younger generation, the Modernist (to which Yeats held wavering allegiance), defines beauty differently, or does not think it can exist any longer.

THE DISCIPLINE AND REWARDS OF BEAUTY

When a beautiful woman loves the wrong man, it becomes an emblem to Yeats of a much deeper disease. In 'To a Young Beauty', he castigates Iseult Gonne for her relationship with those whom he judges to be the wrong people. By seeing her as an artist, Yeats is not only emphasising the physical basis of art but he is also ascribing artistry to being a physically beautiful person. In judging both artists and beautiful people, the efforts, as well as the results, must be selective. This idea is obvious. Yeats covers his obviousness with a reference to a nursery rhyme as if to say that though we are all taught this idea of selection as children, we forget very quickly. These are the old externally imposed hierarchies, however. The idea is so fundamentally applied that it seems reactionary and insufficient in its understanding of the needs of the age, the reasons for bohemianism, the cause of social justice. In the first stanza we miss Blake's social influence on Yeats: the idea that even Jack and Jill have a sweet crystalline cry hidden in their souls if only they would be spiritually attentive. The last two stanzas, where Blake is submerged in the reference to 'Ezekiel's cherubim', are redemptive. They carry the prophetic and Baroque mood of Yeatsian beauty and positive sublimity.

More a man of the seventeenth century than the eighteenth, Blake defended the religious mood against Wollstonecraft, Paine and other rationalist republicans. The mood is also the source of Yeats's best labour to be beautiful. The rarity and loftiness of the beauty is not the result of material aristocracy (a limited type of vision of the beautiful in Blake's vocabulary), but rather it is the result of a more rational progression and visionary, or internally imposed hierarchy. Most people do not see such beauty revealed because they do not aspire to it, rushing instead towards inferior types. For Blake, the Romantic aesthetic is not the artificial grace and decorum of Beauvarlet's society beauties (to his professional detriment Blake avoided such portraiture), but rather it is the image the Book of Ezekiel (chapter 10) presents, of wheels within wheels, of awe-inspiring manifold appearance, of four-faced beings, in which one is of a cherub, another of a man, the next of lion and the fourth of an eagle; in short, it is a vision of the *a priori* precincts of power and the sublime, with the human and the beautiful defined between the divine and the animal realms, defined between God and Nature.

Yeats tellingly avoids such an image of sublimity, for this poem is not about the unpresentable. It is a lesson in the objective discipline of beauty. He ends hoping that the rewards of such discipline may nevertheless lie outside of time and space:

> I know what wages beauty gives,
> How hard a life her servant lives,
> Yet praise the winters gone:
> There is not a fool can call me friend,
> And I may dine at journey's end
> With Landor and with Donne.

The choice of poets is instructive. They were involved in poetic movements of great importance to Yeats: the Romantic and the Baroque. Landor disdained the crowd and easy popularity. Donne wrote poems as ecstatic as the Book of Ezekiel. They represent together that combination of stoicism and passionate ecstasy which Yeats so highly prizes, and towards which he is pushing his new emblem of the beautiful, Iseult Gonne.

Her beauty is the force behind the next poem, 'To a Young Girl'. Although it is addressed to Iseult, the poem is clearly written out of his love for her mother. He remains passionate, heartbroken, and remonstrative. The poem is an unpretentious model of the 'wages beauty gives'. It begins with the overwhelmed repetition of 'My dear, my dear, I know'. By rhyming 'know' with 'so', Yeats displays how his ecstatic knowledge of love borders on the indescribable, 'so' being an emotive but insubstantial word. He even rhymes it twice. The theme is the wisdom that exceeds the bounds of knowledge, for it is a 'wild thought' whose power is so physical the mind cannot follow; it sets her 'blood astir' and 'glitter[s] in her eyes'. Yeats has nothing other than her physical reaction with which to prove her love for him. His knowledge consists only of impression and as such is the emotional equivalent to aesthetic perception. Yeats tries to support his sense that she shares his feeling, despite her denial, by rhyming 'denies' with 'eyes'. He can see by her expression that she shares his feeling, whatever she might say. Ecstasy is the poetic phenomenon, the empirical evidence of the beautiful and sublime. It is the embodiment of the philosophic and poetic idea.

With an image of ecstasy, we are prepared for the encomium 'On Woman'. There is profound sexual insight and human sympathy. Finally, there is fierce unsatisfiable desire. To Yeats, all this is vital not only because it is the way to the positive sublime but also because it illustrates how women continue to confirm the best of pre-Cartesian intellect. They have not been forced to fall passive before a mechanised nature. They have not been put through the mill of examinations which men have created in order to 'destroy the imagination'.[13] In their maternal role, they represent the unity of subject (mother) and object (child). Yeats begins the poem with an image of maternal sympathy:

> May God be praised for woman
> That gives up all her mind,
> A man may find in no man
> A friendship of her kind
> That covers all he has brought
> As with her flesh and bone,
> Nor quarrels with a thought
> Because it is not her own . . .

Yet, he is dissembling when he states that men cannot find this quality in another man. It is not limited to women, for he uses the very phrase to describe Arthur Symons.[14] Like many concurrent theories of lost primitive virtues that have been applied to other races as well as to women, Yeats's theory is meant to make those who are overly sophisticated aware of the instinctual basis of thought. His sweeping essentialist rhetoric merely reinforces his apriorism. He continues to place a zigzagging butterfly genius against the professional systems which mean to keep it flying in a straight line. He proceeds to make the powers of 'The Song of Songs' even more explicitly sexual than they already are. Although the poem is clearly a reification of women as thinking bodies, and implicitly of men, it nevertheless makes an effective point against scientific detachment. Yeats concedes that sexuality is not as important as the beatific figure it provides. He is 'not so bold/To hope a thing so dear' now that he is 'growing old'. He knows that desire is the figurative language for life's search, that sexual torment is like spiritual excitement, that the mystery of sexuality is like the mystery of origins.[15] A Baroque figure of Eros and ecstasy is central to Yeats. He concludes the poem with an image of a desire that leads from one life to another, in the forever-frustrated search for the final subject, and which results in 'an aching head/Gnashing of teeth, despair'. In the sexual search, the object has primacy only in as much as it reveals the subject unto itself, but during the process they change roles and the process begins again, unsatisfiable and unsatisfied.

The image of woman in 'On Woman' is not one of positive maternal sublimity such as Lady Gregory or the Duchess of Urbino represents; rather, it is of the sublime in both its negative and positive forms: frustrated desire violently enacted, highlighting subject–object divisions, and sexuality tenderly consummated, suggesting harmony. Maud Gonne has these sublime qualities because she has 'gazed into the burning sun' ('His Phoenix') and has assumed its destructive and life-giving properties. In 'A Thought from Propertius', we see the sacred violence of the terrible sublime alongside the holy images of the positive sublime, performed at the altar and inspired by wine with both Dionysian and Christian resonance. The definite article of 'the unmixed wine' connects the two sublimities. As is usual with Yeats, one type of knowledge is virginal or world-renouncing, while the other is rapacious and worldly. The next poem, 'Broken Dreams', presents more of the tenderness of positive sublimity: 'Heaven has put away the stroke of doom,/So great her portion in that peace you make/By merely walking in a room.' Both versions of the sublime are quite conscientiously placed in contrasting realms of the *a priori*, so that Maud Gonne can be the Janus-faced head on the threshold of purgation and divinity. She is the face Yeats loved 'before the world was made' ('Before the World was Made'). In his *Memoirs*, he writes that it was as though a gong had sounded when she first entered his life, that same gong that troubles the 'gong-tormented sea' of 'Byzantium'.[16] Yeats reinforces the divine nature of Maud Gonne's countenance in 'A Deep-sworn Vow'. In spite of her betrayal of that vow, he sees her as sustenance to his soul when it hovers over the abyss, is sleepy, or intoxicated. Nearing the margins of consciousness, he confronts their eternal connection. He has now established an aesthetic system that gives shape to an ineffable force in society, in self-understanding, and in relation to God.

He henceforth prepares himself for the fading of that autumn beauty whose passing he has mourned throughout the volume, and he does so, knowing he has constructed his aesthetic. Alfred Pollexfen and Mabel Beardsley are just the most recent of the many people who have died since the turn of the twentieth century. The poems that follow 'Upon a Dying Lady', and which present the system of *A Vision*, are often lamented as another return to his hazy early poetry, although they are but the result of the demise of strength and beauty that we see in the preceding poems. Death and decay provide the introduction to figures of the unseen.

THE AESTHETICS OF DYING

We are reduced to the essentials. Yeats had a love of the heterogeneity of human personality (if, oddly, not of heterogeneous culture) and a belief that what we come to love or hate somehow points in all its contingency to what, in fact, is *a priori*. 'In Memory of Alfred Pollexfen' describes how specific experience become universal. The particulars yield to the necessary at death. The revelation comes in the last four lines, when Pollexfen's death forces Yeats to join the tragic chorus:

> At all these death-beds women heard
> A visionary white sea-bird
> Lamenting that a man should die;
> And with that cry I have raised my cry.

These lines have two functional images: one, a lament of the loss of the individual life, and the other, a revelation of what binds all seafaring families who have lost someone in the banshee-like icon of a seabird announcing death. The society formed during the life of the deceased, the consensual province of the beautiful, achieves sublime status in the universal recognition of the icon. In 'Upon a Dying Lady', there is a similar movement from the particular to the universal, only the movement seems to have begun before the composition of the poem.

As decadent traveller, Mabel Beardsley had already begun to look on life as mere contingency, as a play-thing. She ritualised the playthings of life (the sexuality, the drinking, the dolls) in order to prepare herself for the afterlife. For a decadent demi-monde, society life has religious implications. In her death, the qualities of the beautiful, grace and kindness, together with decadent and religious values, ascend to the *a priori*:

> With the old kindness, the old distinguished grace,
> She lies, her lovely piteous head amid dull red hair
> Propped upon pillows, rouge on the pallor of her face.
> She would not have us sad because she is lying there,
> And when she meets our gaze her eyes are laughter-lit,
> Her speech a wicked tale that we may vie with her,
> Matching our broken-hearted wit against her wit,
> Thinking of saints and of Petronius Arbiter.

With the qualities of the harmonious in society, she endeavours to spare her visitors the pain of her dying and engages them with her wit. Wit and wickedness have provided a method for decadents to stave off death since the days of the Roman Silver Age, when Petronius Arbiter in *The Satyricon* has Trimalchio's servant ring the gong upon the hour as a *carpe diem* to remind the guests that they should indulge because death approaches. The question behind the whole sequence, and indeed implicit in the volume's movement, is: how will the Yeatsian aesthetic of the beautiful weather the eternal changes? Will it be revealed as fundamentally ephemeral? Or will there be a transformation into positive sublimity as is hinted in the final coupling of Petronius and the saints? Taking pleasure in the beautiful is taking pleasure in this world; according to aesthetic theory, there is nothing intrinsically moral in pleasure (pleasure's a sin and sometimes sin's a pleasure). If the 'grounds for pleasure', the 'psychological state par excellence, are converted into a very logical harmony', as Lyotard writes, then the harmony that is established between imagination and understanding, on the one hand, and between theory and practice, on the other, becomes a 'transcendental illusion'.[17] Religious theory and decadent praxis finally agree, according to that illusion. The dissipation and despair that the lives of such decadents as Lionel Johnson and Ernest Dowson have awakened is precisely the result of such a deep-seated 'transcendental illusion'. For the saints, beauty is only found in what is morally beautiful, but this is not true for the decadents.

Ideal beauty may be severed from the real, but we discover how it is severed only when we have enjoyed the latter to the fullest. Saints and decadents are moved by the same aesthetic illusion; and the dying lady's wit is informed by both approaches to the beautiful. The pain of the following part, 'Certain Artists bring her Dolls and Drawings', is felt in the division between the 'Beauty' that Mabel Beardsley represents, and the moral judgement which she awaits. Here 'Beauty' is both sexually and morally ambiguous. The figures patterned on the drawing of her brother Aubrey confirm all the sinfulness which so much of English and French Decadence aimed to purge through art's hypostatisation of sin. There is a sad irony to this for, having spent her passion on toys, she has none left for the ideal forms. The sublime of this part is negative because of the division. The implication of the 'We' in the last two lines is that all objects of beauty, high or low, seemingly moral or not, are nothing but toys. The tension between Petronius and the saints is drawn tighter and is carried into the next number of the sequence.

As a Roman Catholic, Mabel Beardsley turns the ambiguous dolls' faces to the wall when the priest comes to say Mass. The Yeatsian irony is that the priest himself as a member of the institutionalised pack performs a fallen ritual. The next two parts continue Yeats's ironic distance from, but appreciation of the depth of, Beardsley's religious attitudes. For he knows that 'She is playing like a child/And penance is the play' and yet, she has not 'called the pleasures evil/Happier days thought good'. She will have to learn what was immoral or moral about her conception of beauty when she dies; she believes that such knowledge will come but insists that, because she does not possess it, there is no sense in her not acting as she did act. Her courage is what helps her to harmonise her sense of the beautiful with morality and to achieve sublimity in dying.

In Kant's words, 'the intellectual and intrinsically final (moral) good, estimated aesthetically, instead of being represented as beautiful, must rather be represented as sublime'.[18] This is the transformation of which Yeats writes:

> When her soul flies to the predestined dancing-place
> (I have no speech but symbol, the pagan speech I made
> Amid the dreams of youth) let her come face to face,
> Amid that first astonishment, with Grania's shade,
> All but the terrors of the woodland flight forgot
> That made her Diarmuid dear, and some old cardinal
> Pacing with half-closed eyelids in a sunny spot
> Who had murmured of Giorgione at his latest breath—
> Aye, and Achilles, Timor, Babar, Barhaim, all
> Who have lived in joy and laughed into the face of Death.

The 'astonishment', a term so often at the basis of sublime experience in the eighteenth century (for Burke as others), and the terrors of the negative sublime both give way to the forms of positive sublimity. We see the profane illicit love of Grania and Diarmuid given sanction and the cardinal musing in a 'sunny-spot' (i.e. approved place; Reason's, or the Celestial Body's, domain of the redeemed senses) on the profane pleasure of Giorgione. The warriors, hunters and kings also implicitly find a meaning to their bloody but joyful lives.

In the final part of the sequence, 'Her Friends bring her a Christmas Tree', Yeats returns from visions of sublimity to temporal reality so that he may show how the appreciation of beauty, whether moral or not, is indispensable. He also reckons that death and time are the enemy of such beauty. The Christmas tree incorporates the pagan desire to please the senses with a triumphant Christian iconography. It illustrates how the division between the beautiful and the good continues to haunt the living and dying with interdependent, but irreconcilable aesthetic and moral power – that 'she may look from the bed/On pretty things that may/ Please a fantastic head./Give her a little grace'. It is the dying lady's last vision of the world. The closing phrase ('about to die') resounds through-out the following visionary poems, as does the entire meditation on the feminine, making the placement of 'Upon a Dying Lady' in this volume essential, regardless of its earlier date of composition. They are the poems of the afterlife, of the eternal and subconscious dream forces, the Principles that establish the grounds of the beautiful and sublime for the Faculties. They are also concerned with the relationship between morality and aesthetics. These poems look for the 'grace', or forgiveness, that Yeats thinks should be given to the aesthetic of the 'laughing eye'.

Based on the automatic writing of *A Vision*, and on its systems of reality, the closing eight poems try to compress its system to the point of transcendental simplicity. 'Ego Dominus Tuus', 'The Phases of the Moon', and 'The Double Vision of Michael Robartes' illustrate how the subjective and objective interrelate, how art must be based on desire and the struggles of the self and religion be based on renunciation of the self. They illustrate how culture should allow artist and religious to freely interact, as in the highmarks of history: Ancient Greece, Byzantium and the Renaissance. Yet, before we discuss these poems, the mystical system in *A Vision* out of which they were created must be outlined.

8

THE LANGUAGE OF ILLUSION: *A VISION* AND THE TRANSCENDENTAL

Life is an endeavour, made vain by the four sails of its mill, to come to a double contemplation, that of the chosen Image, that of the fated Image.

Yeats, *A Vision*

In *A Vision*, Yeats has erected a complicated geometrical system meant to show how lyric moments illuminate the sexual–religious basis of psychological or historical change. It is not surprising that the automatic writing from which the book was conceived was also intimately connected to improving Yeats's sexual life with the medium, his wife George. Following Nietzsche's idea of the Apollonian and Dionysian, Yeats believes in two realities that are constantly interlocked: the antithetical (subjective) reality and the primary (objective) one. They are constantly interpenetrating, although one or another is usually dominant. When any type of balance is achieved, civilisation reaches its apogee, as for example in Byzantium, when Christ is represented in the pose of Zeus and his primary love also expresses antithetical power. There are moments in history when the gyres turn and one dispensation gives way to another. The most famous Yeatsian examples of this transformation are, first, when Leda, impregnated by the Swan (Zeus), gives birth to Helen, Clytaemnestra, Castor and Pollux creating the age of a Greek antithetical, subjective culture; and second, when the Virgin Mary is impregnated by the Dove (the Holy Ghost), gives birth to Jesus, creating a primary, objective age. The privileged figure in the subject–object relationship is the sexual–religious one.

Yeats schematically renders the difference between the two dispensations thus: 'the primary dispensation look[s] beyond itself towards a transcendent power, [it] is dogmatic, levelling, unifying, feminine, humane, peace its means and end'. Its characteristics are 'necessity, truth, goodness, mechanism, science, democracy, abstraction, peace'. The antithetical dispensation 'obeys imminent power, [it] is expressive, hierarchical, multiple, masculine, harsh, surgical'. Its characteristics are 'freedom, fiction, evil, kindred, art, aristocracy, particularity, war'.[1] As regards our present sense of historical change, of millennialism, Yeats thinks that the Swan shall begin an antithetical age. The aesthetic significance of this is very important. The feminine aspects of the primary and the beautiful shall give way to the masculine aspects of the antithetical and the sublime as the main goal of society.[2] In some ways, Yeats describes the change in terms that have deep implications for the relationship between morality and aesthetics, as well as between civil and natural law.

In *A Vision* he writes of the coming of the rough beast: 'When the old *primary* becomes the new *antithetical*, the old realisation of an objective moral law is changed into a subconscious turbulent instinct. The world of rigid custom and law is broken up by "the uncontrollable mystery upon the bestial floor"'.[3] This breakdown of objective moral law and the rise of turbulent sexual instinct takes place in 'The Second Coming' and 'Leda and the Swan'. In 'Two Songs from a Play' and 'The Mother of God', we see the opposite movement: 'When the old *antithetical* becomes the new *primary*, moral feeling is changed into an organisation of experience which must in its turn seek a unity, the whole of experience.'[4] Christ comes in 'pity for man's darkening thought'. Morality comes again to give shape to sexual instinct; Eros is given a definitively religious dimension. There is in both turning of the gyres what Nietzsche sees as the 'possibility that that peculiar sweetness and plenitude which is characteristic of the aesthetic condition might have its origin in precisely the ingredient "sensuality"'.[5] The interlocking gyres show how Yeatsian aesthetics eroticise the idea of the divine. Traditional genderings of the beautiful and the sublime are thereby subsumed through an ecstatic vision that may momentarily heal the subject–object divide in human consciousness.

Disregarding the chapter addressed to Ezra Pound and the fictional one on Michael Robartes, as they are not essential to laying out Yeats's system, and their most central ideas are dealt with elsewhere in this discussion, we shall concentrate on the five books that constitute *A Vision* proper. Book I, 'The Great Wheel', is Yeats's study of the 28 phases of the moon, from solar primary Godhead to lunar antithetical man, and the various types of poetic incarnation therein. It focuses on the temporal world of the Faculties and helps to illustrate how poetry, society and personality are conceived. Book II, 'The Completed Symbol', illustrates the eternal processes of creation as they are expressed by the eternal Principles and before they are given form in art, being and culture, that is, as they exist in the individual mind before they are put into practice. Here Yeats's concept of the connection between the temporal and eternal in the construction of his larger aesthetic is fully displayed. Book III, 'The Soul in Judgment', is an elaborate analysis of the purgatorial state as it is mirrored in the states of the soul between life and death. Book IV, 'The Great Year of the Ancients', delineates the *Magnus Annus*, in which Christ and Caesar give imaginative shape to history and to the themes of art and literature in selected cultures dating from Rome (and by implication Greece) to the modern era. Finally, Book V, 'Dove or Swan', considers the two primary and antithetical muses that represent Christ and Caesar. In the last book, Yeats posits the Swan as the muse necessary for our age because we are approaching the dawn of a new antithetical age. Throughout these books the aim of the aesthetic is to align the Mask (the ought) with the Body of Fate (the known), the antithetical inner world of desire and imagination with the primary world of outward things and events, in order to achieve the desired ideal.

BOOK I, 'THE GREAT WHEEL'

Book I of *A Vision*, or 'The Great Wheel', is a scheme of literary, personal and social history measured by the 28 phases of the moon. These phases are various incarnations of personality and creativity that move from the complete objectivity of phase 1 to the complete subjectivity of phase 15 only to return cyclically to the objectivity of phase 1. Neither phase 15 nor phase 1 is inhabitable because complete objectivity and subjectivity are impossible to sustain. The cycle has historical, personal and aesthetic implications. Historically, using a Greek frame (Yeats's favourite), one moves from early heroic, or Homeric phases (based in myths of physical and sexual power) to later more refined, aesthetic stages of Greek history (such as the era of Phidias), and then on to more decadent, because more intel-lectual, philosophical and less aesthetic ages (such as those of Hellenistic Greece). In personal terms, the cycle of an individual life moves from the instinctual knowledge of early childhood phases to overly sensuous adolescent ones, to fully aesthetic mature ones, usually highly antithetical, and finally to the more primary phases of old age. In artistic terms, there is a similar transformation: Whitman belongs to phase 6, Keats to 14, Dante to 17, Shakespeare to 20, Newman and Luther to 25, and Socrates and Pascal to 27. This shift is from a highly physical type of poetry to a sensuous one, on to a mature and unified one, and then to an increasingly intellectual form of art that finally gives way to philosophy and religion. To Yeats, the best art is created at or around phase 17 because it synthesises body and mind.

The aim of the system is the Unity of Being and Unity of Culture that exist at the phases surrounding phase 15, which are those of the greatest poetic activity. Each individual, though yearning for another phase, must work within the confines of his or her own condition: 'Man seeks . . . the opposite of his condition [his Mask], attains his object, as far as it is attainable, at phase 15 and returns to phase 1 again'.[6] Those farthest from it (the heroes of Greek myth or Arthurian legend) have very little or no poetic activity, though they are closest to phase 1, the incarnation of God. Such heroes operate as Masks for poets in the antithetical phases of artistic creation. The reasons for this relationship are intricate. For Browning, phase 4 provides a Mask of the 'wisdom of instinct',[7] for in Yeats's view Browning is a man worn out by holding wisdom together with 'labour and uncertainty'.[8] Phase 3, wherein the 'body is still in close contact with the supersensual rhythm'[9] – so close in fact that creativity is not necessary – provides Shelley of phase 17 with his 'wandering lovers and sages', Landor and Theocritus with their shepherds, and Yeats with his fisherman. The Masks of the poets that surround phase 15 are defined by the way in which artistic illumination is experienced in relationship to the primary object. In *Per Amica Silentia Lunae*, Yeats describes the literary inspiration associated with phase 15 as 'that sudden luminous definition of form which makes one understand almost in spite of oneself that one is not merely imagining'.[10]

Phase 15 is a subjective beatific vision of the beautiful, of the thing-in-itself behind the appearance of the physical world: 'Beauty is indeed but bodily life in some ideal condition.'[11] In the moment of illumination, the artist experiences an ecstasy that combines the sacred and profane experiences of saint and lover. The relationship between the poet and the Daimon, his *a priori* amoral guiding angel as it were, is similar to mystical marriage. It aspires to sexual knowledge, while at the same time being a perfection of that experience: '. . . love knows nothing of desire, for desire implies effort, and though there is still separation from the loved object, love accepts the separation as necessary to its own existence.'[12] The relationship becomes explicit, and the separation tellingly bridged, only in the Marriage or Beatitude, the fourth state of the afterlife. Such a vision is significant because of the relationship of reality to Image: 'Nothing is apparent but dreaming Will and the Image that it dreams.'[13] It is that moment when image and event coincide, when desire becomes thought, when the aesthetic reverie ends in creation. The poet unites with the object of contemplation, the object of his 'loss', his Beatrice, or she who blesses. In the strict terms of *A Vision*, it happens when the Will (the is) aligns with the Mask (the ought) and the Creative Mind (the knower) aligns with the Body of Fate (the known). The sensibility, the intellect and perception must be at their most acute to achieve the final marriage of objectivity and subjectivity, God and Nature, the antithetical and the primary, in which Sun is consumed in Moon and 'all is beauty'.[14] This, of course, is a vision of positive sublimity, of the transformation of the tragic loss, because the alienation of the negative sublime experienced by highly lunar phases finds solace in the Mask. The finitude and temporality that isolate them disappear in a transcendental illusion, or at least are deferred in the language of that illusion.

Finally, Yeats places his era in phase 22. As we approach the late primary phases of 'The Hunchback' (26), 'The Saint' (27) and 'The Fool' (28) – figures who are almost unconscious of their belief – and as the poetic act begins to become more and more fragmented, philosophy (analogical thinking) becomes easier to realise than does poetry until, amid the fragmentation, the only way to the transcendental is through renunciation of the world and self. The sustaining figures are Medieval grotesques and saints. These phases are perhaps more central to Yeats's theories of religious inspiration via the objective God, than they are to the poetic inspiration of the subjective dream. 'The Hunchback' is deformed and bitter at the loss of beauty. 'The Fool' is made foolish by the illusory glimpses of poetic truth which he gleans from the snatches of the classics he calls up from the *Anima Mundi*. Seeing the deformity of the world as its definition, the credo of 'The Saint' is that 'Man does not perceive the truth; God perceives the truth in Man'. [15]

BOOK II, 'THE COMPLETED SYMBOL'

'The Completed Symbol', Book II, is Yeats's vision of the eternal Principles of life and thought. The imagination travels through a treasure store of images, communing with the objects of desire and transforming them into riches of personality, social harmony or poetry, during the process of which many travellers are consumed and martyred. In this world of Daimons (creative spirits whose relationship to any individual is like that of a lover, and whom Yeats connects to the Passionate Body[16]), the act of creation again finds its prototype in sexual intercourse (as it did in phase 15). Blake's poem, 'The Mental Traveller', in which the cyclical youth and age of lovers and the conflict and confluence of their sexual energies represent the divisions and unities of history, is Yeats's chief poetic reference for this connection. The terror all feel at the birth of the 'Babe' is like the terror of negative sublimity in the cycles of historical change. In this spiritual-physical land of wounded and wounding creativity, there is a place of artistic incarnation which is very similar to that of the 15th phase: the Thirteenth Cone, God-like mystical locus of the 'Mass'. Again there is a specific sexual reference; we enter the Thirteenth Cone through the cruelty of the beloved and the ignorance of the lover. The Thirteenth

Cone (a cone which is not a cone but a sphere, though we cannot see it as such) exists between where 'the damned have howled away their hearts' and where 'the blessed dance', as Yeats writes in the poem that is the epilogue to *A Vision*, 'All Souls' Night'. Much of what follows in 'The Completed Symbol' is concerned with the eternal implications of the system. Yeats includes these sections as preparation for a fuller treatment in the following books and to give a gyre-like structure to the entire book itself, in which we are constantly looking forward or behind, lost in detail, trying to envision the whole, as Kant notes of a visitor to St Peter's Cathedral in Rome.[17]

In order to understand how the peaceful, humane and unifying forces of a primary dispensation and the violent, inhuman, divisive forces of an antithetical dispensation work within the poems, it is best to examine the relationship between the Faculties and Principles (in Yeats's terminology the Principles are 'the innate ground of the Faculties'[18]), as they provide the axis upon which the dispensations turn. The Principles correspond to the Faculties: 'Husk' is the equivalent of Will (the is); Passionate Body is equivalent of Mask (the ought); Spirit of Creative Mind (the knower); and Celestial Body of Body of Fate (the known). The terms themselves make some of the relationships clear. The reality of the Will, the 'is' or the real, is merely the husk of its former self in the afterlife; it is moulted, shed like an old skin. The Mask, our object of desire, what we hope for, achieves full corporeality in the afterlife; it becomes actual in the Passionate Body. After so many defeats, there is the final victory of Imagination. This is why Yeats, like Shelley, often writes of a vision of reality which artists achieve as some lifting of the veil. In the afterlife, Creative Mind crystallises into its creative essence and the Body of Fate (what is known of this world) achieves its transcendent embodiment and its original state in the Celestial Body. Yeats writes that the latter represents the 'Divine Ideas in their unity'.[19] What makes this complicated system and these unwieldy terms necessary is the light they shed on the relationship between eternal and temporal beauty, and between the negative/positive sublime. Whether positive or negative, Yeatsian sublimity is the interaction of the Principles and Faculties. Yeats implies this when he writes: 'gentleness and violence alike express the gyre's hesitation'.[20] If we replace those terms with positive and negative sublimity, the point is clear. What happens is that the Principles shift, or different aspects are revealed, and the terms of temporal beauty change, as they did at Christ's birth ('The Mother of God' and 'Two Songs from a Play'), at the dawn of the French Revolution, at the rebellion of 1916, or as Yeats imagines they will change in 'Leda and the Swan' and 'The Second Coming'. Any major change in epistemology is the result of such a shift in how people define the beautiful, as well as how they define themselves.

BOOK III, 'THE SOUL IN JUDGMEN.

The period known as 'The Soul in Judgment' in *A Vision* is compos.
six states: (1) The Vision of the Blood Kindred, (2) Meditation, (3) Shifting.,
(4) Marriage or Beatitude, (5) Purification, (6) Foreknowledge. Through
these six stages we are purged of one life and prepared for the next.
During 'The Vision of The Blood Kindred', the real gives way to the
imaginary, substance to shadow, as the spirit leaves the body. Once done,
the aesthetic revelation begins in the three stages of Meditation: Dreaming
Back, Return and Phantasmagoria. In Dreaming Back, the soul comes to
terms with its passions by re-experiencing its most intense experiences,
especially the sexual ones, and those of a sinful or criminal nature. With
the Passionate Body, the soul rises from the genitals after death, in order
that it may find its Celestial Body, its store of Divine Ideas, its heavenly
body of thought. This stage marks the progress to that tranquillity which
must be achieved before we can begin to understand the material of our
existence. In the Return, then, the soul relives its life sequentially, because
the dead must frequent the world of the living in order to find the
language with which they may express their dramas. They themselves
have no language because the Faculties have disappeared with death.
The more complete the Dreaming Back, of course, the better the Return.
The mind can look with serenity into the minds of those alive and may
even read their letters through their living eyes. As the Dreaming Back
exhausted pain and pleasure, the Return exhausts the relations of natural
experience in their natural order. We live our lives again, but now with
eyes that have been spiritualised by death.

In the third stage of the second state, which is Phantasmagoria, we
exhaust emotion in fields of morality and imagination. We are able to do
so through the work of the Teaching Spirits, dwellers in the Thirteenth
Cone. They are most definitely angelic beings who, Yeats insists, are not
like Christian angels existing in the celestial harmony by the grace of
God, but rather they depend upon us, our lives, for 'separation and
solidity'.[21] For 'our actions' lived in life, or remembered in death, continues Yeats, are the food and drink of the Spirits of the Thirteenth Cone.
They are like the Irish fairies who steal human children to restock the
bloodline (they have no blood) in order to write their names in blood and
re-enter heaven. Such vampirish Teaching Spirits (whom Yeats expressly
separates from the 'pure benevolence [that] exhausted Platonism and
Christianity attribute to an angelical being'[22]) enable us to consummate
our im/moral and imaginative inclinations. They enable us to complete
the crimes we have only partially committed and reviewed in the
Dreaming Back and Return, because, through them, we commit acts
which hitherto we have only dared to imagine.

At the height of self-knowledge we are then able to enter the third state called Shiftings, in which if mainly good we learn of evil, and if evil we learn of goodness, so that we are able to regard them impassively. The state prepares the soul for the fourth state of the Soul in Judgment, that is Marriage or Beatitude. It is an ecstatic state very similar in its sexual nature to phase 15 or the Thirteenth Cone. Therein art has begun to be created. In Yeats's terms, remorse yields to harmony and 'good and evil vanish into the whole'.[23] He is of course using Biblical language (the Song of Solomon) in describing a state in which the soul rediscovers innocence, a more 'radical innocence'. The soul, or artist, is now ready for the fifth state, namely, Purification, in which the soul, or mind, can begin its proper work because it is freed of distraction and in touch with the *Anima Mundi*. Purified of the 'complexities of mire and blood', it can see before it the aim of perfection. This is one of Yeats's most evocative versions of the positive sublime.

In the last state, Foreknowledge, a vision of the next life must be completed and accepted if the spirit, or soul, is to be reborn. Yeats's theory of reincarnation, whose truth he insisted on, is predicated on conquering the fear of death (although it seems at times to be an escape from death). Not one of the states of the afterlife is paradisal or final in any way. Paradise is an edge against the real but not a permanent state. As Yeats hauntingly writes, 'Neither between death and birth nor between birth and death can the soul find more than momentary happiness; its object is to pass rapidly round its circle and find freedom from that circle.'[24] If a soul resists this passage, it becomes a frustrator, one of the oracular spirits that lead poets astray, that provide them with false Masks and false objectives. The only way out of that circle is through the amoral work of the inhuman and unpresentable Teaching Spirits of the Thirteenth Cone. Here again we have reached the ineffable God-like locus of personal, artistic, and historical growth.

BOOK IV AND V, 'THE GREAT YEAR OF THE ANCIENTS' AND 'DOVE OR SWAN'

In order to provide some idea of the historical implications of *A Vision*, the last two books, 'The Great Year of the Ancients' and 'Dove or Swan', illustrate how the themes of poetic creation, revealed in the antithetical and primary dispensations, are incarnated in the various gyres and spheres of history. Among the most central examples, because the most balanced, is Byzantium. Yeats writes that in 'early Byzantium, maybe never before or since in recorded history, religious, aesthetic and practical life were one'.[25] They were one because primary worship could express antithetical violence through the delicate skill of the artisan. Most of history is an expression of some imbalance. In 'The Great Year of the Ancients', the ying and yang of antithetical Caesar and primary Christ are revealed on the Ides of March when both of them died. Both achieved apotheosis upon their deaths, therefore displaying the phoenix of self, poetic, social death and creation and their two opposed renderings. Two such different dispensations require two quite different Muses: Dove and Swan. The primary muse, the Dove, is the Holy Ghost, while the antithetical muse is the Swan or Jove, the violent impregnator. They are the separate revelations of faith and desire, of compassion and knowledge, of positive and negative sublimity. In the book entitled 'Dove or Swan', Yeats outlines the oppositions between primary Christian and antithetical Classical forces, charting their courses to the present age. He also examines how what he believes are the best cultures (Greece, Byzantium, and Renaissance Italy) combine the antithetical and primary through what he calls 'Unity of Culture', just as the best individuals combine them in Unity of Being. Believing that we are approaching the end of a Christian age and the beginning of a Classical one, Yeats insists that the Swan must be our muse. This belief is not felt without pain, however. He worries over what knowledge or religion will come of such a violent act of creation. The movement of the interlocking gyres, of the revelation of the Principles in relation to the Faculties, and the demonstrations of antithetical and primary natures are probably best illustrated in those poems that Yeats wrote specifically to accord with *A Vision* and which close the volume, *The Wild Swans at Coole* (1919).

THE POETICS OF *A VISION*

How much *A Vision* has influenced Yeats's poetry, and how essential it might be to understanding the poems, is a subject of some debate. Whether essential or not, it is certainly formative. Some poems, like those at the close of *The Wild Swans at Coole* (1919), are directly inspired by it. The argument of 'Ego Dominus Tuus' is that either the self is fulfilled through absolute sincerity or else through the transcendental illusion of the Mask. In the poem, *Hic* argues the point of absolute sincerity, while *Ille* (whom Ezra Pound called Willie) argues that we find ourselves through the image of our opposite, and that we cannot help but want to be that which we are not. *Hic* argues that Dante's face, the very real outline of it, is so familiar to us, because Dante is so true to himself. *Ille*, on the other hand, argues that Dante fulfils himself in his 'hunger for the apple on the bough/Most out of reach'. Dante becomes great through the agency of 'the most exalted lady loved by a man'. According to *Ille*, Dante finds an outlet for the inhuman, for his lechery, and overcomes the inhumanity of civil strife and exile through the transforming discipline of his love for Beatrice.

Keats is a different case in the poem, as the object-sublime that he achieves is always marked by division. Dante sees Paradise from within; Keats sees it from the irretrievable point of separation. According to Yeats, the reason for this difference lies with *Hic*'s belief in the powers of sincerity. The criticism of modernity is found in one of *Ille's* retorts: 'We have lit upon the gentle, sensitive mind/And lost the old nonchalance of the hand . . . We are but critics'. The Romantics struggle vainly against the separation of heart and intellect, but modern intellectuals have so divorced thought and feeling that they cannot act and by extension cannot create. The 'cult of sincerity', as Yeats would later call it,[26] has made us forget to dissociate the inhuman within, of 'which the soul is hostage',[27] from the inhumanity of industrialised society; it has made us choose the timid rather than the exultant heart.

If the artistic incarnations are most visible in 'Ego Dominus Tuus', the historical theme of subjective (antithetical) and objective (primary) dispensations is more closely examined in other poems at the end of *The Wild Swans at Coole* (1919). Essentially, the subjective dispensation is God made immanent, incarnate; it is a fulfilment of the body and of its divine uses and proportions. The objective dispensation is God made emanate, a transcendence of the body, a denial of the flesh and fulfilment of the spirit through the agency of the primary. Artists usually must look to a subjective dispensation, as their work is a discovery of the self and world, while saints must look to an objective one as their revelation is a renunciation of them. Both illuminations are supernatural, hinted at in human experience, and revealed only in death. In 'The Phases of the Moon', the new moon (phase 1, or solar sign), the lack of reflective subjectivity, is a supernatural manifestation of the primary spirit, while the full moon (phase 15, the lunar sign) is a supernatural manifestation of the antithetical spirit. The approach to these opposing phases of the moon is one of heightening degrees of positive (primary) and negative (antithetical) sublimity. A complete experience of either the inner or the external inhuman sublime means death. The poem is a concise description of the 28 phases of personality in one's combat with the self and with circumstance. Yeats describes the early stages of personality, of culture, of primitive man who is close to the primary, and who acts on instinct because he is in touch with supersensible rhythms: '. . . the dream/But summons to adventure, and the man/Is always happy like a bird or a beast'. As the phases progress, primitive unreflecting man moves towards heroic self-consciousness (like a Turnus, or Hector, debating with himself) in which he will establish himself as antithetical, indeed satanic, analogy to God.

Achilles is referred to thereafter because he is both mortal and immortal, and in his wrath is an ancient precursor to Lucifer. The whole idea of the heroic is based on the idea of achieving a type of glory to rival the immortals. Hence, Nietzsche is mentioned: 'Nietzsche is born,/Because the hero's crescent is the twelfth.' The height of heroism, however, spells its twilight. By phase 13, one begins to experience self-doubt, the self-torment of Satan, 'the soul at war/In its own being'. The soul momentarily finds perfect and complete expression in the body, but in that perfection transcends the phenomenal world which abides neither perfection nor completion. This is '[t]he strange reward of all that discipline': 'Body and soul cast out and cast away/Beyond the visible world.' This is also the perfect incarnation of the immanent God, for '[a]ll dreams of the soul/End in a beautiful man's or woman's body'. As the full moon reflects the sun in its most perfect verisimilitude, so the antithetical body reflects the primary Godhead by giving perfect expression to the soul. The expression of the soul follows Kant's idea that the self is subjective (a point of view) that the soul is an object (an item in the world) and that the sublime moment establishes a bridge between them by illustrating how necessary is the primary movement of the soul in communicating an idea so far beyond the reach of understanding.[28] The subjective Will (is) of phase 15 is perfectly reflected in the objective Mask (ought) of phase 1 and the subjective Creative Mind (knower) of phase 15 is again reflected in its Body of Fate (known) of phase 1.

As Yeats writes of phase 15 in *A Vision*, the sun is consumed by the moon and 'all is beauty'.[29] Complete beauty is supernatural; it is not a human incarnation.[30] Even if they cannot inhabit it, human beings can experience its power. Yeats reaches the pitch of his mystical writing in his description of the sublime moment in phase 15: 'Chance and Choice have become interchangeable without losing their identity . . . [one's] own body possesses the greatest possible beauty, being indeed that body which the soul will permanently inhabit, when all its phases have been repeated according to the number allotted: that which we call the clarified or Celestial Body.'[31] This is an antithetical, completely subjective form of comprehension. Its beauty enters the *a priori* realm of the sublime, and is 'clarified' in the Celestial Body, that organ of Kant's idea of pure reason. What type of sublimity it will be remains to be seen. Is it that negative sublimity which expresses desire and unbridgeable division, a higher form of '. . . beauty dropped out of the loneliness/Of body and soul', where 'the terror in their [the lovers'] eyes/Is memory or foreknowledge of the hour/When all is fed with light and heaven is bare'? Or, is it the positive sublimity which expresses wisdom and divine ideas in their unity? It is both; ideally, if a person experiences the negative sublime, the reason and the resolution for this division should be revealed in the positive sublime. This progression is exactly what Yeats proceeds to imagine after the above passage in *A Vision*: '. . . there is now terror of solitude, its forced, painful and slow acceptance, and a life haunted by terrible dreams. Even for the most perfect, there is a time of pain, a passage through a vision, where evil reveals itself in its final meaning.'[32] The difficulty of the movement from terror to meaning is highlighted by the fact that the word 'terror' was consistently impressed upon Yeats while *A Vision* was being written.[33]

The antithetical progression to complete beauty in the union of body and soul, and its eventual loneliness and longing for the more objective, less self-centred forms of the primary, mirrors the artist's progression in the act of creation. Still, the cruelties of the antithetical must end in primary surrender, else the tragedies of our lonely passionate lives are repeated. In 'The Phases of the Moon', Yeats parodies his own position, and the loneliness and futility of his own antithetical desires. For both the ascetic Aherne (based on Lionel Johnson), and the prophet of the senses Robartes (based on MacGregor Mathers) mock Yeats's ambitions. As author, he pretends to knowledge that he can never possess without the help of revelation. His own characters know that 'He'd crack his head/Day after day, yet never find the meaning'. Like Samuel Palmer, he is an outcast religious artist working in an increasingly secular age. Like Shelley and Milton, Yeats is endeavouring to outline his own cosmography in an age of conflicting world-views, and his attempts have that same lonely quality and the same curse of failure hanging over them. The reason for failure is that Yeats is pulled by his subconscious life as the tides and the cat Minnaloushe are pulled by the moon. Never knowing the answer, he must seek the question 'caught between the pull of the dark moon and the full' in 'The Double Vision of Michael Robartes'.

The poem begins with a description of God's objective will, of the primary dispensation. The key-word is 'obedient'. The body becomes puppet-like, grasping that its will was never its own. In this picture, however, the Other 'Will' is not antagonistic; it is mechanical, working with 'blank eyes'. Lyotard's essays on 'God' and 'Obedience' develop an interesting comparison between the concepts 'to obey' and 'to listen'. 'Nothing', Lyotard writes, '. . . is closer to infinite divine grace than the mechanism these puppets obey'.[34] In the essay entitled 'Obedience', he notes that the word obedience comes from the Latin word meaning 'to listen absolutely'.[35] Listening so, we return to that sound which is original, that does not depend upon harmony, rhythm, and forms. We return to what in the poem Yeats calls that 'hidden magical breath', the Primum Mobile, or pure act, which cannot be repeated. Listen well, Lyotard insists, and the walls of the body will break down like the walls of Jericho. Although Yeats is always ambivalent about such a sacrifice of will, it is nevertheless the '[t]riumph that we obey'. Aesthetically for Lyotard, it is the intuition, the reception of the sound in its flight, that invests the all in one.

Part II of 'The Double Vision of Michael Robartes' hosts Yeats's favourite method for uncovering the indivisible element that contains all reality – the dancer. In this case the woman dancer performs between the Sphinx (the antithetical pagan dispensation of action and power) and Buddha (the Eastern self-effacing God of contemplation whom Yeats later thought should have been Christ).[36] Like Yeats, she is caught between the pull of the dark moon and the full. Her dance takes place on the fifteenth night, the dark moon, the supernatural incarnation of the subjective or antithetical, which is fitting as the artist's work is antithetical by nature. The Sphinx is an emblem of knowledge and power, while the sitting Buddha is a transcendent emblem of love and compassion. The dancer is unconcerned with either force, and yet is moved by both. Her subjective manifestation is a sublime embodiment of the objective soul. She too achieves freedom and grace by moving beyond the 'minute particulars of mankind', and by moving beyond time. The poem's image of the antithetical and primary forces working together upon human endeavour achieves a type of immortal status, a supernatural incarnation. In the antithetical incarnation they are 'dead yet flesh and bone', while in primary transcendence they are 'dead beyond [their] death'. It is clear, then, how art is able to reach, if not inhabit, the complete beauty of phase 15. The soul, if only for the duration of the dance, has found that body which it will permanently inhabit.

The last part of the poem finds Robartes thankful for the scene which has brought about his synthesising vision of the two dispensations. In an internalisation of the quest romance that is worthy of Endymion or Alastor, Robartes sees in the dancer an image of transcendent beauty, a paragon of positive sublimity which is touchstone to his own ideas of the antithetical and the primary. Like Venus, she seems to rise from the waters of his instinctual life, that seat of the Other Will, the object of primary repression which threatens to undo us all. Yet Yeats has not been undone. The power wielded by the dancer is that which unified the Trojans in both the conviction of their strength and of Helen's extraordinary beauty. The negativity of this sublimity only comes after they understand that physical strength and beauty are not sufficient, and when pious Aeneas leads them to establish primary Rome. Robartes, the prophet of the senses, has been given this vision by *Spiritus Mundi*, the collective unconscious. The poem ends as it had begun, with an image of the primary, but now it has been connected to the antithetical. The vision has come in the ruins of an early pre-Roman, Irish Church that to Yeats embodies an Asiatic Unity of Being and Culture, and balances the primary and antithetical.[37] As it had in Byzantium, sexuality and murderousness find a sanctifying voice. It is fitting that Robartes is 'rewarded thus/In Cormac's ruined house' because his vision achieved a similar balance in its presentation of the ineffable world of the Principles behind human endeavour.

Yeats's double vision provides an appropriate introduction to the next volumes entitled *Michael Robartes and the Dancer* (1921) and *The Tower* (1928), which contain such poems of terror as 'Easter, 1916', 'Meditations in Time of Civil War', 'The Second Coming' and 'Leda and the Swan', as well as poems of such positive sublimity as 'Solomon and the Witch', 'A Prayer for my Daughter' and 'Among School Children'. The negative sublime makes us aware of our strengths and of our tendency towards divisiveness, while the positive makes us aware of our weaknesses and of our need for harmony. As always, these themes interpenetrate within the various poems. They are double visions. The historical interaction, the gyring of the antithetical and primary is remarkably interwoven. The aim is to perfect these forces by wedding them. The hope for such a marriage is Eleusinian in its erotic mystery. In the next two volumes there is an obvious awareness of the sexual basis of both forms of sublimity, of destructive and creative ecstasy, of the cyclical rape and return of Persephone, of lamentation and beatitude.

PART III

A Dancer Wound in His Own Entrails: The Negative Sublime

9

THE FRIVOLOUS EYE:
YEATSIAN EPIPHANY AND
THE VIOLENCE OF GOD

The sublime is the child of an unhappy encounter, that of the Idea with form. Unhappy because this Idea is unable to make concessions. The law (the father) is so authoritarian, so unconditional, and the regard the law requires so exclusive that he, the father, will do nothing to obtain consent even through a delicious rivalry with the imagination. He requires the imagination's 'retraction'. He pushes forms aside, or, rather, forms part before his presence, tear themselves apart, extend themselves to inordinate proportions. [. . .] He demands regard only for himself, for the law and its realization. He has no need for a beautiful nature. He desperately needs an imagination that is violated, extended, exhausted.

Jean-François Lyotard, *Lessons on the Analytic of the Sublime*

This erotic cult of the abject makes one think of a perversion, but it must be distinguished at once from what simply dodges castration. [. . .] The eroticization of abjection, and perhaps any abjection to the extent that it is already eroticized is an attempt at stopping the hemorrhage: a threshold before death, a halt or a respite?

Julia Kristeva, *Powers of Horror*

> Oh! sad. And you yourself, yes? feel the pain
> Of this drear picture, though your frivolous eye
> Toys with the gold and crimson butterfly
> Fluttering above the fragments in the lane.

Paul Verlaine, 'Cupid Fallen'

In Yeats's system of historical gyres, 'Leda and the Swan' is set at the significant moment when 'the old *primary* becomes the new *antithetical*, the old realisation of an objective moral law is changed into a sub-conscious turbulent instinct'.[1] Like 'The Second Coming', which in many ways is introductory, 'Leda and the Swan' contains the revolt of Nature and the sensible world against the categorical imperative. The beautiful has moved towards a negative form, a 'terrible beauty', because the underlying standards of taste and ethics, the *sensus communis*, have eroded. The beautiful must be violated in order to be renewed, as in the scenario described by Lyotard above; and yet such 'eroticisation of abjection' may well be, as Kristeva reminds us, 'an attempt at stopping the hemorrhage: a threshold before death'.[2] The attempt to find meaning from the experience moves between the view that the aestheticisation of violence is necessary and the view that such aestheticisation is merely a flight or respite from death. In Burkean terms, Leda is like Job in the mystical moment of confrontation with the Godhead; explanation comes later and is not Burke's concern. In Kantian terms, her internal sense is violated, and the resolution to her crisis must come from within. It is a case of negative, Burkean sublimity seeking a positive Kantian form when 'the abject collapses in a burst of beauty that overwhelms us'.[3] In this reconciliation, the swan itself is an example of what Rudolf Otto in *The Idea of the Holy* names 'divine otherness'.[4]

Besides the poem's empirical and formal questions of sublimity, there is also a strongly rhetorical component that makes Longinus fundamental to an understanding of its dangerous rhetorical implications. Through an examination of the rhetoric we come to the question of what position the reader takes when confronted by the rape. Readers must feel themselves to be like Leda or Job, in order to vindicate the voyeuristic role in which the voyeur poet has placed them. They must be aware of what Verlaine calls their 'frivolous eye'.[5] In 'Leda and the Swan' we may well be said to see 'the uncontrollable mystery on the bestial floor' ('The Magi') from as 'pale' and 'unsatisfied' a perspective as the Magi's own. Vindication relies heavily upon the not unproblematic view of the poem as an epiphany. The close of the chapter examines 'Leda and the Swan' as an example of negative sublimity in light of the positive sublimity of 'Lullaby'. In this comparison, depending upon the central confrontation of Burkean and Kantian aesthetics, we approach an answer to the closing question of Yeats's violent sonnet.

RAPE, SUFFERING AND THE AESTHETICS OF MEANING

'The Second Coming' and 'Leda and the Swan' are two of the most famous and violent poems that enact Yeats's idea of a new antithetical dispensation. They enact an historical moment in which we have lost control of Nature, in which Nature and irrationality revolt when we thought we had hooded and domesticated them. The effort to obtain absolute control over Nature has been mirrored in our move towards absolute control over society, and, since the primary system of self-effacement to outward rule and to material externality has developed, all the repressed forces of irrationality and brute force have struck out against widespread corporate docility. The innocent, however, are left defenceless during this revolt, as the primary system which encouraged their meekness is too ineffectual to defend them from the rape of their souls. In a violent imbalance, power goes to those who can appeal to the bloodlust of the age. Yeats hopes that the artistic freedom and the fictive example-setting imagination of the aristocracy will dominate the scene, but instead arrogant, warmongering brute force is triumphant. Although he laments this murder of the innocents, he sees it as a necessary part of social and self-renewal; the murder of innocents attended the birth of Moses and Christ. His whole system of renewal is at least partly an attempt to embolden the irresolution of those now vulnerable innocent natures which know how to pleasure the soul without bruising the body and to whose suffering he bears lyric witness.

If there ever were an age that would accommodate sensitive natures, the approaching age is certainly not one. The new incarnation evokes the harsh antithetical qualities. It is born in a waste-place, which is typical for many sacred beings. As Christ is a symbol of union, the new opposing incarnation is a symbol of social and animal division; it divisively drives off the 'indignant desert birds' which St Francis would have befriended. Its Sphinx-like form reminds us that the riddle of life ends in destruction whether one answers it correctly or not. It subsumes the sacredness of the violent 'hour of terror that comes to test the soul' ('Hound Voice'), and that is why, in A Vision, Robartes advises that we should '[l]ove war because of its horror, that belief may be changed, civilisation renewed. We desire belief and lack it. Belief comes from shock and is not desired'.[6] Through the experience of terror, we achieve ecstatic understanding of the sublime attributes of the Godhead, as did Mary at the Annunciation, when she envisioned the birth, life and death of Jesus at the very instant of conception.[7] It is through her own terror and the suffering of Christ that the irresistible way towards heaven was revealed, and it is through violence that a society whose underlying standards of taste and ethics have eroded can be renewed. The problems of unjustifiable pain and unfathomable questions of dying are what sustain belief: 'belief is renewed continually in the ordeal of death'.[8]

Yeats is trying to find sublime meaning in Leda's suffering, as Burke tries to find sublime meaning in the suffering of Job. In our confrontation with the Godhead, Burke believes that we

> . . . shrink into the minuteness of our own nature, and are in a manner, annihilated before him. And though a consideration of his other attributes may relieve in some measure our apprehensions; yet no conviction of the

justice with which it is exersised [*sic*], nor the mercy with which it is
tempered, can wholly remove the terror that naturally arises from a force
which nothing can withstand.[9]

Job sees God incarnate in all the diseases and misfortunes that afflict him
and which he is powerless to avoid. Through them, Job experiences a
divine horror at the mysteries of wisdom and understanding, one which
Yeats also perceives as necessary to any profound conception of God
whose advent is imagined as terrifying. The misfortunes are as sublime as
is the invincible storm over the mountain top which constitutes the
conventional idea of the sublime, but in his description Burke is not
concerned with origins or the explanation of suffering. Job perceives
neither justice nor mercy behind his torment. It is a purely psychological
moment. We thereby begin to have a suggestion of what is essentially
incomprehensible, and to see an elusive presentation of what is ultimately
unpresentable: what Hawthorne calls 'dark necessity'.[10] In poems such as
'The Second Coming' and 'Leda and the Swan', however, Yeats attempts
to move from the psychological moment to its origins. Violence functions
in his cosmology in a way very like that suggested in the Psalms; his
poetry is an attempt to interpret the idea that 'the lions, roaring after their
prey, do seek their meat from God' (Psalms 104: 21). For an actual
representation of the shock and terror of belief, which the birth of the
'rough beast' will inflict, we must turn to 'Leda and the Swan'.

   To grasp the poem in the psychological and religious terms of the
Yeatsian sublime, it helps to examine quotations by Rudolf Otto and
Kant on the subject, and to examine the poem in light of them. In *The
Idea of the Holy*, Otto describes divine horror as a *mysterium tremendum*.
He sees the element of awe in this experience as a type of sacred dread, a
'quite specific type of emotional response, wholly distinct from that of
being afraid, though it so resembles it that the analogy of fear may be
used to throw light upon its nature'. In our encounter with the numinous,
he continues, we 'come upon something inherently and "wholly other",
whose kind and character are incommensurable with our own, and before
which we therefore recoil in a wonder that strikes us chill and numb'.[11]
This is a very accurate description of the Yeatsian sublime in its violent,
religious manifestations. It both complements and expands Burke's description of the sublime, and by doing so begins to bridge the gap between
empiricist and formalist, or Burkean and Kantian, ideas of sublimity.
The swan has all those symbolic expressions of power, vitality, will and
movement with which Otto associates the numinous. The swan is 'the
feathered glory', 'that white rush', 'the brute blood of the air', and lastly,
and perhaps most importantly, it is 'the strange heart' whose beating
Leda cannot help but feel. This last phrase is the one that best captures

the divine otherness of the swan. It is what separates it from the swans at Coole Park. The relationship between the mysterious and beautiful wild swans at Coole and the swan that attacks Leda is close to that described by Burke between a draft horse and one of the horses of the Apocalypse.[12] Yeats's description highlights the difference between the swans in 'The Wild Swans at Coole' who 'paddle in the cold' and that one which, in 'Leda and the Swan', is 'the brute blood of the air'. The latter swan's strangeness makes it what Otto describes as 'wholly other', something that so 'masters' her that she is left 'chill and numb'. This sense of divine otherness is momentous. Yeats believes that the experience of the sublime might bridge our temporal experience and the eternal forms outside it: '. . . profound philosophy must come from terror. An abyss opens under our feet; inherited convictions . . . drop into the abyss. Whether we will or no we must ask the ancient questions: Is there reality anywhere? Is there a God? Is there a Soul?'[13] In 'Leda and the Swan' the terror of the sublime demonstrates the psychological realities of existence, and in a richly Kantian mode attempts to connect them to the violent metaphysics of what might lie beyond.

Enlarging upon his ideas of the difference between apprehension and comprehension (that we can apprehend the sublimity of St Peter's Cathedral but never comprehend it), Kant comes to a difficult conclusion as regards the workings of intuition, imagination, time, understanding and reason during an encounter with the mathematical sublime:

> . . . the comprehension of the manifold in the unity, not of thought, but of intuition, and consequently the comprehension of the successively apprehended parts at one glance, is a retrogression that removes the time-condition in the progression of the imagination, and renders *co-existence* intuitable. Therefore, since the time-series is a condition of the internal sense and of an intuition, it is a subjective movement of the imagination by which it does violence to the internal sense – a violence which must be proportionally more striking the greater the quantum which the imagination comprehends in one intuition.[14]

This passage reads like a philosophical exegesis of 'Leda and the Swan'. We identify the reduction of understanding to intuition, the loss of a sense of time, and the internal violence. As Leda recoils 'in wonder', Yeats asks a question that is central to any mystical union: 'Did she put on his knowledge with his power/Before the indifferent beak could let her drop?' Kant addresses the same question in its very mechanism, though he nevertheless leaves us suspended between the means and the aim of the experience, wherein lies the very unpresentable heart of the sublime. He posits that the imagination does violence to our subjectivity because of a rupture in our sense of time. In the very first phrase of the poem ('A sudden blow') we are prepared for just such a rupture, one which the double meaning of 'still' at the end of the line emphasises. It helps to prepare us for the removal of the 'time-condition' that moves us forward to Agamemnon's death – something that perhaps Leda can intuit. And, because the violence that is 'wrought on the subject' is not only wrought 'through the imagination' – or even, as Kant writes in *The Critique of Judgement*, through the 'whole province of the mind'[15] – but on and through Leda's physical being, the parts which are apprehended 'at one glance' are therefore her body parts. Yeats then lists that apprehension which can never be complete comprehension: '. . . her thighs caressed/ By the dark webs, her nape caught in his bill'. Leda is caught in the confusion between the rape and the heart of God the rapist, which represent apprehension and comprehension respectively. Similarly, she is also caught between God's infinite power and knowledge. Her condition and her knowledge are inseparable, which is why Yeats is uncertain whether she may retain the knowledge after the condition has ended. Has she, like Burke's Job, merely confronted and survived an incomprehensible experience, or is she aware of the formal reasons behind it? In Yeats's terms, Leda can *embody* the truth, but she cannot know it.

At this point, Yeats's phallocentric portrayal of the subjective passivity of the female must be noted. The poem 'Lullaby' presents maternal strength and male reliance as a counterpoint to 'Leda and the Swan', but it does not present female strength any more than does the latter, at least not in the way that, for example, Virginia Woolf does in *Between the Acts*.[16] As far as rape, suffering and the aesthetics of meaning are concerned, the poem is not necessarily restricted by gender. One can assume that Ganymede might have fared similarly under like circumstances, and that, during his rape, he would have perceived the eagle as Leda does the swan, as terrifyingly sublime rather than beautiful. The question of both experiences focuses on the nature of a violent confrontation with the godhead. Nevertheless, what significantly separates the two experiences is the poem's very obvious dependence upon Leda's subsequent pregnancy and its elliptical record of her offspring. We must therefore consider ideas of abjection, mysticism and voyeurism in order to comprehend the particularly feminine/female aspects of the poem.

VOYEURISM AND THE RHETORICAL SUBLIME

The world must be confronted with the sacred and the sublime – and violent images of the sacred and the sublime are extremely confrontational – yet none is more confrontational than the theme of rape. For the reading of rape to be an experience that is even remotely sublime, the reader must be made intimately involved, through a sublime style, and through the writer's manipulation of perspective. Yeats's style and voyeurism do precisely that; they impress with rhetoric and manipulate perspective. The voyeuristic writer, what Heaney calls the 'artful voyeur',[17] makes a voyeur of the reader, and the style of the poem forces the reader to recognise the sublimity of what is described. Yeats's sonnet fits Longinus's famous description of the sublime as the echo of a noble mind. In this case, it is as much the echo of the reader's mind that is tested as it is the echo of the author's, from where, M.H. Abrams believes, sublimity echoes.[18] Before interpreting the nature and purpose of Yeats's voyeuristic point of view in terms of the reader's response, the sublime style of 'Leda and the Swan' must be exposed, as so much of the succeeding discussion of the poem depends upon the nature of its dangerous rhetoric.

Longinus lists the five sources of a sublime style as (1) the ability to form a grand conception; (2) a powerful and inspired emotion; (3) the proper formation of the two types of figure, figure of thought and figure of speech; (4) the creation of a noble diction; and, lastly, (5) the source of grandeur which embraces the other four – the total impression resulting from their dignity and elevation. The general and vague first and fifth requirements are made more specific by Longinus's idea that sublimity must strike 'like a thunderbolt'.[19] From the first phrase ('a sudden blow') the poem indeed strikes like a thunderbolt. In the breadth of its religious and historical implications, it is a poem of great thought, of grand conception, of inspired emotion.

Following Longinus's prescription, Yeats 'twist[s] his language, to bring it into conformity with the impending disaster'.[20] He recreates the rhythm of the situation in the rhythm of the poem. He does so in the first stanza not only in the ways that I have shown but also through a type of reverse alliteration, a type of chiasmus: 'A sudden *blow*: the great wings *beating still*'. There is also an interesting use of the double letter (the double 'd' in 'sudden' and the double 'l' in 'still') at the beginning and at the end of the chiasmus whose prolonged linguistic weight highlights the suspended force of the attack. With this verbal device, Yeats stresses both the shock and the repetitive slow motion of the violence. Similarly, in Longinian terms, he mimics the action through asyndeton, the omission of conjunctions.[21] By omitting the smoothening polite quality which conjunctions can give to a poem, he recreates the roughness of the attack:

> A sudden blow: the great wings beating still
> Above the staggering girl, her thighs caressed
> By the dark webs, her nape caught in his bill,
> He holds her helpless breast upon his breast.

Also in lines 9–11, although to a lesser degree, Yeats uses asyndeton when listing the events resulting from the rape and impregnation that will change history (thereby using what Longinus calls 'cosmic differences'[22]), and which themselves imply the stages of sexual violation: 'A shudder in the loins engenders there/The broken wall, the burning roof and tower'. Lines 5 to 8 question the nature of the *mysterium tremendum* that terrorises Leda. While deploying anaphora (repetition of a word or phrase at the beginning of several successive verses, clauses or paragraphs), the appropriate rhetorical figure widely used in the Bible, Yeats also uses conjunctions in order to humanise his sacred questions:

> How can those terrified vague fingers push
> The feathered glory from her loosening thighs,
> And how can body, laid in that white rush,
> But feel the strange heart beating where it lies?

The close of the poem contains the most structurally important rhetorical device in Longinus's list: the polyptoton (an interchange of tenses). Yet, instead of moving from past to present as Longinus advises, Yeats moves from the present of the previous lines to the past:

> Being so caught up,
> So mastered by the brute blood of the air,
> Did she put on his knowledge with his power
> Before the indifferent beak could let her drop?

The shift in tense not only illustrates that he is looking back in time but also shows how the act had been fated to happen, had been in the past before it was in the present. The religious and oracular or prophetic nature of the experience occurs outside of space and time, as in the Kantian sublime.

Yeats is wondering what the nature of ecstasy and religious vision actually is, and whether it will last. Leda has certainly had a vision, and a terrifying one at that. To Bloom, this is the only point of the poem. Yet he is mistaken in preferring an earlier version of the lines 11–12 ('Being so caught up/Did nothing pass before her in the air?') to the later version ('Being so caught up/So mastered by the brute blood of the air . . .') merely because the revision, as he writes, 'adds little in itself and takes away the crucial question: did she have a vision as she was being victimized?'[23] He proves wrong because quite obviously the revision is a much better example of poetic rhetoric; its rhythm, tone and style evoke the brutality of the scene much more effectively. The evocative alliteration of plosive and liquid and dental sounds in ' by the brute blood', emphasised by the labial 'm' and consonant blend in 'mastered', is unrivalled in the tamer early version. Moreover, the rhythm is varied by the spondee of 'brute blood', and what is the anapest of the phrase 'of the air', in comparison to the strict iambs of the early version. The revision even appears to be better in terms of Bloom's last statement. For in 'the brute blood of the air' Leda sees the invisible made horrifyingly and very physically visible, which is exactly what Yeats meant to show. The question is not whether or not she had a vision; that she did is a given, but what is the *nature* of her vision? Is it a divine historical imperative, or is it merely a vision of cruel Nature working at its most random and its worst? Yeats believed in the reality of the unseen, and so he must have believed in all the historical and mythological movements of the sonnet.[24] The poem as a whole is a bold Longinian metaphor of the emotional, philosophical, and religious predicament of the age – what Yeats himself in *A Vision* recognises as an almost religious longing 'for the arbitrary and accidental, for the grotesque, the repulsive and the terrible, that it [the age] may be cured of desire'.[25] Violence has begun to possess a sacred meaning because it can cure us of the agony of obsessive desire. At the end of an era, or the changing of a gyre, the process is 'violent, a breaking of the soul and world into fragments'.[26]

By imitating the experience of the sublime, Yeats would have us relive it. His poem is more than a rhetorical device if it succeeds. It is more than rhetoric or style that recreates the experience. Yeats must manipulate the unwilling reader in such a way that he or she feels the rape on an intimate basis. How he does so has been criticised as voyeurism. Rather than being a mere mindless voyeur to Leda's rape, Yeats is manoeuvring the reader's response into a position very analogous to his, so that we must witness him in the act of voyeurism, and become voyeurs as well.[27] If we accept this, then Yeats's voyeurism, and our role as readers, take on a different meaning. We must remember that the poem is an enactment of a crucial moment in the movement of the gyres, when, as Yeats writes of 'Leda and the Swan', 'the [cultural] soil is so exhausted that . . . nothing is possible but some movement from above preceded by some violent annunciation'.[28] And, because the symbol of the gyres has a vaginal and sexual basis, we are all made witnesses to the terrible forced creation of historical destiny, a destiny of which, no less than Leda, we all are victims. When reading of Leda's fate, we are confronting our own. Yeats's depiction of the rape is aimed at making us realise this identification with the subjectivity of Leda and the terrible otherness of the swan. This aim is bound to be difficult to reach. The result is inevitably unstable.

In the depiction of rape, the emotions of reader and writer are extremely volatile. There are multiple reasons for this. The writer must choose words to describe the rape and the victim that either do not sound voyeuristic or, as Yeats chooses, purposefully do. The writer must describe the mechanism of the rape, especially the penetration, without seeming to enjoy either the violence or the sexual nature of the assault. The author's attitude towards the victim is also problematic because he is her creator and is therefore the one who victimises her. Lastly, the writer must treat the reader as a participant in the rape, or as an audience with a conscience. We must be aware of our position of safety as readers and of our aesthetic response to the sublime; a position and a response which are central to both Kant's and Burke's ideas of the sublime.[29] In this instance, whether consciously or not, Yeats has exposed the duplicity of the reader of the sublime. If Leda is a 'reader' of 'signs' who tries to take on their knowledge and power, every reader of her efforts, he seems to imply, must inevitably share her plight.

Choosing words to depict rape is unmanageable in comparison to choosing words to depict any other act of violence that is without obvious sexual characteristics. The writer who is describing rape, describing the unscriptable, is not simply discussing arms, legs and other generic body parts, as one does when describing battle. The writer is now discussing breasts, thighs, lips, and male and female genitals; he is discussing the erogenous zones. In so doing, the literary treatment of rape must be placed in the context, or somehow opposed to the context, of erotic literature. The chief difficulty in portraying rape is that the words provoke a type of sexual response, whether one wants them to or not. To use generic and polite terms of a clinical nature such as groin, privates and even mouth, in order not to mention genitals and lips, for example, would sound less than sympathetic towards the victim's plight. Certain literary conventions for the description of breasts and female genitalia, such as orbs and gates, which may sound affectionate and polished in love poems, at least in the Renaissance, can simply sound callous in a description of rape, as they often do even in certain Renaissance descriptions.[30]

Another comparable difficulty is that the vocabulary of the action, not only the description of the participants, is different in the description of rape than it is in the description of any other act of violence. In the description of armed combat, for instance, one is describing strategic battle manoeuvres, the movement of the weapons, the angle of the body. In rape, the movements are uncomfortably similar to consenting sexual intercourse; the only way to separate them is the rather dubious choice of accentuating the violence. In the instance of rape, one is no longer fascinated by violence, as questionable an activity as that is. One is bringing it into an intimate aspect of life, which, because of its emotional and physical power and importance, must stand in contrast to brutality, as the sacred stands in contrast to the profane, if it is to absorb its power and redefine its terms. Consequently, violence becomes crucial to the description of rape, especially if the writer is to contrast clearly the emotional and physical power of sexuality with that of violence. Its savagery is especially central to Yeats's illustration of the rupture between God and human beings. As there are two types of ecstatic sublime, the blessed and destructive, so there are two types of sexual manifestations of God's presence: the angelic rapture experienced by St John, St Catherine and St Teresa, and that which, quoting Mallarmé, Yeats at the end of the 'Tragic Generation' calls the advent of 'the savage god'.[31] Like Wordsworth's concepts of joy and fear, incarnations of positive and negative sublimity, these manifestations are the twin embodiments of sublimity and of otherness.

In order to realise this sublimity and otherness, Yeats wants to manipulate the reader's response to the rape, especially with respect to the will of the victim, but the literary devices which are available are by nature erratic. For Leda, the experience must manifest the condition of society's faith. Her society and ours 'desire belief and lack it.' The poem aims to show how 'belief comes from shock and is not desired',[32] that is, the belief we desire is not the one we need, while the one that we need is not the belief we desire. The absence of any article (a, an or the) or possessive pronoun (her, in this instance) before 'body' underlines the disorientation, the strange otherness of this body; the experience shows how estrangingly separate body and soul can be and how they crave union. This absence also places 'body' between the reader and writer as some representative figure that is shared by both of them. Rather than merely reifying Leda's body, as in some ways he is doing, Yeats endeavours to upset any easy detachment on the part of the perceiving eye. The reader should feel an uneasy subjectivity. We want understanding and yet fear that the ultimate type of discipline, which might lead to it, would not be true to our ideal of understanding, that the means would not do justice to the ends. Yet this is often exactly what constitutes revelation. This is the paradoxical knowledge which we need but cannot contain beyond the moment of apprehension. This is the truth we can embody but cannot know. Yeats makes us voyeurs to the spectacle of the unfolding of her (and by constant implication the unfolding of our) desire. We see 'her thighs caressed', 'her helpless breast upon his breast', 'her loosening thighs' and are left to imagine the rest: the breaking of her hymen, an orgasm that, uncomfortably unattributed, could be his or hers or both, and then the detumescence of his phallus. This is not so much a description of her learning to desire the rape, as it is a description of a revelation which is like a rape, of a dawning of desire for a belief one does not understand.

By making us voyeurs to the rape of Leda, as he himself is a voyeur, Yeats is fracturing imagination from understanding (we imagine what we cannot understand) and is forcing us to intuit the monstrousness of the creation of love and war (Leda's offspring) which, like good and evil, continue to haunt the philosophic mind.[33] Not being Zeus, both poet and reader must identify with Leda and not with the swan; if, that is, they can avoid demonising themselves in an effort towards self-aggrandisement. For the reader to avoid any defensive self-aggrandisement, or for one not to attack the poem for its treatment of gender, it is necessary to read 'Leda and the Swan' as an epiphanic experience. Though not all critics agree with an epiphanic reading, most do allow the poem its visionary qualities.[34] Behind Yeats's poem lies a demonstration of Teresan mysticism, one which includes Kristevan abjection and powers of horror. The reader must play the role of mystic. In Kristeva's words:

> The mystic's familiarity with abjection is a fount of infinite *jouissance*. One may stress the masochistic economy of that *jouissance* only if one points out at once that the Christian mystic, far from using it to the benefit of a symbolic or institutional power, displaces it indefinitely (as happens with dreams, for instance) within a discourse where the subject is resorbed (is that grace?) into communication with the Other and with others.[35]

The only other choice is to choose the negative, or even false sublimity of the violator, and remain trapped within the active but blind self, which knows none of the divine heterogeneity and otherness of abjection. Yeats ultimately avoids this false alternative, as he leaves to Leda the focus of the final question in the sonnet. The poem is what Kristeva terms 'an unveiling of the abject; an elaboration, a discharge, and a hollowing out of abjection through the Crisis of the Word'[36] – one which in any version of psychoanalytical sublimity must lie in the reconciliation of knowledge to power, in the resolution of 'the Crisis of the Word', which is a type of 'grace'. To conceive of the poem as a working example of negative sublimity that moves towards a positive epiphany it is best to compare it with 'Lullaby', its complement and an example of positive sublimity.

THE DEFILED AND EXALTED BODY

A good juxtaposition of 'Lullaby' and 'Leda and the Swan' requires an examination of sexuality as a basis for the beautiful and the positive sublime in opposition to the negative sublime. Donne's poem 'The Ecstasy' presents an image of perfected sexuality and usurps the seventeenth-century belief that the body was too sensual, too animalistic to have any connection with the soul. Donne writes that 'Love's mysteries in souls do grow,/But yet the body is his book'.[37] This image has the harmony of the senses and the pure essence of objective form which underlie all notions of the beautiful. In its power and final morality, such beauty tests the limits of the infinite and the ultimate. It approaches the positive sublime, one well known in the seventeenth and eighteenth centuries, a sublime

Kant called 'grand', or 'noble', Addison called 'great', and Burke referred to as 'magnificent' – a positive sublime which partially compensates for the negativity usually associated with sublimity. According to Kant, when moral good is aesthetically represented, it must be sublime even if it started as a representation of the beautiful, for such a 'final end' goes beyond the form of the beautiful.

In this way, the morality of 'The Ecstasy' finds its counterpart in 'Lullaby', for in the latter, the image of Tristram and Iseult, like that of Baile and Aillinn in 'Supernatural Songs', is one of an eternal ecstatic reconciliation akin to Donne's. While 'Lullaby' is like 'The Ecstasy', 'Leda and the Swan' parallels the Holy Sonnet 14, or 'Batter my heart, three-personed God'. In fact, Yeats often openly alludes to the seventeenth-century reading of the soul as the Bride of Christ that underlies Donne's sonnet ('Supernatural Songs'). An epiphanic reading of 'Leda and the Swan' is therefore very apt. If the first two poems are of the beautiful, or positive sublime, the latter two are of the negative, dynamic sublime. Jupiter's descent is violent. As sufferers beneath his descent we are all Ledas. The passion, no matter how hideous, has potential to exalt the sufferer, as the 'ravished' in Barthes's economy is an exalted mystical intermediary reflecting on both subject and object positions.[38] The very term 'put on' in the last couplet of 'Leda' ('Did she put on his knowledge with his power/ Before the indifferent beak could let her drop') resembles Donne's paradoxical plea to be ravished so that he might be chaste. The phrase 'put on' itself has clear echoes of the resurrected body of the New Testament.[39]

'Lullaby' displays a complicated reflection of an absolute unity (in late Wordsworthian terms, an absolute unity is a sublime unity).[40] The poem is concerned with the absolute unity which can be found only in sleep or death:

> Beloved, may your sleep be sound
> That have found it where you fed.
> What were all the world's alarms
> To mighty Paris when he found
> Sleep upon a golden bed
> That first dawn in Helen's arms?

As Curtis B. Bradford shows, Yeats believed that this poem was worth meticulously reworking.[41] Yeats even included it in his edition of *The Oxford Book of Modern Verse*. In a very quiet way, it tells a great deal about how the antithetical cruelty that the swan inflicts must lead to some sort of primary submission in the end. It embodies that redefinition of the relationship between the sacred and profane which Yeats increasingly asserted. A holy lullaby concerned with rape is not so incongruous as it appears, especially when seen from Yeats's perspective that, with the rise of *amour courtois,* wisdom is found in profane and in sacred passion.[42] It also makes sense when viewed in light of Barthes's mystical ideas of ravishment and *jouissance* (or bliss), of love-as-passion (and passion's root in suffering) which are taken directly from the Christian tradition of *amour courtois*.[43] Historically, the illicit, impossible passion of *amour courtois* becomes fused with the notion of ideal love, and then later becomes a part of the cult of the Virgin. Through antithetical cruelty (that of the cold, unreachable woman, and of the adulterous lover), one comes to fathom the terrible nature of ideal love.

This idea directly refers to Leda's transformation into a mystical subject with god-like powers. 'Leda and the Swan' was once entitled 'Annunciation'; its resemblance to 'The Mother of God' is obvious and intentional. The chief difference is that Leda comes in the midst of *The Tower* (1928) as the embodiment of the negative sublimity of an antithetical dispensation, while the Virgin Mary comes in *The Winding Stair* (1933) as the embodiment of the positive sublimity of a primary dispensation. Yeats's placement of 'Lullaby' in *Words for Music Perhaps* (1932) – a collection that is attached to the latter primary volume – is revealing in its ambiguity, in what it could *perhaps* be stating. Leda's gentleness makes her a perfect picture of primary mildness. Yeats is thinking of some sort of ultimate reconciliation, of heavenly atonement, however hesitant he is to make a final assent to any form of belief (other than reincarnation). He tellingly places the poem of atonement within this ambiguous collection of lyrical forays into the possibilities of *a priori* truth. For Yeats, lyrics are based in the realm of the *a priori*, whether lamenting its uncertainty or witnessing its existence. Within his system of violent and gentle turning of the gyres, there is equal reason to think that after the attack Leda will become a vision of antithetical terror, as there is to see her as a protective mother.[44] Though he imagines the latter in 'Lullaby', in other poems he has sufficiently avoided the traditional conception of gender roles to make Leda's terrible transformation a real possibility (one which befits his system). Leda gives birth to a 'terrible beauty'. It is no coincidence that Helen is left out of the list of consequences of the poem, for in her we have a vision of female antithetical strength. She is a woman who can impart most 'violent ways', whom Yeats wanted to impress, and before whom he felt threatened. She would praise violence, as did Gonne (Helen's living image), purely for excitement's sake.[45]

In 'Lullaby', however, Leda is that familial female aspect of the godhead which Yeats heralds in 'Supernatural Songs'. She is an emblem of the Mother-Goddess, a deity of the irrational, the blood-stained, the body, the transgressive (especially in the context of Crazy Jane), the Earth, who, after suffering (as in Shelley's view of Prometheus) at the hands of the most tyrannical and patriarchal of the gods, attains her full maternal powers and uses them tenderly and forgivingly. She has put on the power and knowledge of love's magic potion. The antithetical cruelty of the swan has finally surrendered to the primary rule of maternal love. Two earlier drafts of the last lines stress the connection to the Mother-Goddess, for Yeats had written 'Did the famous Leda guard', and then 'Did the king of heaven guard' before he decided on the final version.'[46] That the 'king' becomes Leda is a contradiction befitting the contradictory relationship of the two poems. At this stage, Leda has taken on the crucial role that the swan had previously played. The last four lines of the final version of the poem read:

> When the holy bird, that there
> Accomplished his predestined will,
> From the limbs of Leda sank
> But not from her protecting care.

With this triumphant image of the long-suffering soul, Yeats, like Donne, usurps the conventional notions of the body as too debased to be a vehicle for transcendence. The bird in these lines is the object of two different clauses: its 'will' has been 'predestined' by the gods and it is under Leda's 'protecting care'. Leda now protects the animal, bodily side of sexuality (the holy bird is now an empty passive vessel of Jupiter, having 'accomplished' his 'will') and understands that it is the anguish of the soul that often perverts the body's uses, that makes the book of the body bear the flowers of evil. 'Leda and the Swan' and 'Lullaby' thus mediate the debate on aesthetics, morality and sexual politics by showing how abject subjectivity can overcome the reifying will. In the end, however, Leda has only partially put on the knowledge with the power; as a survivor, her sublime visions must remain partial – only the mythological figures (Paris, Helen, and the others) can achieve absolute unity, because they do so in death.

The difference between death's vision of unity and life's partial epiphanic vision further emphasises the place of Leda as image of the soul. Sleep to the soul, in such an instance, means death. She would enter that 'quarter where all thought is done' ('A Dialogue of Self and Soul'). Ecstasy is never really complete for the soul, at least not when within the body. It is not to Yeats, because 'the tragedy of sexual intercourse is the perpetual virginity of the soul',[47] and not to St Teresa. Her images of ecstasy, rapture, and their effects explain the relationship between the rapture of 'Leda and the Swan' and the ecstasies of 'Lullaby'. Ecstasy, to the sixteenth-century Carmelite nun, is the result of a long contemplation of an object, when the subject comes relatively painlessly out of the self and becomes one with the object. On the other hand, rapture

... comes in general as a shock, quick and sharp, before you can collect
your thoughts, or help yourself in any way; and you see and feel it as a
cloud, or a strong eagle rising upwards and carrying you away on its wings;
I repeat it: you feel and see yourself carried away, you know not whither.[48]

Apart from the difference of the type of bird, this passage could be a
prose summary of 'Leda and the Swan', especially if the poem is read as
an epiphany. The passage even has much of the apocalyptic language
Yeats uses in *A Vision*. Describing the aftermath of the experience,
St Teresa writes:

Sometimes the person is at once deprived of all the senses, the hands and
body becoming as cold as if the soul had fled; occasionally no breathing can
be detected. This condition lasts but a short while; I mean in the same
degree, for when this profound suspension diminishes the body seems to
come to itself and gain strength to return again to his *death* which gives
more vigorous *life* to the soul.[49]

That Leda stays awake in the 'Lullaby' may be because she is in such a
state: in a stage between the diminishment of the suspension and the final
gaining of strength (even if the *final* gaining of strength is an *a priori* final
end). It appears that the idea of returning to the *death*, to the scene of the
crime, is clearly a part of coming to terms with an experience of rapture
and an experience of rape. One comes to terms with the amorality of God
(as of destiny) that even devout thinkers equate with Jehovah. To achieve
this, however, requires a surrender of the type the mystics always describe.
Defiled or exalted, the body remains a divine expression of the soul; the
return to *death* finally gives more 'vigorous *life* to the soul' (in Yeats's
words, 'Belief is renewed constantly in the ordeal of death').[50] These are
certainly some of the truths that occupy Yeats. As St Teresa has her male
counterpart in St John of the Cross and his concept of the Dark Night of
the Soul, it is obvious that the experience of rapture is cross-gendered.
When reading 'Leda and the Swan' it is essential to remember the human
basis of our relation to the figure of the abject sublime.

Whether or not one imagines revenge as the solution to the historical
problem of reification and brutality, surely there is as extreme a danger
(for women as for men) in rejecting the idea that the innocent one *who
suffers* is the subject as there is in rejecting any possibility of revenge. The
mythological figure of Leda, and the victims she represents, remains a
poetic emblem of our age. The epiphanic experience of the poem is rooted
in the abjection which it utters; the strained relationship between the
individual and the collective, as between the individual and God, herein
finds a powerful voice and witness to despairing violence and the need for
ecstatic fulfilment.

10

DESIRE AND THE
FASCIST DREAM:
DESTRUCTIVE/CREATIVE
VIOLENCE IN SOCIETY

Not the least among the tasks now confronting thought is that of placing
all the reactionary arguments in the service of progressive enlightenment.
[. . .] True thoughts are those which do not understand themselves.
  Violence, on which civilisation is based, means the persecution of all
by all in a helpless attempt to make the incommensurable commensurable.
[. . .] 'Horror is beyond the reach of psychology'.

Theodor W. Adorno, *Minima Moralia*

A society that is being pulled by historical forces into a new era in which
the terms of existence will be radically different, as were the Romans at
the time of Christ, creates individuals who suffer or flower under the
same forces as the state, and the greater the individual, the more indicative is his or her suffering or flowering of the larger society's predicament.
This relationship is evident in Yeats's famous descriptions of Niobe and of
a Byzantine worker in *A Vision*. In Yeats's image of Niobe,[1] the confusion
of the whole is defined by the greatness of the effort to stem it, while, in
his image of the Byzantine worker, the unity of the society is contained in
the unity of the smallest part. The collective and the individual, the
impersonal and the personal, find such unified expression that 'the work
of many . . . seemed the work of one'. Through his artistic skill and with
much more ease and with much less apparent contradiction than does
Yeats in fact, the worker sanctifies the violence that is inherent in the
workings of society: ' . . . the pride of his delicate skill would make what
was an instrument of power to princes and clerics, a murderousness in the
mob, show as a lovely flexible presence like that of a perfect human body'.[2]
  In this image of Byzantium, Yeats imagines a Unity of Being and
Culture that would embody human violence; it stands in extreme contrast
to the later brutal manifestation or call for manifestation in 'On the
Boiler'. Yet the embodiment of violence is not unusual, nor is it restricted
to Yeats's later poetry. He had been haunted by the idea since the early

sublimations in *The Wanderings of Oisin* (1889). It is also seen in the Athenian bow, the image of Heraclitean strife and contending opposites to which Maud Gonne is compared in 'No Second Troy' as Helen-like maker and breaker of kingdoms. The germ for the idea of social violence in Yeats is traceable back to Baudelaire and to Wilde, although it is Nietzsche who gives him the most philosophical exposition in *Beyond Good and Evil* and *The Birth of Tragedy*. In these works, the drive towards aggrandisement and augmentation of power is recognised as organic, because the loftiest expressions of culture are sublimations of such passions as selfishness, cruelty and lust.[3] Yeats's most obvious treatment of this theme is 'Meditations in Time of Civil War'.

While 'Meditations' is a poem of institutionalised or collective violence, and poems like 'Leda and the Swan' and 'The Second Coming' are poems of God's violence, poems such as 'Hound Voice', 'Her Vision in the Wood', 'Man and the Echo', and 'The Death of the Hare' are poems of the meaning of internal violence in the making of the self. In Yeats's verse, violence is a part of the individual struggle towards transcendence against a system of obstacles set by a combination of society and Fate. It is for this reason that Yeats's evocations of violence in one's relationship with God, and his evocations of violence in one's relationship with oneself are usually positive ones. It is also why, inversely, his poetic evocations of violence in a more social realm are usually negative ones. Once violence is taken out of the actual demands for survival, desolate reality makes it destructive beyond redemption. The collective vision (the effects of shared experience) is inevitably destructive. The exceptions to this rule, such as 'Easter, 1916', shall be noted as they appear. The end of 'Nineteen Hundred and Nineteen' illustrates how the Beatific Vision that is experienced when the soul meets its Bridegroom is transformed by social pressures into the grotesqueries of the evil incubus Artisson and his witch Lady Kyteler.

THE AMBIGUITIES OF VIOLENCE: 'EASTER, 1916' AND 'THE TOWER'

Before Yeats reaches overarching meditation on his career, and the perversion of his ideals and systems of being, he must pass through the several insights of the volumes *Michael Robartes and the Dancer* (1921) and *The Tower* (1928). He must sail towards Byzantium. Not having reached the sometime blessed states and 'starlit air' of *The Winding Stair and Other Poems* (1933), especially of the poem 'Byzantium', he cannot retrieve the sense of beauty that he felt so deeply in *The Wild Swans at Coole* (1919). This is not to say that the beatific states are purely demonstrations of transcendent faith untroubled by doubt. Like the sense of fading beauty that haunts *The Wild Swans at Coole* (1919), the ecstasies he experiences while in states of vacillation are the closest he knows to the heights of transcendence, although they are not in themselves transcendent. He attains only a glimpse of a transcendent vision, and remains haunted by the absence of any form of permanent transcendence that does not entail death. In many ways, certain poems are stricken by the thought that there is no transcendence at all.

'Easter, 1916' is the closest Yeats comes to transcendence through social or revolutionary violence. Yet, even its treatment is ambiguous. If, on the one hand, the aim is worthy of excessive feeling and bloodshed, it may produce a 'terrible beauty' (the quality that makes the poem serve as palinode to 'September 1913', to the place where motley is worn). If, on the other hand, either the goal or the means is unworthy of great passion and sacrifice, or else is misconstrued by those possessed of the dream, then the character and the nation can be deformed, as were Markiewicz during the rebellion, the British during colonial rule, and many Irish during the Civil War. For the Irish, in particular, the inability to achieve a positive version of the sublime is traced to unfamiliarity with the beautiful. According to Yeats, this lack gives them a 'hopeless levity' and makes them seem 'the harlequins of the earth'.[4] The aesthetic of independence, of the freeing of desire from the constant mistaking of the goal, is bound to be 'a terrible beauty'.

In the third stanza of 'Easter, 1916', desire is detailed in all its metamorphoses, and before it again reaches the violent climax of the refrain, it finds telling analogies in the ever-present water and high-flying birds, the furiously galloping horse and rider, and the ever-changing weather of Ireland:

> Hearts with one purpose alone
> Through summer and winter seem
> Enchanted to a stone
> To trouble the living stream.
> The horse that comes from the road,
> The rider, the birds that range
> From cloud to tumbling cloud,
> Minute by minute they change;
> A shadow of cloud on the stream
> Changes minute by minute;
> A horse-hoof slides on the brim,
> And a horse plashes within it;
> The long-legged moor-hens dive,
> And hens to moor-cocks call;
> Minute by minute they live:
> The stone's in the midst of it all.

This passage refers to the current, the state of being, that gives birth to the terrible beauty. In its constant metamorphoses, it is chaotic. The rider of the horse in this stanza is Pearse, the poet-warrior upon his 'wingéd horse'. Yet horse and rider, in this stanza, are anonymous, generalised, soliciting questions such as: whose horse? what rider? going where and for what purpose? The transition of Pearse and his horse into Perseus and Pegasus, into a mythological setting is, in fact, the beginning of the transformation of the collective violence of 'The Rising' into the world of forms, into the world which drives destructive and creative violence. The transformation can either be no more than a Platonic escape from the facts of the violence or it can be a further step towards final definition. Likewise, it can lead to all the ceaseless changes of Ovid's *Metamorphoses* or it can lead to the Crucifixion that is meant to be the end of violence.

Amidst the unsteady violent flux of a sensual world that chases after elusive desires, the heart must try to find some form of permanence, even though it troubles 'the living stream'. The heart goes against the grain, for even the most insubstantial form, such as a 'shadow of cloud on the stream', changes 'minute by minute'. Although the horse is shod and ridden, and therefore under human influence, both rider and horse, symbols of passion, 'plash' within the flowing stream. Civilisation cannot escape. Like the moor-hen and moor-cocks, they are swept up in the general tide of desire. The desire that drives us drives us to its source, to find the instinct, the stigmata of experience, to dwell amid the Ideal. The stone is not an entirely negative symbol; it is the result of an 'enchanted' heart. The heart, then, should remain enchanted, but not forever immovable. It is not that the heart has purpose which is wrong, but that the purpose is static. It should inflect the fluctuating forms of our desire to know why, to answer eschatological and teleological questions, and not become doctrinaire. A heart of stone has lost the spell.

It is fitting that 'Sailing to Byzantium', a poem in which Yeats sails to the source of desire, should come before 'Meditations' and 'Nineteen Hundred and Nineteen'. If Byzantium is both the land of Unity of Culture and Unity of Being that is portrayed in *A Vision*, and if it is also that realm of the soul's purification, portrayed in the poem entitled 'Byzantium', then it makes sense that in a time of civil war which to Yeats is an untranscendent war, he should be caught between this world and one of unity and purity. He recollects in the poem 'The Tower' all that he had created to lead him towards unity, to choosing Plato and Plotinus for a friend, as well as all that ever impeded his progression there. There is the old fight between body and soul and, as in many mystical works, it is desire that both links and separates them. There is the 'horrible splendour of desire' that leads the man to drown in the bog of Cloone and that sends Hanrahan to all his discoveries in the grave.

Desire, especially its possessive authoritarian forms, is one of the most significant roots of violence. It clips the farmer's ears and drives the '[r]ough men at arms, cross-gartered to the knees' to 'break upon a sleeper's rest'. The sublime nature of violence is twin-sided: creative and destructive. Violence gives us the 'mighty memories' of Hanrahan or merely breaks upon a sleeper's rest. The violence embodied in fascism is every child's nightmare, as Adorno writes, but it is also – Yeats knew well, having suffered its truths in childhood – every child's ambitious dream.[5] Rooted in desire, sexuality, like violence, needs to be given shape and value. This chapter's epigram by Adorno seems highly relevant to the brutal blindness and insight of Yeats's politics, and sets out the goal of the entire section on negative sublimity. Yeats's 'true thought',[6] the meaning of which he could never comprehend, is that desire cannot be turned aside, whether out of cowardice, pride or 'some silly over-subtle thought' or 'anything called conscience once'. Otherwise, when 'memory recur, the sun's/Under eclipse and the day blotted out'. The consequences of this state are dire for Yeats; such a man is 'bankrupt master' of the house because 'neither love/Nor music nor an enemy's clipped ear/Could, he was so harried, cheer'. Like Nietzsche, Yeats was always afraid of being overcome by that nervous ethical nature which destroys the sense of tragic joy that is ours by instinct, of being overcome by what the former calls the 'subtle servility of the categorical imperative'.[7]

In the third part of 'The Tower', the violence of desire is given shape and value in the 'people of Burke and of Grattan', with 'learned Italian things' and the 'proud stones of Greece'. Each of these groups was a conquering and conquered race, and was successful because it gave form and utterance to the violence it both suffered and inflicted, as Yeats believed a ruling class should do. Yeats explains this idea in 'On the Boiler':

> If human violence is not embodied in our institutions the young will not give them their affection, nor the young and old their loyalty. A government is legitimate because some instinct has compelled us to give it the right to take life in defence of its laws and its shores.
> Desire some just war, that big house and hovel, college and public-house, civil servant – his Gaelic certificate in his pocket – and international bridge-playing woman, may know that they belong to one nation.[8]

To him, civilisation is based on violence; we should therefore make it a unifying force. In order to appeal to the 'instinct' which compels us 'to give [government] the right to take life', the ruling class should focus the powers of bravery. Yeats wants to give a form and utterance to violence in a way that would make it palpable, that is, a violence that would have a physical sense of faith which denies the existence of death, as does Cuchulain, that 'violent and famous' man. Also in the self-sacrifice required in war, we lay ourselves down for an ideal, with a distinct faith in immortality (one of the 'three essentials', Freedom, God, and Immortality, which Yeats borrows from Kant to 'make life liveable'[9]). It is a faith that we should willingly put to the ultimate test, as he later tries to show in the poem 'Death'. Done with faith in God and nation, this would join the believer to the nation at large. The morality of the 'just war' would ensure the morality of the fighting. This is how Yeats imagines the ideal enaction of violence, but to give him his due, most of his depictions of violence expose it as less than ideal.

In 'The Tower', desire is not presented in its most violent forms, except, of course, in the present of Mrs French's ear. The force of the title poem is violent and sexual, and leads Yeats to the edge of his own existence, to where, facing death, desire is at its most extreme; here, the desire to survive and create intensifies into the lust and rage that spur an old man into song. Denying both the reality and his fear of death, Yeats is approaching its extreme violence of change and all its most powerful physical metamorphoses. He fears that death will transmute those great objects of desire beyond recognition; that the death 'of every brilliant eye/That made a catch in the breath' shall

> Seem but the clouds of the sky
> When the horizon fades;
> Or a bird's sleepy cry
> Among the deepening shades.

The violence of change after death makes Yeats fear for the existence of the '[t]ranslunar paradise', which he had just heralded as imminent. He confronts that faith by which he lives or dies. Perpetual change threatens all that he has loved, and so threatens his faith in immortality. In 'Meditations in Time of Civil War' and 'Nineteen Hundred and Nineteen', Yeats meditates on the violence of change in its most rupturing temporal and amoral terms; and only the force of desire can possibly survive it. The confusing moral premises of the fighting are mirrored in the moral compromise of the types of warfare that emerge.

THE HIERARCHY OF VIOLENCE: 'MEDITATIONS IN TIME OF CIVIL WAR'

In the first part of 'Meditations', Yeats wonders if society could exist without expressing violence or hierarchy (which in his view are united), if the image of supper at a resplendent table is the result of a long and contentious swilling at the trough. He begins with an ideal image of the spirit being as beautifully moulded as is water in a fountain, without the violence of restraint, and merely under the gardener's guidance:

> Surely among a rich man's flowering lawns,
> Amid the rustle of his planted hills,
> Life overflows without ambitious pains;
> And rains down life until the basin spills,
> And mounts more dizzy high the more it rains
> As though to choose whatever shape it wills
> And never stoop to a mechanical
> Or servile shape, at others' beck and call.

This effect must be the result of someone's work, of the labour to be beautiful, though in Yeats's presentation it seems the work of magic. In his vision of the spiritual realm, this is the perfect synthesis of the antithetical subjective force and the primary objective order. The hierarchic violence between ruled and ruler finds its emblem in the very arrogance of the spiritual stream of water and in the order of the lawns and hills. The spirit does not rebel, however, and the order of the garden does not oppress in this vision of paradise. In the wasteland outside, both unceremoniously do.

In ironical old age, Yeats parodies the reconciliatory truth or sooth of the early poem 'The Song of the Happy Shepherd' as 'mere dreams'. He nevertheless insists that the dream is pure at the source; for both the ruler and the ruled, as two sides of any struggle, possess the spirit that is not servile, that is moved by Kant's idea of essential 'Freedom'.[10] Yeats knows that, though the fractiousness of society and the unification of spirit are equally and anciently real,

> Yet Homer had not sung
> Had he not found it certain beyond dreams
> That out of life's own self-delight had sprung
> The abounding glittering jet . . .

This is the purity of the place of the spirit or soul. Life's self-delight is the transcendental promise that continuously transforms the actual, although it is so seldom realised. As for the self and society, their place is one of stone in which the heart must try to remain enchanted. Either it is a secret place in which one who is bred to a harder thing than triumph must learn to exult, or it is the tower that has been built to be a place from which to rule. Both places have their share of violence and bitterness and require bitterness and violence to withstand the elements. The separation of historical necessity, of an indifferent fate, and the necessity for transcendence is of prime importance for Yeats. The rupture that is often between them haunts his work as much as it does Beckett's, only, being in the main a tragic poet and not a tragic-comic one, Yeats is less able to parody the cruelty of the former and to satirise the persistent delay, or impossibility, of the latter. Yeats essentially tries to unite them in the transcendent dream of the beggar and the nobleman on the opposite ends of the economic divide.

In 'Meditations' he endeavours to grasp the reason for the related divide between transcendent sensual beauty and the grim but durable characteristics that combat reality:

> O what if levelled lawns and gravelled ways
> Where slippered Contemplation finds his ease
> And Childhood a delight for every sense,
> But take our greatness with our violence?
>
> . . . What if those things the greatest of mankind
> Consider most to magnify, or to bless,
> But take our greatness with our bitterness?

Though he may be in many ways referring to his version of the rise of Protestant Ireland, he is also aware that any Platonic system like his requires a division of labour. The division between self (or body) and soul mirrors that between the working and the upper classes.[11] In Yeats's idea of Byzantium, the division of labour would not be so divisive as to make every document of civilisation one of barbarism as well. Whether or not one accepts Yeats's compensatory vision of a hierarchical but harmonious order, in which the artist would serve no less than any other in order to find a unifying form of expression, one feels that his poetry is rife with the pain of present misunderstanding, disunity and divide. It is not surprising, then, that Yeats's vision of the reasons for violent civil or class disorder, for the root of the evil, as it were, was powerful enough to make him an example to Louis MacNeice and W. H. Auden, and in a sense precursor to their themes of class-suffering.

Between self and soul, or working and upper class, Yeats's transcendent hierarchical system hopes to control the effects of the violating divide, as the fountain controls the water. In this harmonious hierarchical ordering of free will, Yeats has not moved far away from Milton's idea of those beings who freely serve because they freely love. It is a structure in which no one should willingly escape service, and one which is so pervasive that genius itself labours under its sway. 'Il Penseroso's Platonist' must also suffer the rage of his Daimon if he is to imagine anything effectively. Again, Yeats illustrates how, if it is to be freed of self-destructive passion, even the most powerful antithetical subjective and self-serving force must surrender at last to a primary rule, to mercy, pity and understanding. The Daimon itself is under an equivalent rule. Harsh reality is what makes for transcendence, while the war between self and soul, or lower and upper classes, prepares the way for eventual peace. As in the work of many poets, this dialectic between reality and transcendence, which is like that between suffering and knowledge, exists in much of Yeats's work. The hardness of the terrain is what makes 'the symbolic rose . . . break in flower'. Only '[b]efitting emblems of adversity' can 'exalt a lonely mind', and 'only an aching heart/Conceives a changeless work of art'. As pain is given definition and meaning by religious ideas of suffering, so the general run of violence should ideally be transformed into a higher form through liberating acts of self-sacrifice and violence.

Violence in the relation with God, as seen in 'Leda and the Swan' and 'The Second Coming', runs like a vein through human violence, and it is usually misunderstood when externally directed. The semblance of God's violence is best crystallised in internal warfare because self and God are so intimately connected. This idea is ever present in the 'Meditations' and finds counter-expression in the last stanza, when Yeats is haunted by a sense that mistakenly society values the outward show of battle, but not *Il Penseroso*'s lonely, conscience-stricken struggle against the rage of daemonic images:

> I turn away and shut the door, and on the stair
> Wonder how many times I could have proved my worth
> In something that all others understood or share;
> But O! ambitious heart, had such a proof drawn forth
> A company of friends, a conscience set at ease,
> It had but made us pine the more. The abstract joy,
> The half-read wisdom of daemonic images,
> Suffice the ageing man as once the growing boy.

Others do not share his view of the courage and violence involved in deep introspection, which to him match any shown on the battlefield. The violence of self-scrutiny is as necessary as the violence of what he calls 'necessary war'.[12] Emphasising the internal gaze as he does, Yeats is therefore thought an idler by the noisy set, and so, when an 'affable . . . Falstaffian man/Comes cracking jokes of civil war', he must turn to the feminine principle in order to soothe himself. In Weiskel's model of the Romantic Sublime, Yeats turns away from the Oedipal confrontation with the father and towards the pre-Oedipal sense of the mother.[13] He seeks the sexual release of violence that takes place in the pull between opposites. Yeats presents an image of violent male subjectivity ('As though to die by gunshot were/The finest play under the sun') and a contrasting one of the feminine object-sublime ('I count those feathered balls of soot/The moor-hen guides upon the stream'), which is one of nearness and nurturing.[14] He also gives us a unified image of the associative dream-state, of the imaginary world of the 'cold snows' in which the symbolic order of a fixed mathematical reality (his counting the chicks) finds bliss in the eternal-ideal. During this *coincidentia oppositorum*, his envy is carried away by the moor-hen down the stream. The image of the hen carries Yeats to a positive sublime like Goethe's 'Eternal Feminine' where his violent desire is pacified. Yet, Yeats achieves this peace through envy at his own failure to be violent. He ascends with Mephistopheles at his back.

We come to the most sexual and redemptive moment of the poem in which bees – symbol of the honey of sexuality – build in the empty house of the stare (a warring and rapacious bird[15]). Violence has proved to be random and has led only to more violence, with no clear fact to be discerned except for the violent act. The lyric redemptive moment of the poem is accomplished under female supervision:

> The bees build in the crevices
> Of loosening masonry, and there
> The mother birds bring grubs and flies.
> My wall is loosening; honey-bees,
> Come build in the empty house of the stare.

The moor-hen is like Leda who gathers the violence of Jove under her protecting care. What had seemed real to the Falstaffian man achieve the meaningless reality of spectacle. Not being real in any imaginative sense, not unifying disparate parts, or creating some new perspective (as Coleridge defines the function of imagination), fantasy only makes the heart grow brutal.

In the last part of 'Meditations', the relationship between violence, imaginative vision and deluding reality reaches full proportion. The snow that had earlier eclipsed Yeats's envious desire is now the mist eclipsing the desire of the decaying West, as symbolised by the broken stone of his tower, while desire is rising in the form of a sword in the East. The images that come to him are full of the Ovidian violence of change. In the midst of this imagery, Yeats almost joins in the bloodthirstiness, if only because he is so driven by despair over the end of the Medieval rule of faith which the knights of the Templar represented, and which, in his view, fell before the scientific humanism of the Renaissance. Restraining himself from becoming murderous, Yeats rises on the imaginative power that had tempted him to kill. He harnesses the violence. This is the perfection of desire, the ecstatic heights of the profane perfection of mankind, which leads to the sacred image. This is the blood and vinegar on the way to Calvary. The '[f]renzies' that 'bewilder', the 'reveries' that 'perturb the mind', the '[m]onstrous familiar images' that 'swim to the mind's eye' evoke one of his most passionate Pre-Raphaelite images of ecstatic sacred beauty:

> Their legs long, delicate and slender, aquamarine their eyes,
> Magical unicorns bear ladies on their backs.
> The ladies close their musing eyes. No prophecies,
> Remembered out of Babylonian almanacs,

Have closed the ladies' eyes, their minds are but a pool
Where even longing drowns under its own excess;
Nothing but stillness can remain when hearts are full
Of their own sweetness, bodies of their loveliness.

Yeats's Vision of Evil and theory of violent desire are dependent upon a vision of beauty that perfects profane desire and achieves the religious dimension of the positive sublime. The potential violence of the unicorn (unicorns are famous for their capacity for violence) finds calm in the beauty of sexual fulfilment. In the traditional lore of the unicorn, only a virgin can lure the potentially violent unicorn. Yeats, however, dislikes the idea of parthenogenesis, or virginal conception, and so neither learning nor prophecy crosses the women's minds, but on the backs of a mythical beast whose horn was reputed to be a powerful aphrodisiac, their eyes close out of longing.

In its progenitive or transformative aspects, this higher form of violence, then, is like sexuality, as it breeds another form which is both like and unlike those forms initially involved. In 'A Dialogue of Self and Soul' and the 'My Table' section of 'Meditations', we see violence and sexuality connected in the image of the 'changeless sword' covered by a 'bit of an embroidered dress'. Both are expressions of desire. The right sexuality, in Yeats's cosmology, is like a just war with the right outlet for violence, in that it transforms violence into a transcendent end. Sexuality is not the expression of violence; it is its release in a different form. In its most naked expression, sexuality, as Girard states in *Violence and the Sacred*, is violent chiefly because violence can be sexual.[16] To summarise Girard's argument: when we are most passionate, the primal scene seems violent; nevertheless, sexuality is only wholly violent when its transformation of violence is deformed. We are not violent when truly sexual but we can be sexual when blindly and senselessly violent. Sexuality can be an effect of violence, but only when it is thwarted can it be the cause.

Violence is here perfected in the 'eyes that rage has brightened', and the 'arms it has made lean'. The light of that moon which had 'seem[ed] unlike itself', of a moon that seemed to be a part of the immutable world, and not the division between mutability and immutability, is soon put out 'by the innumerable clanging wings' of birds of prey. Yeats is surrounded by the cruder, untempered forms of violent desire that have not been baptised by water or fire, that have not been sensually or spiritually purified by a redemptive vision. This predicament makes him wonder about his own material success or lack of success in the world's terms. He is again left sailing to Byzantium. He has only the 'abstract joy' and 'half-read wisdom of daemonic images' that come of his search for the purgative dancing floor. He is left in that place of sensual purification where the choir of love tender their sacred laurels, while the foul goat-head of pan-sexuality appears in order to throw off the repressive rule of Jupiter, the Olympian of hated rationality. The eventual overthrow and spiritual purification, however, will be described in later volumes of poetry.

SELF-PERPETUATING VIOLENCE: 'NINETEEN HUNDRED AND NINETEEN'

The next poem in *The Tower* (1928), 'Nineteen Hundred and Nineteen', also discusses the effects of Jupiter's tyranny. Those things that had seemed 'sheer miracle to the multitude' now seem commonplace. In this poem, however, we view the ill effects of a barbarous and Shelleyean overthrow, in which the sacred role of violence is subverted. As in 'Meditations', Yeats still wonders if violence is essential for a society to prosper both culturally and materially. The 'we' of the poem extends the guilt to all those Late Victorians and Edwardians who do not take the final step towards purity, as envisioned in Isaiah, and who do not turn the unused cannon into a ploughshare. For they too must wonder with parliament and king that

> . . . unless a little powder burned
> The trumpeter might burst with trumpeting
> And yet it lack all glory; and perchance
> The guardsmen's drowsy chargers would not prance.

This fear exists because there is no beautiful image with which to vent violence (something which Yeats believes is necessary to accomplish fate), as there once had been in the 'sheer miracle' of the warrior-goddess, Athena. As a warrior-virgin-goddess, she provides an image of the 'fierce warres and faithfull loves' that moralise Spenser's song.[17] Without her, there is no 'Queene' in the 'faerie land' of the subconscious.

The inconspicuous word 'perchance' is central to the above quotation. In order for the chargers to prance, for them to keep awake, they must feel this tension: perchance violence is inevitable. In Yeats's cosmology, we establish ourselves in our tense kill-or-be-killed relationship with the spectre of our own destiny. The violent centrifugal force in Yeats's Vision of Evil has not been addressed by the society at large. The philosophy that has been pieced together during the hour of terror which comes to test the soul has not been included in society's expression of itself. There was neither gladiator nor slave to represent all that Stoicism or Platonism repressed. Consequently, pre-philosophic barbarism has returned:

Now days are dragon-ridden, the nightmare
Rides upon sleep: a drunken soldiery
Can leave the mother, murdered at her door,
To crawl in her own blood, and go scot-free;
The night can sweat with terror as before
We pieced our thoughts into philosophy,
And planned to bring the world under a rule,
Who are but weasels fighting in a hole.

The consequences of the inability to express the fury make Yeats question the aim and purpose of art. If the art of a unified culture is destined to be destroyed by another succeeding one that has no unity, that is barbaric, what is the purpose, where is the 'comfort to be found'? Yeats proceeds to answer this question: the spiritual comfort is in the ghostly solitude that survives the vanishing of the object of desire.

Art captures the spirit, and though an object of art like the statue of Athena may disappear in time, the spirit that the artist captures in ghostly solitude will outlast any incendiary bigot who would destroy it because the spirit of art can subjugate terror. The spirit is captured in the next part of the poem. That 'shining web' woven out of the bowels of subjectivity cannot escape the objective reality of terror, even with as great a length of time as the Platonic Year affords. It is the body (the outward show of the spirit, or soul) that, represented in the swan's flight, is forced to meet the winds that 'clamour of approaching night.' It has to face the undeniable terror that reaches through perception and makes the external world – the world of complete and terrifying otherness – insistently real to the perceiver, almost to the point of banishing subjectivity. In this instance, the subject either mimics the madness of terror and becomes equally bloodthirsty, or else he or she transcends that terror by reflecting back another more powerful image of its pathos. This is the conventional image of the Romantic Sublime. With Yeats, it is more complex than liberating oneself from fear through confrontation with Oedipal-like power. For him, a transcendental *a priori* form is sought through an image of pain and surrender, or of self-purification, as in the following instance. The fantasy of transcendence becomes an integral part of the design – though even it can be a hopeless compromise, a moral disappointment, a fantasy that only makes the heart grow brutal. The ghostly solitude, the transcendent spirit might itself become deformed in the process towards any worldly victory. It might become a malignant shape in the contending mirror of malicious eyes, one which in 'A Dialogue of Self and Soul' Yeats hopes to avoid.

In the society that Yeats has outlined thus far in 'Nineteen Hundred and Nineteen', we have little hope. Violence is not sacred, but is a self-perpetuating blood-lust. The sacred image of Athena born ready for battle, who is also a symbol of purity and wisdom, does not exist any more. Meaningless violence is imitated with an apocalyptic fervour in order paradoxically to find the meaning of violence: 'The swan has leaped into the desolate heaven:/That image can bring us wildness, bring a rage/To end all things'. All of Yeats's art and philosophy is threatened and, if destroyed, will be no more than the product of a diseased mind. The violence threatens

> . . . to end
> What my laborious life imagined, even
> The half-imagined, the half-written page;
> O but we dreamed to mend
> Whatever mischief seemed
> To afflict mankind, but now
> That winds of winter blow
> Learn that we were crack-pated when we dreamed.

His mind is revealed to be no more than a mechanism engaged with the patterns of language, which themselves have no more meaningful reference to what they refer than does his mind to the dreams it has dreamed. It cannot make amends. Yeats is left with an explicitly empiricist nightmare, in which the Burkean psychology of pain and terror is the beginning and end of the sublime, in which violence is revealed to be a 'helpless attempt to make the incommensurable commensurable'.[18]

In the fifth part of 'Nineteen Hundred and Nineteen', Yeats returns to the satirical spirit that was prominent in the late seventeenth and the eighteenth century in order to find what he regards as the source and worst symptom of the empiricist malady. As he attacks Locke, Newton and Descartes for leaving us with the dross of the physical world, and for underestimating the source of their own inspiration (in 'Fragments' and *Explorations*), he here attacks the satirical mind, born of Voltaire and Rousseau, for satirising the sanctities of Blake's 'beams divine'. It is important to note, however, that Yeats does not attack satire as a whole. He attacks forms of satire which do not implicitly serve to further some end as Swift's satire serves human liberty; he attacks the forms of satire which do 'not lift a hand to help the wise or great'. Heartless mockery fractures unity, and, in mood, is like the random violence upon the roads. Fraught with the meaninglessness of the world, all it can do is to attack any attempt to establish meaning.

Yeats believes that, regardless of motive, mockery and violence are prophetic of change, that, in other words, 'Heaven suffereth violence and the violent bear it away' (Matthew 11:12). He believes that a new era begins in this violent, mocking and indeed sensual atmosphere. He uses images of Herodias's daughters (i.e. those like Salome) to suggest the coming of a prophet like John the Baptist, whose violent death at the whim of Salome's desire makes way for the Messiah. In the images that follow, Yeats reveals much of the pressure of present violence. He reveals the wayward sexual license and heightened sexual expression which sometimes characterise the furore of an age of transition, and which, as Girard writes, take on violent forms as long as the violent and the sacred remain separate.[19] Sexuality seeks salvation, but instead it becomes as obsessive, dangerous and foreboding as Salome's; its purpose is subordinate to the winds of prophecy:

> A sudden blast of dusty wind and after
> Thunder of feet, tumult of images,
> Their purpose in the labyrinth of the wind;
> And should some crazy hand dare touch a daughter
> All turn with amorous cries, or angry cries,
> According to the wind, for all are blind.

After this image of lust-driven universal blindness, the last image of the poem illustrates how the idea of ecstasy changes under the pressure of the external world of violence. Like Blake's 'A Vision of the Daughters of Albion', it is a perversion of the idea of sacred beatitude between God and the soul. Whereas in Blake's poem only Oothoon, the victim of rape who will not surrender the beauty of desire, still understands the sacredness of beatitude (her lover and her rapist do not), in Yeats's rendering the witch Lady Kyteler brings symbols of revelation and sexuality to her incubus, Robert Artisson. The undoing of the old order is complete. The very names are perversions – though perhaps unconscious ones – of Lady Gregory and her son Robert Gregory, and of the Unity of Culture and Being they provided for Yeats, which he describes in 'Coole Park, 1929' and 'Coole and Ballylee, 1931'. In the light of an apocalyptic beginning of a new world, the relationship between Artisson and Kyteler takes on incestuous meaning when placed beside the Gregorys, and leads the questioning mind, Oedipus-like, against the travail of the blind prophet, to the monstrousness at the beginning of creation, to the monstrousness of the incestuous first family's progeny (à la Kyteler and Artisson). Yeats is describing the blind ambition that sires civil war, or that ambition which will inherit the age that comes after it. Either way, it is part of a vicious circle of self-perpetuating violence and violation:

> But now wind drops, dust settles; thereupon
> There lurches past, his great eyes without thought
> Under the shadow of stupid straw-pale locks,
> That insolent fiend Robert Artisson
> To whom the love-lorn Lady Kyteler brought
> Bronzed peacock feathers, red combs of her cocks.

The self-perpetuating nature of the violence that results from the Civil War in Ireland gives Yeats reasons to condemn it. One has to look to other more intimate self-wounding evocations of violence in the Yeatsian ecstatic sublime in order to find the acts of violence which are creative and renewing, those volcanic eruptions that make the seemingly devastated land more fertile.

11

HEART'S VICTIM AND ITS TORTURER: WOUNDS OF THE SUBJECT–OBJECT MYSTERY

For in love's field was never found
A nobler weapon than a wound.
Love's passives are his activ'st part,
The wounded is the wounding heart.

Richard Crashaw, 'The Flaming Heart'

In terms of the sublime, the destructive and creative relationships of the self take on very specific importance as regards any notion of stability in the subject. For Burke, it is a matter of the delightful feeling of self-preservation that follows a terrifying experience of the sublime. To have survived the experience is the ultimate test of the self's stability and power.[1] Yeats believes that 'profound philosophy must come from terror',[2] and that the proof of such philosophy is not simply mere survival and power, but rather it is some more permanent or *a priori* sense of the transcendent currency of self and soul. Kant's idea of violence and the self is more to Yeats's point. The terror of Kant's sublime leads to transcendence, to the supersensible.[3] It is a positive sublime. As Lyotard states of the synthesis in the Kantian sublime: 'Thus sensation must be double, or split into two heterogeneous yet indissociable sensations. We are of course referring to terror, which has to do with the presentable, and to exaltation, which refers to the unpresentable.'[4] If terror does not synthesise with a transcendent exaltation (in contrast to the limited exaltation of self-preservation), as at certain points in Yeats's poems of violence and society, then it is an example of negative sublimity. If it does lead to transcendence, or to the unpresentable, as a result of its terror, it is an example of positive sublimity. These twin poles of negative and positive sublimity provide much of the charge to Yeats's poetry. At either pole, sublimity is formed in subjective feeling; it is at the base of any discussion of the relative stability or instability of the self and its relationship to presentable or unpresentable worlds.

The formal idealist Kant answers Locke's empiricist point on the instability of the self with a complicated theory of apperception, or self-consciousness, which is based in the belief that what we think we feel is ours *a priori* because no one else reasonably could feel it. To doubt unity of consciousness is to cease to be self-conscious. Apperception, then, is transcendental in that it depends upon unknown and ultimately unprovable values for existence. To Kant, as to Yeats, it is sensible, presentable proof of an unpresentable, supersensible world. In its extreme cases, the argument eventually leads to a glorification of sensation as proof of subjective unity, to a valorisation of suffering as proof of transcendent morality, to Kant's concept of the sublime sacrifice, in which, against the rule of self-preservation, one sacrifices oneself for the larger good. Yeats valorises self-wounding for one's own good and self-sacrifice for another's good nearly as much as he valorises conflict and violence towards the other. Each in some way tempers knowledge of the self's powers. Yeats's chief metaphors of the sublime experience that contains all the qualities just mentioned (selfishness, sacrifice, valorisation of suffering, glorification of the senses, violence and creation) are sexual in nature. Kantian aesthetic disinterestedness (that is, the lack of desire which is prerequisite for true aesthetic appreciation) plays no real role in the Yeatsian sublime, except perhaps in his concepts of 'tragic joy' or 'heroic reverie'. Even these terms refer to heightened moments of ironic distance from the greatness of one's passionate life more than to any pure concept of disinterest. For both the German philosopher and the Irish poet, the aesthetic solution to the philosophical mystery is most certainly contained in the subject–object relationship. Yeats insists upon sexualising the mystery. He does so both because sexuality is itself mysterious and because it is inherently dangerous (which is a quality that it shares with all sublime experience). He subscribes to Crashaw's view that 'in love's field was never found/A nobler weapon than a wound'.[5] Ecstasy results from the wounds of love as well as from those of war; the aim is to find the most fertile ones and to cultivate the relationships in which they are inflicted.

SELF'S CREATIVE/DESTRUCTIVE VIOLENCE

The search for the destructive *and* creative violence of the Yeatsian ecstatic sublime is not an easy one, as Yeats never quite disconnects private from social acts of violence, and therefore, as a consequence, any manifestation of violence to him seems always to be corrupted and untranscendent. The exceptions prove the rule. Like many of the poems of *The Winding Stair* (1933) (the stair being the symbol of the soul's transcendence as the tower is symbol of the self's violence), 'Remorse for

Intemperate Speech' is filled with remorse, only in most of the other poems in the volume remorse results in intellectual love. In 'Remorse for Intemperate Speech', Yeats rants to knave and fool, turns hatred into sport, because 'Great hatred, little room,/Maimed [him] at the start'. He feels he can achieve nothing more; he remains untranscendent and condemned to the self's unresolved conflicts. The case is similar in many other poems of violence. They volley between the private and the public realms, looking for the meaning of the blood-sacrifice, for the source of the penchant for violence, and the poetry of violence in its most unadulterated forms. Yeats has a 'fanatic heart' and cannot live like the monks at Glendalough who in the 'gleam' of Christian ecstasy 'seem/Self-born, born anew' ('Stream and Sun at Glendalough'). He cannot renounce violence; he must ritualise it. To him, 'good strong blows are delights to the mind' ('Three Marching Songs'). The ritual has its basis in both public and private sacrificial ceremony ('Hound Voice', 'Her Vision in a Wood', and the fifth part of 'Under Ben Bulben'). 'Hound Voice' is particularly striking in its confusion of public and private realms of violence. In the confusion, another equally important aspect of violence emerges; we see that any perpetrator is also the victim, that, as Crashaw states, 'the wounded is the wounding heart'.[6] Finally, Yeats concludes that only a quasi-sadomasochistic union of subject and object lends meaning to violence, and makes it both creative and destructive.

This belief overarches the later, more virulent poems of violence and is best expressed in part V of the 'Supernatural Songs', in the play *Purgatory* (1939), and in *A Vision*, when Yeats explains that in his conception of the purgatorial nature of the afterlife, in the objective world of the godhead, the good discover the evil of their nature and the evil discover the good. Seeing that there is more ill than good in the world, Yeats asks in 'Ribh Considers Christian Love Insufficient': 'Why should I seek for love or study it?/It is of God and passes human wit'. Equally, seeing that the best antidote to poison is the poison itself, he views hate as 'A sort of besom that can clear the soul/Of everything that is not mind or sense'. He understands, as he writes in *A Vision*, that '*antithetical* [or subjective] cruelty and deceit must be expiated in *primary* [or objective] suffering and submission'[7] – an expiation which is denied the murderous old man in *Purgatory* (1939) – and so asks:

> Why do I hate man, woman or event?
> That is a light my jealous soul has sent.
> From terror and deception freed it can
> Discover impurities, can show at last
> How soul may walk when all such things are past,
> How soul could walk before such things began.

When soul walks, reality is inverted: the evil of hatred becomes the hatred of evil. In a mortal world whose wisdom is foolishness to God, whose tragedy will be but a dance to us in the afterlife, as Yeats writes in *A Vision*,[8] even the highest ideals are implicated in the evil, and have to be hated as well. The 'delivered soul' turns in hatred from 'every thought of God mankind has had'. Indeed, to Yeats, the very structures in which we do our thinking are suspect of being built merely for fashion's sake, of being temporal misrepresentations of the eternal soul and, as such, they are rather faithlessly accepted as *a posteriori* facts only because they have proved to be useful. The social utility of organised religion is a case in point. The Bishop of the Crazy Jane poems is an example of temporal misrepresentation; he impedes Crazy Jane from expressing the profane, essential passions that would perfect her soul. She ideally should discover what Lyotard calls the 'infinitely secret' inhumanity to 'which the soul is hostage'. Her craziness, her 'anguish', as Lyotard continues, 'is that of a mind haunted by a familiar and unknown guest which is agitating it, sending it delirious but also making it think – if one claims to exclude it, if one doesn't give it an outlet, one aggravates it'. Endeavouring to exclude her secret inhumanity, the bishop is an unjust representative of 'the inhumanity of the system'. We must keep these two sorts of inhuman 'dissociated', claims Lyotard.[9] Crazy Jane and the Bishop, pagan and Christian values, antithetical and primary inhuman incarnations, are at odds. The aim of Yeats's sublime is the release of the unpresentably inhuman within us. The freedom of the soul is pre-emptive.

Thought itself must be hated because it can embody truth only temporarily. Hatred reduces all thought to the heat of its original desire, which is as close as one can be to any permanent form of truth: 'Thought is a garment and the soul's a bride/That cannot in that trash and tinsel hide:/Hatred of God may bring the soul to God.' By so doing, we find the substance that will survive the final baptism by fire: 'At stroke of midnight soul cannot endure/A bodily or mental furniture.' Through *'antithetical* cruelty and deceit' we come to that moment of *'primary* suffering and submission' which Yeats envisages as the movement towards a redemptive, exclamatory surrender of the self to the greater Genius or self within, to God's final revelation of the self:

> What can she take until her Master give!
> Where can she look until He make the show!
> What can she know until He bid her know!
> How can she live till in her blood He live!

The last line is of particular significance for the present discussion, both because of the presence of the Godhead and because it introduces Dionysian/

Christian terms of violence, violation, blood-sacrifice, and sanctity. The
emphasis on violence is designed to release those secret images that
waken in the blood, which lead to that type of purification that Yeats
describes in 'Supernatural Songs' and of which St Matthew is speaking
when he writes that Christ 'baptises you with the Holy Ghost, and *with*
fire' (Matthew 3:11). In this regard, Yeats has all the apocalyptic and
somewhat mystical 'end of man' rhetoric of the postmodernists, although
he allows more possibility of metaphysical truth. This uncertain, twofold
nature of Yeats's work in many instances provides the 'terror' that he
defines as the source of 'profound philosophy'.

To understand the underlying theme of baptism by fire, let us compare
lines from 'A Bronze Head',

> A vision of terror that it must live through
> Had shattered her soul. Propinquity had brought
> Imagination to that pitch where it casts out
> All that is not itself.

to these from 'Under Ben Bulben',

> Know that when all words are said
> And a man is fighting mad,
> Something drops from eyes long blind,
> He completes his partial mind,
> For an instant stands at ease,
> Laughs aloud, his heart at peace.
> Even the wisest man grows tense
> With some sort of violence
> Before he can accomplish fate,
> Know his work or choose his mate.

and to these of 'Hound Voice':

> The women that I picked spoke sweet and low
> And yet gave tongue. 'Hound voices' were they all.
> We picked each other from afar and knew
> What hour of terror comes to test the soul,
> And in that terror's name obeyed the call,
> And understood, what none have understood,
> Those images that waken in the blood.

Let us also compare them to the last age of man in the section entitled
'The Four Ages of Man' of 'Supernatural Songs': 'Now his wars on God
begin;/At stroke of midnight God shall win.' We can see that all the
quotations are very like the previous poem from 'Supernatural Songs',
'Ribh Considers Christian Love Insufficient', and that they all suggest
how a consummating act of violence results in redemption. They prove
not only that the victorious God on whom we have made war actually

exists but that the private space can either be violated as Leda is violated, or it can be the source from whence purifying violence comes. Being thus sensitive or powerful, the private space can be said in a philosophically final sense to exist, in all its mystery.

SELF-DISCOVERY, MOURNING, AND THE DANCE OF DEATH

It is this private space, which is best symbolised by blood, that provides the strength of the poem 'Hound Voice'. For not only is it a poem of fascist blood-lust, of the violent bitter creed of the Anglo-Irish hunt club, or of colonial oppression, but it is also a poem of self-discovery. 'Her Vision in a Wood' is a poem by which to judge 'Hound Voice'; the hunter and the hunted of the latter poem merge like heart's victim and its torturer, or wounded and wounding heart into one and the same entity. In psycho-analytical terms, it is a poem of the unleashing of the libido; in Yeatsian terms, it is a poem of purgatorial wisdom. In the first stanza, Yeats seeks salvation in savage contrast to the dull round of daily existence, and amid those images ('bare hills and stunted trees') that constitute the wild, and which have a profound basis in our 'slumber bound' dreams. He sets the stage for the violent release of *a priori*, subconscious or instinctual desires and fears of the soul into the reconciling transcendent realm, in the 'hour of terror' that is described above. One wonders whether Yeats hints that he and his chosen women understood what no other can understand, that he and the women understood it momentarily, or that no one else was intimate enough to find the pulse of the *Spiritus Mundi* (that storehouse of images in the blood). The ending of the poem is purposely vague, because it outlines the quest to solve a mystery that cannot be solved.

The poem is a dream-hunt, on the verge or over the verge of death. That is why it seems that neither he nor his women have risen early enough to hunt. Being slumber bound, they are not fully conscious, and do not give chase as some others may. Also, they are more susceptible to the deepest consciousness of all, which is the associative consciousness of dreams. The hunt is the essence of the process of Becoming, and the hunted Beast is Being, or the private inward self. When Yeats and his women are on its trail, they are therefore 'wide awake'. Perhaps this reading concentrates too much on the self, but then again this is an intentionally solipsistic poem. At the end, the hunters are injured in the fray and must care for themselves while the hounds encircle their prey. The hounds form the Platonic circle which is God (as Yeats describes God in 'Discoveries'[10]) and enact the 'profane perfection of mankind' like that 'half-awakened Adam' who set the woman's bowels 'in heat' under the Sistine roof:

> Some day we shall get up before the dawn
> And find our ancient hounds before the door,
> And wide awake know that the hunt is on;
> Stumbling upon the blood-dark track once more,
> Then stumbling to the kill beside the shore;
> Then cleaning out and bandaging of wounds,
> And chants of victory amid the encircling hounds.

The animals and hunters experience a type of ecstasy, a sublime frenzy full of the blindness, appetite and insight of all religious experience. As Yeats proclaims in 'Under Ben Bulben', those who experience this type of ecstasy, whose bowels are 'in heat', will find 'Proof that there's a purpose set/Before the secret working mind'. This blindness to their own brutality provides ultimate insight into their own motivations, although only after the crime has been committed.

In 'A Dialogue of Self and Soul', the sword enwound in a lady's dress is like the looking-glass in which Self can reflect. Symbolically, self-understanding in its imperfect temporal forms is wounding. Soul envisions a world free of these symbols and wounds. Self sees that they still have the ability to give profound insights and so will not abandon them even though they cause it so much pain. Self must be free to commit the crime once more until the '*antithetical* cruelty and deceit' of crime can be 'expiated in *primary* suffering and submission'. The implication of Self's conflicts in this world is that they prepare it for ultimate judgement in the next. The greater the temporal conflicts of Self, the more extensive, severe, and perhaps perfecting is the judgement of Soul in the afterlife. Fearfully, Yeats craves as much freedom as possible from this cyclical process. In the section of 'A Man Young and Old' entitled 'The Death of the Hare', he describes in autobiographical terms this need to free himself, at least partially, from what he feared was the violence of self-discovery – whether to oneself or to others – and from the infinite pain of self-realisation.

In the poem Yeats is walking with Iseult Gonne, and points out that men chase her as hunting dogs chase the hare. He places this scene directly in the Renaissance tradition of venery and Venus, of the chase and the chaste (he had already identified Iseult with the hare in 'Two Songs of a Fool'), except there is something amiss.[11] The system goes awry. Her negative reaction exposes him to the 'manic gaze'[12] of the dogs as they kill the victim:

> I have pointed out the yelling pack,
> The hare leap to the wood,
> And when I pass a compliment
> Rejoice as lover should
> At the drooping of an eye,
> At the mantling of the blood.

Then suddenly my heart is wrung
By her distracted air
And I remember wildness lost
And after, swept from there,
Am set down standing in the wood
At the death of the hare.

Yeats is conscience-stricken. We recall that, when he was a boy, he had
seen a hare being killed and, haunted by its cry, had resolved never to kill
anything other than fish.[13] Here is the root of his sense of wildness lost.
Brought back to his own fear of death, Yeats sympathises with another
being's fear, in spite of his view that violent imagery is what makes our
blood mantle.

The guilt-inducing cry of a rabbit at the moment of its death also
occurs in the late poem 'Man and the Echo'. Through the mirroring
mocking echo, the search for the self reveals the violence that Yeats has
inflicted or has helped to cause. He wonders whether there might be
neither an aim nor an end to the violence, and asks the oracle of poetry if
the pain of the empirical is all we are bound to know:

O rocky voice
Shall we in that great night rejoice?
What do we know but that we face
One another in this place?
But hush, for I have lost the theme,
Its joy or night seem but a dream;
Up there some hawk or owl has struck
Dropping out of sky or rock,
A stricken rabbit is crying out
And its cry distracts my thought.

This act of violence returns us to one of the central components of his
imagery, one he often associates with Maud Gonne, especially in 'A
Bronze Head', that is, to the idea of the soul as a hawk, or as a raptor,
searching for its prey. In this hunting motif the word 'raptor', with its
root in the Latin *rapere*, to seize (which is significantly the same root for
rape and rapture), and the word prey, with its religious homonym, combine
to underline the destructive/creative nature of any act of self-discovery.
They also continue to emphasise the violent terrifying aspect of the
negative sublime.

It is this violent aspect of existence that awaits judgement. This is our
original sin; this is what spurs us into song. On the brink of death we
listen for some sign from the abyss as to what final significance our behaviour will have; we listen to hear if the echo will join in the judgements of
our own actions or whether it will invest what we have said with a different
meaning. Whether the echo is ours or not is as questionable as whether

the ego is the subject or the object of its dreams. We are left in ignorance, certain only of the mystery of suffering and our complicity in its causes. Paraphrasing Montaigne, Yeats argues that the crimes we commit we must mourn over for the rest of our lives, adding that he hates those who do not mourn.[14] He continues to struggle with the reasons for the crime and the quality of his mourning without a conclusive answer. The difficulty arises, however, when we do not know whether we have committed a crime; then, the flowering of the self is blighted.

The errors of self-analysis must be traced back to the process of self-discovery. The basis for the process is that we do battle with ourselves until we are wounded and unseal the secret of our angst. This is why Yeats insists that it takes as much courage to look into oneself as it does to die on the battlefield. To find that secret place and exult is 'of all things known . . . most difficult' ('To a Friend whose Work has come to Nothing'). In a collectivist age as ours, the source of self-renewal can only be found in what Adorno calls the 'ancient wound'.[15] When Horkheimer parabolically states in *The Eclipse of Reason* that all our hopes for salvation lie with those who died in the Holocaust,[16] he means that if those oppressed are finally able to describe the meaning of their own unspeakable experience, and the sublime horror of our 'ancient wound' whose bleeding they witnessed, they will provide the key to the present metaphysical breakdown. Through pain, they will find the *a priori* reason for pain. Here is the penultimate meaning of the Yeatsian sublime, of which there is no ultimate meaning that can be represented to the living. Like Foucault, Yeats tests the limits of experience in order to prove, in complete freedom, the actual rather than the imposed limits of the self. The self's suffering for expression conversely reveals the absolute freedom and authority of the immortal soul. After listening for God's dread voice through storm and fire, we find in the quiet aftermath the 'still small voice' (I Kings 19:11–12), and thereby unite the self's material and the soul's spiritual understanding. This is the process of creative violence in the self's romances. Yeats had very specific reasons to explain why violence and meditations on violence are not creative.

In his introduction to *The Oxford Book of Modern Verse* (1936), Yeats expresses what then became a famous condemnation of the First World War poets for the poetry they wrote out of 'passive suffering'.[17] That they made poetry out of being the victim was to Yeats a one-sided example of conflict and, as such, was not truly creative. To him, the question of whether or not violence is necessary is more fertile than its ill effects or pity. Thus, he delves into the ethical and moral centre of any question of violence. If it is requisite, he continues, we should view its passion with an ironic detachment, as did the Connaught Rangers who had just returned from the Boer War. In his essay, Yeats states that the soldiers

> ... described an incident over and over, and always with loud laughter: an unpopular sergeant struck by a shell turned round and round like a dancer wound in his own entrails. That too may be a right way of seeing war, if war is necessary; the way of the Cockney slums, of Patrick Street, of the *Kilmainham Minut*, of *Johnny I hardly knew ye*, of the *Medieval Dance of Death*.[18]

In the safe, aesthetic distance of Yeats's mind, this vision gave an energy to the experience of violence which made it more tolerable than a more pathetic rendering might have done. In his scheme, the soldiers were aware that the sergeant was their spiritual enemy, if not their physical one, and faced a rough version of their Mask when they confronted the sergeant's comic, grisly death. The soldiers' 'manic gaze'[19] expresses a tragic joy that has learned to accept violence. It is the epitome of the distance and self-preservation vital to an experience of the sublime.

Their tragic joy is not like that of Cuchulain, or of the ancient Chinese in 'Lapis Lazuli'; it is not heroic, because on that particular battlefield they were not in an heroic situation. Their perfectly suitable acerbic black humour comes from the slums of Dublin and London, and derives its courage and wisdom from folk song, street slang and ritual. It is a coarse method of coping with the maimed and diseased, seeing suffering as a dance of death. The concept of not being able to know the dancer from the dance, the movement of the body from the thought that inspires it, finds here its most macabre expression of unity. The soldiers survive the image's inversion of the dance of beauty because they are accustomed to such a parody. As Yeats writes in 'Lapis Lazuli', we see 'gaiety transforming all that dread.' Their attitude, though not as elevated as Cuchulain's – in the poem 'Cuchulain's Fight with the Sea' and in the play *On Baile's Strand* (1904) – or Kevin Higgins's attitude towards death in the poem entitled 'Death', is nevertheless far above those who murder the woman in 'Nineteen Hundred and Nineteen'. Such ignominious battle makes us no more than 'weasels fighting in a hole'.

How does Yeats's violent vision of opposites result from and shed light on the battle within the self? In the section of 'A Woman Young and Old' entitled 'Her Vision in the Wood', the manic gaze is turned exultantly upon that part of the self which is revealed in the other. In fact, the reason for which the manic gaze is cast on both self and other is due to their mutual victimisation, by virtue of which subject and object are seen as the same.

REVELATIONS AND DREAMING EGO

At the most sensual moment of the night, at 'wine-dark midnight', the speaker realises that she is no longer attractive, that, as an old woman, she has become sexually irrelevant, that under the 'rich foliage' of her pubic hair, of her sexual being, she is 'dry timber'. So she obtains the sole satisfaction she can, the 'lesser pang' which is revenge upon herself for her sexual irrelevance. She is in a sacred wood because she seeks the sexual ecstasy, the 'greater' pang that borders on religious experience, and that comes closest to a perception of God the more it becomes an impossible desire. That is why she states:

> Too old for a man's love I stood in rage
> Imagining men. Imagining that I could
> A greater with a lesser pang assuage
> Or but to find if withered vein ran blood,
> I tore my body that its wine might cover
> Whatever could recall the lip of lover.

Her subsequent self-laceration, which she has inflicted on herself in order to be attractive, to bleed as fertilely as she did when she was young, introduces a procession that bears a wounded Adonis/Attis-like figure upon a litter. The psycho-sexual wounds are symbols of a mystery whose rites require the secret message of blood if the mystery is to be plumbed. They are the last hope of understanding the enigma of the self and of the subject–object division, before it has been entirely glossed over by the facts of daily life. The relationship between the woman and the man is mirrored in the relationship between the hunter and the hunted – though this time it reverses the order of 'The Death of the Hare'. For each, it is a surrendering of oneself to the seductive mark of the beast. The beast on whom off-stage, as it were, all have turned their manic gaze has returned the gaze, and then fatally struck back. And again, like the sergeant wound in his own entrails, the violence is given a musical setting to capture the *a priori* rhythm of the mystery. Only now the music is a lament sung by 'stately' women:

> All stately women moving to a song
> With loosened hair or foreheads grief-distraught,
> It seemed a Quattrocento painter's throng,
> A thoughtless image of Mantegna's thought –
> Why should they think that are for ever young?
> Till suddenly in grief's contagion caught,
> I stared upon his blood-bedabbled breast
> And sang my malediction with the rest.

Two reactions to the wounding connected with the subject–object mystery are represented in the poem. The first is that of art's selfless universality, its secret inhumanity, represented by those who travel with and mourn for the wounded man, who have 'bodies from a picture or a coin', who seem a 'thoughtless image of Mantegna's thought', and who are 'for ever young'. They may be seen as pagan deities, Daimons, or the immortal aspect of the artist who feels, perhaps grievously laments, but who nevertheless remains untouched. The second reaction is the other more personal and intimately mortal aspect of the self which is represented by the woman who bears witness at the centre of the poem.

She is the one who also bleeds for beauty in that slaughterhouse of the imagination's eye where the wounds had been inflicted. Although she is also wounded, she is so moved by the detached immortal view of the event that she joins in their curse. She nevertheless remains sympathetic to the man, as an image of humanity caught in the throes of its own ecstatic self-wounding nature; that is, she remains sympathetic to *la pietà*, to the pathos of the self-sacrifice we make in our efforts to gain self-knowledge and to be whole. This is 'love's bitter-sweet': 'That thing all blood and mire, that beast-torn wreck,/Half turned and fixed a glazing eye on mine, / . . . love's bitter-sweet had all come back'. Like Adonis in Spenser's 'Garden of Adonis', this figure on the litter is the image of the perpetual cycle of decay and resurrection implicit in both violence and sexuality, the pulse of life that dies while giving birth to another.

Again we return to the sexual nature of beauty and violence, that image which, to Yeats, haunts the imagination, like the piece of woman's clothing on a sword from 'A Dialogue of Self and Soul'. Around this image circle immortal and mortal longings, which are as interdependent as they ever were opposed. Yeats's story of the interdependence of mortal and immortal dates back to *The Wanderings of Oisin* (1889). The immortals here would have no one to carry and lament if not for the blood and desire of the old woman. Likewise, she needs those who are 'for ever young', those immortal elements who thrive on mortal conflict, if she is to see the completion of her self-image carried through the wood. The immortals will not witness her ecstasy, for they too are swept away by their own ecstasy; if they had witnessed it, they implicitly would understand why she felt as she felt (and perhaps she in turn would understand their feelings). That would mean that a transcendent understanding of the scene, an apotheosis, could come about, but she cannot achieve that, she can glimpse it only because she is still alive. There is brief transcendence for the living. Thus, we see how the ultimate insight offered in the ecstatic sublime is always eclipsed by the loss of self-possession, by the swooning or orgiastic shutting of the eye:

And, though love's bitter-sweet had all come back,
Those bodies from a picture or a coin
Nor saw my body fall nor heard it shriek,
Nor knew, drunken with singing as with wine,
That they had brought no fabulous symbol there
But my heart's victim and its torturer.

All long for beauty and lament that violence has been done, but the ritual goes on because sexual violence is born of sexual despair and needs ritual assuaging. With the god-like mourners lost in Dionysiac ritual, the old woman has touched her most ancient and deepest wound, her 'dark declivities', that source of suffering which is described in the previous section of the lyric sequence ('Parting'). Unlike the mourners, she has found in the image of the wounded man 'no fabulous symbol there'. Instead, she has found 'her heart's victim and its torturer'. That, however, is only the tangled image of the mystery and not its resolution. Through these wounds, she has plumbed the subject–object mystery, that relationship of the internal and external worlds, of the primary and secondary qualities; for she has moved from subject to object, and she has seen how, at their most intimate, they are indistinguishable.

By so doing, she comes into 'eternal possession' of herself 'in one single moment' – an action which to Yeats, as to Aquinas, is the purpose of the eternal scheme.[20] In a world without objective truth, one has to go deep into the subjective dream in order to find the source of self, or the essence of the objective world, which flowed in and shall flow out again. The external and internal struggles are finally no different. The essence of each is neither the one nor the other, neither subject nor object, but is one and the same. The tragedy of the poem is that she can never understand the basis of this mystery, but she can embody the ultimate unity of its paradox in the ironic distance from her passions that is afforded by moments of tragic ecstasy or tragic joy. Subject and object are joined, although separate, in the same way that the Trinity is one and the same, although separate – the Holy Ghost being that entity that unites Father to Son, as in Christian mystical thought the ecstatic experience and Holy Ghost are that which unite subject and object.[21] In Yeats's version of the Trinity, however, the uniting power of the Holy Ghost is as sexual as is the power of mystic ecstasy; and the union is that between Man and Woman, or the male and female aspects of the Godhead, rather than between Father and Son.[22] Like the figure of sexuality, the Holy Ghost bears great resemblance to the double nature of the Yeatsian ecstatic sublime, in that it can be the divine image both of beatific love and of apocalyptic fury.

In the poem's image of subject and object, there is neither opposition nor dialectic, only the double image and the mystery underlying its creation. Regarding the subjective dream that guides one to the object, Adorno states:

> Between 'there came to me in a dream' and 'I dreamt' lie the ages of the world. But which is the more true? No more than it is spirits who send the dream, is it the ego that dreams.[23]

The ultimate significance of the poem's violent religious imagery may possibly be the awareness that the suffering we inflict and the suffering we undergo are extensions of the supreme violence of our own desire, a desire which is essentially insatiable, except perhaps in dreams. Yeats writes of dreams and desire in *The Shadowy Waters* (1906):

> All would be well
> Could we but give us wholly to the dreams,
> And get into their world that to the sense
> Is shadow, and not linger wretchedly
> Among substantial things; for it is dreams
> That lift us to the flowing, changing world
> That the heart longs for. (lines 177–83)

In such a state, as he concludes later in the narrative poem, when the 'body has begun to dream', everything external becomes a 'burning sod in the imagination and intellect (lines 486–8)' consumed by the violence of desire and by the flames of the empyrean.

PART IV

Whence Did All That Fury Come?

12

STARLIT AIR: THE POSITIVE SUBLIME

> . . . it is a question of processes that, even if they do not originate in the heavens, certainly go beyond our intentions and our control, acquiring – with respect to the individual – a kind of transcendence.
>
> Italo Calvino, *Six Memos for the Next Millennium*

Some critics do not grant the positive sublime its full Kantian value. Jahan Ramazani, for instance, calls the positive sublime a psychological 'movement from terror to joy'. In Burkean fashion, the 'joy' is one of self-preservation, of triumph, of a cure; it is a strategy to avoid death and is called 'the psychological sublime'.[1] Though this discussion is effective and revealing, it does not allow the full religious or mystical value that Yeats intends. The tension between the negative and positive sublime, between terror and joy, gives force to his verse. Yeats constantly insists that mere survival is not enough. The 'something more' of the Kantian sublime, the transcendent possibilities on the immaterial edge of the material real, is as much a part of life's constellation of values as is one's sense of power.

THE NECESSITY OF TRANSCENDENCE

To lay all stress on the psychological aspect of the subjective imagination is to simplify the cause of the *frisson* experienced during an encounter with complete otherness, with the imaginary – a highly relevant moment for Yeats, who sees the confrontation with the imaginary as central to the task of replenishing the exhausted imagination. Western civilisation stands like Leda on the banks of the Eurotas, ready to take on both the antithetical knowledge and power of a new dispensation, in order to find new primary terms of wisdom and love. Though Yeats places artistic powers firmly in the self, he does know that those powers are derived from the object world, that the way to the subject is through the object. Suffering finds meaning through consciousness of objective reality. Yeats believes that, except perhaps for modernised versions of Christianity such as Kierkegaard's, the problem with the psychology of his time is that it has no positive place for suffering.[2] Furthermore, he holds that any reality becomes ultimate at the moment of the confluence of subject and object, antithetical and primary, as the poem 'Long-legged Fly' suggests. Ramazani has tellingly reached the right conclusion when he writes that,

> Without such heroic self-assertion, the poet would remain, like Sappho in Longinus's treatise, broken-tongued, in the same condition as Soul in 'A Dialogue of Self and Soul,' whose 'tongue's a stone,' or like Soul in 'Vacillation,' 'Struck-dumb in the simplicity of fire!' In the dialectic of the sublime, the poet must rise from this momentary death, the tongue recover from its muteness.[3]

His premise is nevertheless unnecessarily reductive in that he insists self-assertion must diminish the importance of transcendence and of Soul:[4] 'However much the extra-poetic Yeats succeeds in being a mystic, the lyric self in his poems is rarely the passive vessel of the Daimon. Self asserts its prerogatives over mystic Soul in many more lyrics than "A Dialogue of Self and Soul"'.[5] Proceeding to admit the Bloomian idea that 'poetic identity is generated by their [Self's and Soul's] agon', Ramazani concludes that the closing 'we' of 'A Dialogue of Self and Soul' is the unleashing of the Freudian libido. By insisting on this formulation, Ramazani is basing the Yeatsian sublime in Burkean psychological modes of experience, although his is a highly subtle rendering which avoids too strict a psychological reading by supplementing it 'with a Heideggerian emphasis on the ecstatic encounter with death.'[6]

The Kantian positive sublime is crucial to Yeats because, rather than merely being a threat to identity, the mystical moment that Soul represents is a completion of identity. Though the sexual force of Ramazani's statement that the closing 'we' is an expression of the libido is very apt, that 'we' also illustrates how dependent Self is upon Soul for plenitude. The libido of Self is perfected by the moral, religious vision of Soul, of that part of our psyche that, rather than merely reflecting our own appetites, connects us to others in consummating primary ecstasy through our surrender to a religious imperative; if there is no surrender, as Yeats writes in *A Vision*, 'the old tragedy will be repeated'.[7] The sublimity of selfhood threatens to be purely destructive; it must meet the demands of Soul to find its consummation. For if Self is subject, Soul, as item in the world, is an object that is consubstantial with Self. Their union is the subject–object mystery at the vanishing point. It underlies creation, artistic and otherwise. The mystery of the aesthetic eludes materialist readings that do not allow it its place. The type of absolute freedom and transcendence that is consistently posited by Yeats demands an irreducible space – a space with roots in the empirical and in the light of the ideal. The present reading of Yeats, though admitting the undeniable force of a more empirical perspective, is closer to Italo Calvino's emphasis in *Six Memos for the Next Millennium* than it is to Ramazani's:

> Writers . . . establish their contacts through earthly transmitters, such as the individual or the collective unconscious; the time regained in feelings that reemerges from time lost; or 'epiphanies', concentrations of being in a single spot or point of time. In short, it is a question of processes that, even if they do not originate in the heavens, certainly go beyond our intentions and our control, acquiring – with respect to the individual – a kind of transcendence.[8]

The confrontation of idealism and empiricism, of the Kantian and Burkean sublime, is implicit in the phrase 'a kind of transcendence'. It receives Yeats's fullest expression in 'A Dialogue of Self and Soul' and throughout much of the volume *The Winding Stair and Other Poems* (1933). The question Yeats asks in the poem 'In Memory of Eva Gore-Booth and Con Markiewicz' is what will survive the conflagration of time and the autumn of the beautiful. What will prove that '[m]an has created death' ('Death'), that the world of pure forms does indeed exist beyond castration, semiotic collapse, the annihilation of the ego?[9] For Yeats, as for Kant, the world is concerned with morality; but while, for Kant, the moral sense associated with the sublime affirms certain categorical standards of behaviour, for Yeats, the moral sense transcends ethical standards. Morality's relationship to experience is always divisible by new experience; the moral is a quotient, not a formula. Absolutes must be deferred. Yeats's ideas of good and evil (ideas rather than assertions or doctrines) are revealed through experience. They are moral in so much as they give meaning and purpose to the crime of death and birth, to the original sin that has been the theme of poets since the age of Homer. In Yeats's opinion, 'There is too much talk of the moral law, surely the tongue of the poet is for other teaching. Is there not a pulpited million of disconsolate voices shouting the moral law for so much a day?'[10] The word 'moral' has been adopted here at times for the sake of comparison with Kant. Yeats uses the word 'religious' more instructively as regards questions of belief. To him, religion must be reconciled with natural emotions, and particularly with sexual love. Morality, as such, is the snare of convention and is at odds with religion because its formal rules stifle both the freedom of self-expression and the moral vision of the soul. Yeats's religion sets out to unify these two forces, rather than to repress the one for the sake of the other.

Kant also deems that the formal idealist heights of the soul must be proved in the empirical grounds of the self. He writes:

> These two conceptions, both that of God and that of the Soul (in respect of its immortality), can only be defined by means of predicates which, although they themselves derive their possibility entirely from a supersensible source, must, for all that, prove their reality in experience, for this is the only way in which they can make possible a cognition of a wholly supersensible being.[11]

Having based his conception of the soul in the sphere of the self, Kant proceeds to describe the concepts necessary to metaphysical proof: 'Now the only conception of this kind to be found in human reason is that of the freedom of man subject to moral laws and, in conjunction therewith, to the final end which freedom prescribes by means of these laws.'[12] Similarly, Yeats's 'A Dialogue of Self and Soul' is fundamentally an effort to establish the relationship between Soul's morality and the freedom of Self. Whereas Kant feels that aesthetic disinterest, objective distance, is the occasion for that moral circumscription of freedom, Yeats instead takes Burke's emphasis on power, self-preservation and desire for procreation, as the basis of the self's salvation and the path towards establishing the moral scope of freedom. In this, Burke's safe aesthetic distance is different from Kant's idea of disinterest. The soul is disinterested in a way that the self can never be. In Kant's aesthetic register, any pure judgement of taste is disinterested and therefore dependent on the soul, for it is the 'animating principle in the mind . . . the faculty for presenting aesthetic ideas'.[13] In the second part of 'A Dialogue', Self achieves distance through the agency of Soul (which remains disinterested throughout). Soul's morality is thereby found in the desires of Self. Its discovery is essentially a religious-erotic experience – an ecstasy of the religious and sexual order – in short, the Baroque figure of the saints in ecstasy or one of Beardsley's Decadent sinners, an image which potentially reconciles the Burkean and Kantian sublime.

SELF AND SOUL: BURKE AND KANT

From the beginning of 'A Dialogue of Self and Soul', the respective statements by Self and Soul make this poem a confrontation of Burkean and Kantian sublimes. Soul presents the simultaneous destruction of the empirical world, the 'crumbling battlement' and the revelation of the ideal. Ramazani maintains that here Soul is doing the summoning, is engaging in the work of Self, is using the same language that Yeats uses in 'All Souls' Night', when he summons spirits to him at midnight. In such a scenario, Kant's transcendental extra is merely more of the same empirical reality. Soul is only different in that it is a negation of Self. Clearly, Self and Soul are interrelated; each can do the work of the other. This blurring does not erase the lines between them, however, nor does it make Soul less powerful than Self. All formal knowledge is based on inferences that empirical reality can give. Soul needs the language of Self in order to find expression; Self needs the perspective of Soul in order to find meaning. That the horizon of Soul, Kant's transcendental point of view, is constantly deferred does not make its presence any less powerful. Soul is therefore bound to appear spectral, indistinguishable from darkness. At midnight between sleep and dreams, Soul moves in from the margins to the centre of experience. In this belief, Yeats objects to Nietzsche's exclusion of Socratic-Christian spirituality, asking: 'But why does Nietzsche think that the night has no stars, nothing but bats and owls and the insane moon?'[14] The 'breathless starlit air' and 'the star that marks the hidden pole' are meant to mark the sphere and goal of an important human mood.

Burke's attitude towards the night is similarly sceptical of any meta-physical enchantment. In a chapter of the *Enquiry* entitled 'Magnificence', Burke allows for one of his rare blurrings of the line between positive and negative sublimity. In his reference to the stars, we see no element of Platonism and pure forms, of the starry firmament that reveals *a priori* truths. In fact, we see a refutation of those elements:

> The starry heaven, though it occurs so very frequently to our view, never fails to excite an idea of grandeur. This cannot be owing to any thing in the stars themselves, separately considered. The number is certainly the cause. The apparent disorder augments the grandeur, for the appearance of care is highly contrary to our ideas of magnificence. Besides, the stars lye [sic] in such apparent confusion, as makes it impossible on ordinary occasions to reckon them. This gives them the advantage of a sort of infinity.[15]

Burke equates the stars' magnificence with the mathematical sublime, but, unlike Kant, he gives it no metaphysical significance. In terms of Soul, Yeats's discussion is closer to Kant's famous statement: 'Two things fill the heart with ever renewed and increasing awe and reverence, the more often and the more steadily we meditate upon them: *the starry firmament above and the moral law within*.'[16] From the moral law within to the starry sky above, we are surely ascending 'breathless starlit air' in order to come to 'that quarter where all thought is done', to the supersensible faculty of Reason. Though for Yeats conventional morality is at odds with true religious vision, his idea of Soul is very like Kant's.

Concerning Self, however, Yeats's ideas are highly Burkean. The pain of self-understanding comes through temporal conflict, while the pleasure of society is found in the civilised company of women, in the highly cultured life centred round ceremonies of instinct and procreation. The

Self's opening remark contains all these elements. Self discovers itself in the speculum of conflict, in the 'looking-glass' of the phallic sword, whilst the vaginal protective image of the 'court-lady's dress' gives solace. This is the essential gendered tension that Burke famously forms in the *Enquiry* and in the *Reflections*. The masculine and feminine principles provide the conceptual basis for the union between masculine Self and feminine Soul, and for the antithetical and primary qualities Self and Soul represent. Soul promptly rebukes Self. Here Ramazani is particularly insightful. The concerns of superego Soul work antagonistically against the libido of Self. In the first part of the poem there is no mediating Ego. Contrary to Ramazani's reading, the uniting 'we' of the end of the poem is not so much an unleashing of the libido as the fashioning of an Ego that is able to balance the needs of the libido with the imperatives of the Superego – needs and imperatives which in the next remarks of Self and Soul are evident:

> *My Soul.* Why should the imagination of a man
> Long past his prime remember things that are
> Emblematical of love and war?
> Think of ancestral night that can,
> If but imagination scorn the earth
> And intellect its wandering
> To this and that and t'other thing,
> Deliver from the crime of death and birth.

> *My Self.* Montashigi, third of his family, fashioned it
> Five hundred years ago, about it lie
> Flowers from I know not what embroidery –
> Heart's purple – and all these I set
> For emblems of the day against the tower
> Emblematical of the night,
> And claim as by a soldier's right
> A charter to commit the crime once more.

Soul wants renunciation, a return to our ancestry, to the divine glory whence we came, our primary home, while Self insists on its carnal antithetical needs. Self resists union with Soul because it spells the death of selfhood. The tower is the work of Self, while the winding stair is the path of Soul – a path which ascends the ruin of selfhood, the 'crumbling battlement'. The opposition has been set. There seems to be no possibility of accommodation for either of them.

Soul ends with the siren-cry of the primary, positive sublime, meant to lure Self towards its reconciling sphere. Soul offers the essential unity of subject and object, human and supernatural, of the real (Will, or is) and the ideal (Mask, or ought) that Self craves, but the price is death:

My Soul. Such fullness in that quarter overflows
And falls into the basin of the mind
That man is stricken deaf and dumb and blind,
For intellect no longer knows
Is from the *Ought*, or *Knower* from the *Known* –
That is to say, ascends to Heaven;
Only the dead can be forgiven;
But when I think of that my tongue's a stone.

The chief problem is that Soul presents the domination, then the anni-hilation of sensible desire at the behest of supersensible morality. For Yeats, the way towards the supersensible never relinquishes the sensible – rather, it fulfils it. Following Blake, Yeats sees that at the limits of sensible experience lies the chance of supersensible fulfilment. When Soul presents its image, it is not enough. Self stays behind. The basin of the mind shall find its corresponding image in the fountains of rich flowering lawns which have been built by violent bitter men who longed for the gentleness and sweetness they did not possess. In other words, the violent path of Self leads to the Garden of Soul where, surrounded by objects of its desire, it can rest now self-delighting. The truest sublime is the synthesis of opposites. Self must stay behind in 'A Dialogue' because it must beat out its path to the Garden. Part of the process of so doing involves recounting its failures, disappointments, the infinite pain of self-realisation. It recounts the stages of human development in the fashion of the famous speech in *As You Like It*. The acquisition of selfhood is marked by 'ignominy', 'distress', 'clumsiness' and 'a disfigured shape'. The close of the third stanza subtly emphasises the sacred and erotic aspect of the marriage of sensible and supersensible reality. The empirical fallen path of Self is paradoxically meant to discover the formal idealist truth that is 'kindred of his soul', but its fallen nature frustrates its efforts to achieve this realisation. Hence, left on its own without the help of Soul, Self is consis-tently stripped to bare essentials. Through the course of self-destruction and renewal, Self eventually uncovers the occasion for the union of Self and Soul, of empirical and idealist realms, and it does this as the sublime and the beautiful, the masculine and feminine principles combine in the perfected individual.

The last stanza of the poem describes this intermingling: the ego fulfils both the demands of conscience and the desire of the libido, the union of sacred and profane, the remorse that ends in intellectual love:

I am content to follow to its source
Every event in action or in thought;
Measure the lot; forgive myself the lot!
When such as I cast out remorse
So great a sweetness flows into the breast
We must laugh and we must sing,
We are blest by everything,
Everything we look upon is blest.

The beatific individual extends the sense of beatitude to the external world, to those objects of sense, to the otherness that is bedevilled by division – otherness which is more often a threat than a complement to Self. Self finds all this in its connection with what Kant calls the 'psychic substance' of Soul.[17] That the formal reality of the soul must be proved in the empirical reality of the self, that primary wholeness must be found in antithetical division is the source of all our torment.

Yeats evokes the harshness of the friction between the self and soul in the following poem, 'Blood and the Moon', wherein he elaborates a series of poetic, philosophical, political and religious variations on the theme. From Swift's 'sibylline frenzy', through Burke's organic (against Newton's mechanical) conception of society, to Berkeley's subjective and self-consciously Irish rendering of reality (versus Locke's and Johnson's objective, English rendering), we see the play of primary and antithetical truths in the seventeenth- and eighteenth-century setting in which those truths were fought out. The emphasis on blood and the subjective imagination can be misleading; Yeats is attempting a balancing act of antithetical means and primary ends. Two passages are of particular relevance. The subjective passage on Berkeley is balanced by the next stanza in which the subjective will finds objective meaning: 'The strength that gives our blood and state magnanimity of its own desire;/Everything that is not God consumed with intellectual fire.' Magnanimity is that quality in government which Yeats thinks is lacking in Nietzsche's philosophy.[18] Without it, the 'glories of our blood and state' are, in the original lines of James Shirley (of which Yeats quotes a phrase here), 'shadows, not substantial things'. Never does the division between the needs of the self and the requirements of the soul, between Burkean and Kantian sublimes, between the antithetical qualities of knowledge and power and the primary ones of wisdom and love seem so broad. The last lines of the poem nevertheless do quite suddenly and effectually show how the hidden reality of the soul plays on the margins of consciousness and reality. There is hope of harmony between the opposing forces on those margins, and there is something miraculous, something beyond the scope of human endeavour:

> For wisdom is the property of the dead,
> A something incompatible with life; and power,
> Like everything that has the stain of blood,
> A property of the living; but no stain
> Can come upon the visage of the moon
> When it has looked in glory from a cloud.

The positive sublime is quite fittingly seen through the semicolon between the phrases 'property of the living; but no stain'. It is a connected thought that requires a shift in grammar, an adverbial clause precipitously balanced as a possible occurrence that is not happening at that moment. The moon is a changeable demarcation between the mutable sphere of earth and the immutable heavenly sphere. The Elizabethan world-picture still holds for Yeats as pre-Lockean and therefore prelapsarian model. The moon can be either symbol of the *a priori* (as it is here) or it can reflect the madness of the mutable world (as it does in another poem from this volume, 'The Crazed Moon'). This changeability, this blurring border, is at the heart of the questions which are explored in *The Winding Stair* (1933) volume.

THE SYNTHESIS OF LADY GREGORY

To use Yeatsian syntax, the volume balances profane and sacred, sacred and profane, mutable and immutable, immutable and mutable, never certain of the order. The balance is struck in 'Oil and Blood' and 'Veronica's Napkin'. The only certainty is that the sacred and profane must exist together. The Coole Park poems, 'Coole Park, 1929' and 'Coole and Ballylee, 1931', are monuments to Lady Gregory's Unity of Culture, her ability in running a demesne, to maintain the balance between the Yeatsian oppositions. They are ballast to all the various questions that are asked in the volume. Yeats's statement in 'Coole Park, 1929' that 'Thoughts long knitted into a single thought,/A dance-like glory that those walls begot' reveals the Unity of Being and Culture towards which his historical system of antithetical and primary movements aims. The congeries of being ('Thoughts long knitted') disappears into the single being that is God ('a single thought'). The dance is the chief Yeatsian symbol of the union of body (or self) and soul; it lapses, however, as soon as the dance is done. The exalting fusion that the dance represents is unpresentable, except through metaphor of the dance. The move from metaphor to meaning is reductive. Transcendental signification depends upon the metaphorical dance for any meaning to be distilled. Yeats characterises the mystery of the dance thus:

They came like swallows and like swallows went,
And yet a woman's powerful character
Could keep a swallow to its first intent;
And half a dozen in formation there,
That seemed to whirl upon a compass-point,
Found certainty upon the dreaming air . . .

The compass-point is that hidden pole which marks the soul and which the self's wandering thoughts should be fixed upon. Gregory's maternal authority is that hidden pole.[19] As the confluence of feminine beauty and masculine sublimity, she is able to achieve an extraordinary synthesis between antithetical power and primary wisdom. She is the exception to Burke's rule that the authority of the sublime and the partiality of the beautiful have solely male and female embodiments. Gregory achieves immortality; her 'laurelled head', for which all appropriate dedication must neither be directed to the primary wisdom of the sun nor to the antithetical power of the shade, is the harmonising object to which Yeats surrenders. In order to pay the proper homage, to give 'a moment's memory to that laurelled head', the eye must be bent upon the grounds of being, the *a priori*, formal truths moving beneath empirical earth-bound reality. This is the momentary mingling of primary wisdom and antithetical power that informs the Yeatsian dialectic.

In 'Coole and Ballylee, 1931', Yeats meditates on how he can continue to embody the experience of the Unity of Being and Culture which he had known at Coole Park. From the embattled position of Thoor Ballylee, he bears witness to the signs of dark, barbaric forces reasserting themselves throughout Europe. He is aware of the connection between the divisive force of the tower and the unifying force of Coole Park, and knows that the tension between them is what bears fruit; it is the space in which flows the 'generated soul'. The force inside the dark womb, the antithetical psychic power of the poet Raftery's cellar, seeks to rise to Coole Park's unity. Yeats's tone is tragic, as the effort in this age is increasingly difficult: 'Nature's pulled her tragic buskin on'. The tragedy is that the specific type of dance-like glory is no longer possible. When the poet suddenly sees a swan, which is emblem of the soul, he is aware of the loss of primary expiation and of the intellectual love that works in 'nature's spite'. The swan is 'so lovely that it sets to right/What knowledge or its lack had set awry'. The reconciling force whose comings and goings are so mysterious, whose purity borders on the superhuman, whose existence may be palpable but is always unverifiable, is also very fragile. A child without the benefits of ceremony and the knowledge of tradition could easily destroy or at least dangerously disregard something of so tenuous a beauty, and do so merely out of an untutored, spiteful nature: 'So arrogantly pure, a child might think/It can be murdered with a spot of ink.'

The implication is that only ceremony and tradition, 'Marriages, alliances and families,/And every bride's ambition satisfied', will protect the tenuous powers of reconciliation – the soulfulness that can set 'to right' what knowledge, or ignorance, had 'set awry'. Yeats, like Burke, believes that the soul can achieve a great deal if it is protected by tradition, ceremony and custom. Yeats feels that he is the last of an issue, the last of the Romantics who believes this; the tradition that dates back to Homer and that 'chose for a theme/Traditional sanctity and loveliness' has been forsaken. Passion is left unguided; the soul, which the swan represents, is powerless before the 'darkening flood'. Though poets derive their material from the fallen empirical world, from Original Sin, they nevertheless seek that which can 'bless/The mind of man or elevate a rhyme', that is, they seek beatitude both for its ability to positively influence society and to give poetic form its transcendent beauty. The positive sublime is threatened by the destructive force of the deluge, by the terrifying force of waters above their banks like those which first gave Burke the subject of terror as the basis for his *Enquiry*.[20] At such moments in the volume, Yeats's version of a cultural, Kantian sublime seems to have little chance of survival. Amidst the intensely elegiac major poems of the volume, many of the minor poems seek to offset the tragic tone.

'For Anne Gregory' presents a playful erotic image of *agape*, the most primary image of God. It comes as light relief to the elegiac end of 'Coole and Ballylee, 1931'. 'Swift's Epitaph' presents an heroic image of self-sacrifice. 'Mohini Chatterjee' is an image of reincarnation ('Men dance on deathless feet') that counters the death and ruin which haunt the great elegies. 'The Choice', on the other hand, a stanza taken out of 'Coole and Ballylee, 1931' deepens the darkness. The choice of the antithetical over the primary method may have that tension which is vital to poetry, but it also may not lead to the final reconciliation of the positive sublime. The poem 'At Algeciras – A Meditation upon Death' is one that asks the question to which the others provide the negative or positive answers. It is a poem worth considering as introduction to the themes of the major ones that follow ('Byzantium' and 'Vacillation').

It begins with an image of southern heat and decay hanging over the meeting of the Atlantic and Mediterranean, the 'narrow Straits', the pillars of Hercules – limit of the known world in Classical times. It is the threshold which Yeats, when ill, felt he was approaching, and in which this world's reality mingles with the transcendent, as do the Atlantic and the Mediterranean, the beautiful and the sublime. The migratory birds flying across this threshold are emblems of the soul's passage from life through decay and death to the afterlife, when the dawn of that new light breaks. The poet then recollects when as a boy he presented shells to an 'older mind' in the hope of finding wisdom. This act of gift-giving is appropriate to one's relationship with God, and it contains the relevant idea of the getting of wisdom through self-sacrifice. The wisdom Yeats hopes to have is not Newton's, not the barrenness of abstractly metaphorical knowledge, but that combination of abstract and concrete, of intellectual and sensual knowledge which the metaphors of poetry can best give. The aspect of the poem most pertinent to this discussion is in the last stanza:

> Greater glory in the sun,
> An evening chill upon the air,
> Bid imagination run
> Much on the Great Questioner;
> What He can question, what if questioned I
> Can with a fitting confidence reply.

In this poem Yeats clearly shows how, confronted by the objective reality of the Deity, the primary characteristics of humanity, peace, love, and surrender, predominate. We are reduced to child-like dependence. There is 'Greater glory' in the primary sun, rather than in the antithetical moon. The self has lost confidence and wonders what faith it can give that God will commend. This testing of faith is the substance of the next two great poems.

TESTING FAITH

In 'Byzantium', we are presented with the smell of the fire, the trace of the negative sublime that always hangs upon the positive sublime, and therefore with the sense that we might lapse again into terror, that the bottom will fall out from what seem *a priori* truths, that we are left with nothing but the abyss. It is well known that Yeats wrote this poem in answer to T. Sturge Moore's criticism of 'Sailing to Byzantium'. Moore felt that the latter poem never moves out of Nature, as it promises, because such a movement is impossible. In his explanation he alludes to Wittgenstein's idea that 'nothing at all can be said about ultimates, or reality in an ultimate sense'.[21] 'Byzantium' is Yeats's effort to present the unpresentable. His method is of great importance, as the poem hovers between Burkean and Kantian definitions of the sublime. The poem is concerned with images that move among vague definitions and blurred relationships between words: 'Miracle, or bird or golden handiwork, /More miracle than bird or handiwork'. And it is concerned with images that break the laws of physics: 'An agony of flame that cannot singe a sleeve'. The effort to frustrate the powers of language brings to mind Burke's belief that, in order for language to be sublime, words and images must challenge the limits of sense.[22] Words must play with the relationship between objects and between subject and object. Such play with referentiality establishes that the way to ultimate reality, to the transcendence of the material world, while always referring to material objects, is nevertheless revealed in the interrelationship of objects with the mind; in other words, there is transcendence in the act of aesthetic perception.

Essentially, Yeats places shades moving through images of sex and death, moving through a purgatorial scene of shifting relationships, of mutable forms, of various planes of perception of reality; the shades are searching for the purity that has been denied them when they were held by '[t]he fury and the mire of human veins'. The first stanza illustrates how, still burdened with corrupted sense, and still prone to lustful and warring passions, to the rawest forms of love and hate, we move between the supernatural incarnations of the purely subjective (the antithetical 'moonlit dome') and of the purely objective (the primary 'starlit dome'). We are denied purgation unless we find in Byzantium's Unity of Being and Culture a fusion of the antithetical qualities of power, desire, war and the primary qualities of wisdom, love, peace – a fusion which the art of the Byzantine worker in *A Vision* represents. In Byzantium, 'religious, aesthetic and practical life were one'. The primary imperatives of religious thought and the antithetical needs of aesthetic life found expression in the everyday life of its citizens. If through the pride of his 'delicate skill', the 'philosophical worker in mosaic' can vent the 'murderous madness of the mob', it is because such Unity of Being and Culture allows him to give it transcendent expression.[23] The fire of his invention is a purgatorial version of God's 'intellectual fire'. More 'miracle than bird or handiwork', his 'golden handiwork' combines Nature and artifice, and transcends the 'complexities of mire and blood'.

The eidola (or phantasmal images of the ideal) move through the profane and sacred images, seeking purification. The purification is a moral one, implicitly engaging and redefining Kant's ideas of sublimity. Instead of annihilating or abandoning the sensible, Yeats lifts it up in all its profanity in order to find in its passion the force of all sacred images. The dolphins that come to offer 'their backs to the wailing dead that they may carry them to Paradise',[24] as Yeats writes out the conception of the poem in prose, are sexual water-symbols. They are images of the sensual purification that complements the spiritual purification by fire. The gyring movement of life must be unwound so that one returns to simplicity and 'unwind[s] the winding path'. The antithetical mood, 'by the moon embittered', must scorn the empirical world from which it draws power. This is what breaks the 'bitter furies of complexity' and results in the 'condition of fire where all is music and rest', as Yeats writes in his *Memoirs*.[25] The inference is that fire burns us only because we are made of base material. At the close of the poem, however, there is still the smell of the fire; neither music nor rest has begun:

> Astraddle on the dolphin's mire and blood,
> Spirit after spirit! The smithies break the flood,
> The golden smithies of the Emperor!
> Marbles of the dancing floor
> Break bitter furies of complexity,
> Those images that yet
> Fresh images beget,
> That dolphin-torn, that gong-tormented sea.

There is no single image that contains all images and ends the search, or a creative gesture that contains all creation in itself and ends the engendering. The last line tells us that we are still on the threshold between the negative and positive sublime, suffering the last and perhaps keenest throes of sexual torment before we are spiritually redeemed.

'Vacillation' takes up many of the themes discussed in 'A Dialogue of Self and Soul' and in 'Byzantium', but deals with them more explicitly. The first two sections present the choice between subjective antithetical power and objective primary wisdom, between the swordsman and the saint. For Yeats, self-negation ('Attis' image') is only an escape from the course of life, which remains tormented between the half of the tree burning with God's ascetic intellectual fire and the half of 'abounding foliage moistened with dew', moistened with the water of sensuality. Though from his youth Yeats understands the merit of religious sensuality and ascetic purity (of Robartes's way, alias MacGregor Mathers and of Ahern's, alias Lionel Johnson), he knows that the best artists suffer the middle way in order to create lasting works of 'intellect or faith'. To do so, the artist must stand the test and terror of death, withstand the experience of the negative sublime. Maintaining this balance allows him or her to experience the type of primary ecstasy of which Soul spoke in 'A Dialogue of Self and Soul'. Part IV of 'Vacillation' presents a union of subject and object in which the subject is made aware of the unique, final end of all surrounding objects. The ordinariness of the setting gives it a decidedly primary ambiance full of goodness – humane, democratic and unifying. It is an example of Christian beatitude, like that which Yeats experienced at various times throughout his life.[26] Here is Yeats's poetic description of such a moment:

> My fiftieth year had come and gone,
> I sat, a solitary man,
> In a crowded London shop,
> An open book and empty cup
> On the marble table-top.

While on the shop and street I gazed
My body of a sudden blazed;
And twenty minutes more or less
It seemed, so great my happiness,
That I was blessèd and could bless.

Christian blessedness is what causes Yeats to vacillate between his pagan speech and an acceptance of Von Hügel's Christian mysticism. Some form of blessedness is also the aim of Yeats's search. In the prose description of primary illumination, he ceases to be aware of the empirical critical necessities of his craft, while flushed by an understanding of the metaphysical content of his lyric verse: 'instead of discovering new technical flaws, I read with all the excitement of the first writing.'[27] As we use rules for poetry in order to be free of rules, or craft in order to be free of craft, we use the antithetical harshness of the critical mind in order to find a primary harmony of parts of speech. According to Yeats, this lack of critical instinct is paralleled by the lack of any critical attitude towards others. If 'the natural condition of our life is hatred', as Yeats continues in *Per Amica Silentia Lunae*, it is because we are irritated with those facts, people and circumstances that trouble this pure and extended image of the soul, of the *Anima Mundi*.[28]

Part V of 'Vacillation' works in conjunction with part IV. It is the appalled conscience driving Yeats towards Christianity, and the remorse, the self-criticism, that ends in the above intellectual love. The warriors of part VI have to admit the full significance of remorse, if they are to experience intellectual love, the extended image of the soul. For all their antithetical war they must surrender to primary peace. The refrain of 'Let all things pass away' refers to the insignificance of the temporal, empirical world in the light of the moral, *a priori* realm. This dominance of the eternal introduces us to part VII, and to another internal Yeatsian dialogue, between Soul and Heart, which also moves between Kantian and Burkean sublimes. Soul insists upon the predominance of formal ideals ('Seek out reality, leave things that seem'), while Heart maintains that the empirical world of appearance is the basis for all artistic endeavour ('What, be a singer born and lack a theme?'). Soul insists upon Kant's moral imperative, referring to the sublimity that is Hebrew by birth ('Isaiah's coal, what more can man desire?'). Heart resists the loss of personality and individual voice that occurs when one stands in the empyrean ('Struck dumb in the simplicity of fire?'). It resists the consensus of opinion that Burke feels is so detrimental to judgement, and it resists the sway of pure theory over the practicalities of existence. Soul insists that salvation is there and Heart makes a fundamental statement for Yeats's position as a poet: 'What theme had Homer but original sin?'

Having established the basis in literary tradition for his decision not to become Christian, Yeats concludes with a vision that balances primary sanctity and wisdom with antithetical power and knowledge:

> Must we part Von Hügel, though much alike, for we
> Accept the miracles of the saints and honour sanctity?
> The body of Saint Teresa lies undecayed in tomb,
> Bathed in miraculous oil, sweet odours from it come,
> Healing from its lettered slab. Those self-same hands perchance
> Eternalised the body of a modern saint that once
> Had scooped out Pharaoh's mummy. I – though heart might find relief
> Did I become a Christian man and choose for my belief
> What seems most welcome in the tomb – play a predestined part.
> Homer is my example and his unchristened heart.
> The lion and the honeycomb, what has Scripture said?
> So get you gone, Von Hügel, though with blessings on your head.

Yeats accepts the miracles of the saints' lives and of the resurrection, although, of course, within the perimeters of reincarnation in which he devoutly believes. He sees that both Homer's and Von Hügel's ways are valid. Swordsmen and saints worship images that break hearts, as opposed to those followers of Attis who castrate themselves and therefore know not what they know but know 'not grief'. The life of swordsmen and saints are each other's Mask. The mummy is a symbol of the gyring movement of personality and history between them. Modern saint and Pharaoh return to the same gyring images of antithetical and primary dispensations, whether in sin or in sanctity, driven by the same desiring body that is enwound in preparation for death. The succour that Christian intellectual love can give is not enough for Yeats. He must draw sweetness from strength, tread the path of evil, of antithetical cruelty and deceit, of Burkean sublimity until, in Dionysian pilgrimage, he surrenders to primary suffering and love and gives full credence to the sacramental object. His sexual wound is then healed by Apollonian illusion, by the Kantian sublime. This is the force driving Yeats up the winding stair to the 'breathless starlit air' of the supersensible world. Rather than relinquish the sensible, or put away the flesh, he will carry forth some of the strength of the flesh into a religious vision which affirms its sensible power.

THE METAPHYSICS OF THE YEATSIAN LYRIC

Yeats ends the volume wondering, in 'Stream and Sun at Glendalough', what 'hidden pole' keeps him futilely seeking the peaceful resolution of the Christian world at Glendalough:

What motion of the sun or stream
Or eyelid shot the gleam
That pierced my body through?
What made me live like these that seem
Self-born, born anew?

He knows that his way is one of sexual-spiritual torment, as the Crazy
Jane poems so aptly show. 'Crazy Jane and the Bishop' is a further confrontation of sensible desires and supersensible imperatives. This is a recurrent
theme, of course, as poems dating back to *The Wanderings of Oisin* (1889)
illustrate. For Yeats, body and soul must be united in Paradise. The
Bishop, willingly and mistakenly, deforms the body for the sake of the
supersensible. The gist of *Words for Music Perhaps* (1932) is that antithetical wounding and primary kindness are necessarily interdependent. It
takes but a sampling to prove this: 'Fair and foul are near of kin'; and
'nothing can be sole or whole/That has not been rent' ('Crazy Jane talks
with the Bishop'). In 'Crazy Jane grown old looks at the Dancers', he
notes that '*Love is like the lion's tooth*', while in 'His Confidence' he insists
that 'Out of a desolate source,/Love leaps upon its course'. In 'Mad as the
Mist and Snow', he wonders if this dangerous antinomy has not caused
the madness of the mad race of poets. Madness grows out of the search
for permanence in a transient world. Crazy Jane is their speaker.

The anxious search for permanence at the heart of the ambiguous
relationship between negative and positive sublimity is tellingly presented
in part X, 'Her Anxiety'. The source of anxiety is the struggle between
negative and positive sublimity for supremacy. An advantage is suggested
by the varying tone of the refrain, and is consequently forever elusive,
forever unverifiable as one cannot be sure of the tone. Tone is perhaps the
most uncertain aspect of the pattern and rhythm of grammar. Yeats's
change of tone becomes apparent:

> Earth in beauty dressed
> Awaits returning spring.
> All true love must die,
> Alter at the best
> Into some lesser thing.
> *Prove that I lie.*
>
> Such body lovers have,
> Such exacting breath,
> That they touch or sigh.
> Every touch they give,
> Love is nearer death.
> *Prove that I lie.*

Yeats is discussing whether love (the highest human experience) and the
beautiful (love's social expression) can survive the onslaught of death, can

survive the terrible inhuman, negative sublime. Change and decay are seasonal. As flowers wither, so must love; we await spring in the hope of love resurrected and the body transfigured. The tone in which we read the refrain seems to be a matter of choice. We can read both instances in a tone of accusation, as a challenge; we can read them as a lament; or, finally, we can read them in some combination of both tones. To read them without emotion, flatly, would run counter to the poem's high evocation of the relationship between love and death.

In the frame of negative and positive sublimity, it would be most appropriate to read the first refrain in a challenging manner, highlighting the empirical truth of the poem's theme of evanescence, and to read the second in a tone of lament, emphasising the poem's need for some metaphysical certainty in the face of death. To read both lines as a challenge would make the poem a dark statement of the negative sublime, of the loss of origins and the non-existence of the *a priori*. The delicacy of the opening lines at least partially belies such complete desolation. To read them both as plaintive requests would be somewhat better as, although the force of the poem is very dark and deathly, at the same time it is very sensual. The poem is a lover's lament. This reading, however, would rather too simply resist the darkness of the theme. Likewise, we could not read the first as lament and the second as challenge because the power of sexual love is premised on the belief that, in its gesture suspended over the abyss, love will not die. The combination of first challenge and then lament is best, for it reading starkly outlines both the division between formal need and empirical fact, and love's attempts to establish a bridge. The poem is among those lyrics that best accord with his metaphysical conception of poetry. It has a rhetorical balance worthy of Longinus's idea of the sublime and one representative of Yeats's best lyrics.

According to Longinus, style is sublime because the rhythm of the moment which is being described is caught in the rhythm of the sentence describing it. He believes that there are innate communicative structures underlying the relationship between the signifier and signified; the sublime is the revelation of those structures, if not their final determination. Not being a final determination, the relationship between writing and the real can be disrupted by the potential violence of their difference. The divergence accounts for various contemporary views. Sublimity is the potential violence and/or the potential revelation. In the divergence, we also see the relationship between negative and positive sublimity. Art has become the testing ground of such ideas. Yeats looks to the lyric, with its roots in rhythm, as the best expression of our relation to *a priori* structures. He illustrates this conviction in a letter written in 1901, during the transformative years between the composition of *The Wind Among the Reeds* (1899) and *In the Seven Woods* (1904):

. . . a play or a novel necessarily describes people in their relation to one another, and is, therefore, frequently concerned with the conscience in the ordinary sense of that word, but lyric poetry is the voice of what metaphysicians call innate knowledge, that is to say, of conscience, for it expresses the relation of the soul to eternal beauty and truth as no other writing can express it.[29]

Although Yeats uses one of his early highly transcendental terms, 'eternal beauty', the more sophisticated terms of the beautiful which he is then formulating are reflected in his ideas of metaphysical knowledge and conscience. Like Longinus, Yeats thinks that sublimely lyrical writing transcends the human and brings one close to the mind of God, that the harmony of well-written material echoes the inherent harmony of the soul. According to Modernist fashion, Yeats fully explores the sexual nature of the metaphysics of sublimity. In *Words for Music Perhaps* (1932), we are presented with complete and systematic representation of how sensible desire is given supersensible expression. Along with 'Supernatural Songs' from *Parnell's Funeral and Other Poems* (1935), it acts as a frame, indeed a rather hopeful credo, for the violently alternating visions of negative and positive sublimity that follow in the last two volumes, *New Poems* (1938) and *Last Poems* (1939).

13

THE STREAM THAT'S ROARING BY: THE TRAGEDY OF HISTORY

Even the presentation of the sublime, so far as it belongs to fine art, may be brought into union with beauty in a *tragedy in verse* . . .

Kant, *Critique of Judgement*

Sexual intercourse is an attempt to solve the eternal antinomy, doomed to failure because it takes place only on one side of the gulf. The gulf is that which separates the one and the many, or if you like, God and man.

Yeats, *Letters*

But if the historical view is taken to mean a simple chronological approach to life, that will not answer (though it might help solve some knotty problems of dates of composition and strategies of publication), because the life was lived on so many levels, in bursts of parallel intensity.

Roy Foster, *Paddy and Mr Punch*

At the beginning of Yeats's 'Supernatural Songs' – one of those poems, like 'Fragments', that are millennia in miniature – the monk Ribh reads by the light shed from the sexual union of two immortal lovers, Baile and Aillinn. Throughout the rest of the poem's extrapolation of Ribh's philosophy, ecstasy accordingly takes a central position in the vast interrelationship of history, religion and myth, and reveals some of the most difficult aspects of the distinction between the beautiful and the sublime. It presents Yeats's historical and mythological ideas of subjectivity, objectivity, of the individual and society – ideas which underlie the distinction between these two aesthetic terms. In the lovers' tragic tale, the distinction between the sublime and the beautiful turns on the troubled relationship between human love and sexuality, and God's love and sexuality. As is evident in the above epigraph from Yeats's *Letters*, his metaphysics and aesthetics are based upon the correspondence between divine and human love.[1] The aim of love for him is consummating harmony – the balance of object and subject, the concord of individual and society, the correspondence between the antithetical, subjective human world and the primary, objective divine. The chief and traditional difference is that God's love is whole and self-begetting, while human love is marred by division and discord. Human problems can be overcome, it seems, only during ecstatic moments of insight or in the transcendental terms of the afterlife. The history of the profane world, East and West, is a history of illusions. Civilisations have tried to align subject and object, individual and collective, to create a mythic or fictive world of redemption, to search for a relevant analogy 'in bursts of parallel intensity.'[2] In short, history is the larger reflection of the much more intimate illusion that lovers can unite in transcendental sexual ecstasy.

The connection between East and West is implicit from the beginning. Yeats holds that, before the Battle of the Boyne, Ireland was an Asiatic country, and that the Gaelic world Ribh inhabited was still closely connected spiritually to the East.[3] In order to tap this hereditary ecstatic connection, Yeats uses the folktale of Baile and Aillinn; folktale combines the universal and the particular, the temporal and the eternal, being an ancient story developed in the collective memory that bears the impress of each individual storyteller. In Yeats's opinion, ' . . . all know what leaf and twig,/What juncture of the apple and the yew,/Surmount their bones'. The lovers' happiness is symbolised by Nature. The 'miracle', as Yeats writes, is performed by Aengus, the god of ecstasy and love. The theme of the sequence is struck: subjective temporal love finds its best expression in the objective, eternal fecundity of both God and Nature. Love, in the terms of A Vision, is the union of emotion (the particular or individual) with instinct (the universal or collective demonstration of the supersensible).[4] In this tale, we are confronted with a type of beauty (very close to the Kantian sublime) that considers questions of a definitively *a priori* and eschatological type – we see the beauty and meaning of the lovemaking of Baile and Aillinn in the afterlife.

UNION OF SUBLIME AND BEAUTIFUL IN TRAGEDY

The combination of sublimity and beauty is not unexpected (though not deeply expanded upon) by either Burke or Kant. The latter writes very suggestively in the *Critique of Judgement* of the union of sublimity and beauty in tragedy.[5] He suggests that the slight to beauty is worth the sacred and tragic meanings which are imparted by the conjunction of the sublime and the beautiful. Consubstantial with the self and combining subjectivity and objectivity, the soul is considerably moved by the synthesis of the two aesthetic categories. The tragic element seems to make such a union more clearly an attempt to bridge morality and aesthetics, to bridge the moral, transcendent soul and the empirical embattled self. The unity is what the sublime moment and what, in particular, the sexual force of 'Supernatural Songs' aim to achieve. In the application of this rapprochement between the sublime and beautiful, art is most definitely a provocation, yet it is one that is nevertheless part of the division.

Art as beautiful object becomes sublime because it proves the imagination inadequate to the subjective ideas of reason, as well as to the purposiveness of what is being dramatised or described. The terror and pity of tragedy have always united beauty and sublimity, and liberated rather than repressed the senses. In his subjugation of the sensible, Kant forgets the possibilities that the birth of aesthetics suggested: the freedom not only to think as one wishes but to feel as one wishes. One thereby may find that morality which, in Blake's reckoning, exists at the limits of desire. Still, natural and moral law must be balanced. The balance is the object of Yeats's religious vision and the cause of his hatred of any conventional morality that merely seeks to subdue the sensible portion of our being. By converting Kant's idea of reason into the Celestial Body as sensible, sexual expression of the divine ideas in their unity, and as transcendent form of the objects of mind, Yeats seeks to balance the empirical needs of the self and the moral imperatives of the soul. 'Supernatural Songs' describes how this has been historically and cyclically achieved, destroyed and resurrected again.

That said, it still remains to apply this idea to the story of the lovers, and to how and why they had to suffer and die in order to achieve their angelic form of consummation. Of this elevation of specific temporal suffering onto a supersensible plane, Nietzsche writes in *The Birth of Tragedy*:

> The metaphysical delight in tragedy is a translation of instinctive Dionysiac wisdom into image: the hero, the highest manifestation of the will, is destroyed, and we assent, since he too is merely a phenomenon; and the eternal life of the will remains unaffected. Tragedy cries: 'We believe that life is eternal . . . here beauty vanishes the suffering that inheres in all existence'.[6]

In the poem, the beauty of the lovers in the afterlife is the result of their by now sublime suffering – sublimity being the aesthetic of suffering. To achieve the beauty of their immortal love, the lovers had to be 'purified by tragedy', as Ribh notes; each had to hear the story of the other's death, and to die of grief as a result, before they could be happy together. If the image of their suffering and death is sublimely tragic, the image of their lovemaking moves beyond the mere outward physical form of the body and the subjectivity of the sublime, beyond the tragic split in human consciousness which makes sexuality a straining joy. The lovers in death achieve the objective finality of the beautiful; they become its eternal concept:

> The miracle that gave them such a death
> Transfigured to pure substance what had once
> Been bone and sinew; when such bodies join
> There is no touching here, nor touching there,
> Nor straining joy, but whole is joined to whole;
> For the intercourse of angels is a light
> Where for its moment both seem lost, consumed.

This type of beauty provides the bridge between negative and positive sublimity, for not only is it a result of their suffering but it is also the transcendental signifier of relief and meaning.

In the 'Estrangement' section of the *Autobiographies*, Yeats the mystic defines ecstasy as an essentially tragic vision of eternal beauty. What starts as a subjective moment of elevated emotion ends in a vision of objective reality:

> A poet creates tragedy from his own soul, that soul which is alike in all men. It has not joy, as we understand that word, but ecstasy, which is from the contemplation of things vaster than the individual and imperfectly seen, perhaps, by all those that still live. The masks of tragedy contain neither character nor personal energy . . . Before the mind can look out of their eyes the active will perishes, hence their sorrowful calm. Joy is of the will which labours, which overcomes obstacles, which knows triumph. The soul knows its changes of state alone, and I think the motives of tragedy are not related to action but to changes of state . . . Yet is not ecstasy some fulfilment of the soul in itself, some slow or sudden expansion of it like an overflowing well? Is not this what is meant by beauty?[7]

The division between the empirical world, wherein the will labours, and the formal ideal world of the soul is, for a moment, overcome. The sorrowful tragedy is that such fulfilment is imperfectly understood by the living, and that it implies the death, or radical transformation, of the will and empirical world. The chief and consequent difficulty for a culture seeking consistent aesthetic standards, especially for tragedy, lies in how one defines an ideal spectator, or tragic poet for that matter, one whose understanding and perception of subjective suffering must form the basis for any type of shared or objective vision.

SENSUS/DISSENSUS COMMUNIS

The difficulty encountered in the attempt to achieve a standard of taste underlies any debate over the place of the beautiful and the sublime in criticism because the idea of an ideal spectator implies an objective norm, and such objectivity forms a basis for distinction between the two aesthetic terms. In other words, how can one be objective about the sublime, or what, if anything, does sublimity have to do with objectivity? Yeats uses the ecstatic sublime as one of his most vital emotional figures. For him, the Unity of Culture that presupposes the feeling of the beautiful is exactly what the freedom of the sublime both disrupts and re-establishes. He problematises the relationship of the *sensus communis* of the beautiful (what society as a whole believes to be beautiful) to the incommensurable subjective quality of the sublime. At the shifting bottom of the *dissensus* or the *sensus communis* lies the question of how taste and morality are defined; and both the feeling of sublimity and of beauty are part of their continually developing definition. Finally, one might say that, through the act of perception, the sublime paradoxically helps to establish the objective terms of the beautiful without losing its basis in subjectivity.

As Christopher Norris states in the chapter entitled 'Kant Disfigured' from *The Truth about Postmodernism*, the dynamics of historical change are almost impossible to reduce solely to cultural norms of behaviour.[8] Someone at some time must disagree with the *sensus communis* without a ready group to provide the social construct, and perhaps without any example to follow. The decision is not always easy to trace. The controversy over the ending of *Huckleberry Finn* – whose main character's relatively enlightened treatment of the African-American Jim is what Norris cites as example for the irreducibility of moral rebellion against immoral cultural norms – illustrates just how difficult is the task of tracing the origins and transformations of morality. Is morality an *a priori* sense, or is it socially determined? Did Huck treat Jim well when he was alone with him and badly when back in 'civilisation' merely out of social convenience, or was a permanent moral sense awakened when they floated up the Mississippi? Yeats maintains that the faculty for such a decision is inherent, that we are not entirely influenced by our environment, and that new ideas overwhelm individual and society as sexuality overwhelms the conscious mind. In his words, 'History is necessity until it takes fire in someone's head and becomes freedom or virtue.'[9] We cannot verify the source of such ideas because we are as ignorant of their derivation in God's 'intellectual fire' ('Blood and the Moon') as we are of our own sexuality:

> Eternity is passion, girl or boy
> Cry at the onset of their sexual joy
> 'For ever and for ever'; then awake
> Ignorant what Dramatis Personae spake . . .

This conception of how the *sensus communis* is transformed by the sublimating discourse of ecstasy, of innate faculties and their influences on social standards of taste, highlights certain issues in the union of beauty and sublimity in tragedy. Yeats insists that tragedy depends on what unites us, and comedy depends on what separates us.[10] Seen in this light, the union of the sublime and beautiful in tragedy provides an artistic figure for those rebellions against the old exhausted consensus which in turn may establish the new. Though the terms of our experience may be different, our ability to experience tragedy is a shared one. As quoted in 'Estrangement' above, Yeats believes that 'the soul . . . is alike in all men'. Struck by the sublimating discourse of ecstasy, the lovers in the tale are 'purified by tragedy'. The predicament is a tragic figure because the moral perfection which the union of the beautiful and the sublime seeks is as essentially unachievable as the mortal love of Baile and Aillinn, and remains to be perfected in death.

In the end, what makes Yeats's idea of sexual ecstasy so much more sublime than beautiful is that in his system of belief complete union cannot be achieved in this life: 'The tragedy of sexual intercourse is the perpetual virginity of the soul.' He held that 'sexual torment' is much like 'spiritual excitement.'[11] In the 'Supernatural Songs', Yeats uses a favourite idea, gleaned from the Song of Songs, to express the torment: the Baroque idea of the soul awaiting Christ as a bride awaits her groom. It is a perfect expression of how we aspire to the condition of God's love. In part II ('Ribh denounces Patrick'), Yeats attacks Christianity's repression of the feminine as a repression of the sensible:

> An abstract Greek absurdity has crazed the man –
> Recall that masculine Trinity. Man, woman, child, (a
>   daughter or a son)
> That's how all natural or supernatural stories run.
>
> Natural and supernatural with the self-same ring are wed.
> As man, as beast, as an ephemeral fly begets, Godhead begets
>   Godhead.
> For things below are copies, the Great Smaragdine Tablet
>   said.

He then proceeds to describe the tragedy of sexual intercourse:

> Yet all must copy copies, all increase their kind;
> When the conflagration of their passion sinks, damped by the
>   body or the mind,
> That juggling nature mounts, her coil in their embraces
>   twined.
>
> The mirror-scalèd serpent is multiplicity,
> But all that run in couples, on earth, in flood or air, share
>   God that is but three,
> And could beget or bear themselves could they but love
>   as He.

Juxtaposed with the description of Baile and Aillinn's lovemaking, where 'whole is joined to whole', Yeats's idea of the wholeness of supernatural love (combining male and female aspects) illustrates the incompleteness of human love, and why the soul needs to be united with God.

Part V of the sequence describes such a relationship. The soul must be prepared by opposing the world's understanding of God:

> . . . delivered soul herself shall learn
> A darker knowledge and in hatred turn
> From every thought of God mankind has had.
> Thought is a garment and the soul's a bride
> That cannot in that trash and tinsel hide:
> Hatred of God may bring the soul to God.

The soul is prepared, and eternity enters at the end of the life as at the end of the day. Midnight, like consciousness between sleep and waking, or between life and death, is the occult moment for union:

> At stroke of midnight soul cannot endure
> A bodily or mental furniture.
> What can she take until her Master give!
> Where can she look until He make the show!
> What can she know until He bid her know!
> How can she live till in her blood He live!

Yeats's vision is of utter human abjection, as is enacted in 'Leda and the Swan'. It is the moment of *jouissance* for the mystic, when abject love of God expresses the crisis between subject and object, between the two spheres of being and knowledge – the abject being neither subject nor object.[12] To Yeats, 'the world begins to long . . . for the terrible that it may be cured of desire',[13] that it may cast itself out in ecstasy. Or, as he writes later in the sequence, desire first begins with a girl and boy's innocent relationship to the ecstatic creative source and moves to sadomasochistic extremes:

> A passion-driven exultant man sings out
> Sentences that he has never thought;
> The Flagellant lashes those submissive loins
> Ignorant what that dramatist enjoins . . .

Like tenderness and love, violence and hatred also can provide moments of ecstatic insight. Deriving pleasure from pain, sadomasochism mimics the mystical experience of union with the Godhead, except that it pre-empts realisation in assuming a failure to find any true fixed value. The assumption of failure, the disbelief in any fixed value, makes sadomasochism a powerful example of the world's longing for a terrible cure. Sadomasochism, then, is the most extreme example of the 'profane perfection of mankind' ('Under Ben Bulben').

Yeats tellingly describes the human dimension of masochism in *A Vision*:

> . . . one finds men and women who love those who rob them and beat
> them, as though the soul were intoxicated by its discovery of human
> nature, or found even a secret delight in the shattering of the image of its
> desire. It is as though it cried, 'I would be possessed by' or 'I would possess
> that which is Human. What do I care if it is good or bad.' There is no
> disillusionment for they have found that which they have sought, but that
> which they have sought and found is a fragment.[14]

This passage captures the ascetic self-abnegating quality, the terrible
sublimity of the masochist's amoral search for a fragmented human image
of the creative source. In this respect, the masochist is no different from
the sadist, as Yeats's recurrent images of Salome attest. Both desires are so
violent that they must see their will mercilessly executed, on themselves or
on others. In the latter instance of the story of Salome and John the
Baptist, as described in 'Nineteen Hundred and Nineteen', we see the
result of sublime sacred violence on the *sensus communis* in the grand
historical and religious perspective of the coming of Christ.

The stanza from 'Supernatural Songs' quoted above places these sexual
extremes in an historical dimension, and also introduces in the sequence
Yeats's idea that the *sensus communis* can be radically changed by the
revelation of supernatural meaning – that a community, or historical
period may, in fact, need such change and that this need, if extreme enough,
will find sadomasochistic expression. The historical dimension, in this
case, is the effect which ecstatic Christianity had on Rome, and helps to
envision how later Rome and Christianity were combined in the Holy
Roman Empire:

> The Flagellant lashes those submissive loins
> Ignorant what that dramatist enjoins,
> What master made the lash. Whence had they come,
> The hand and lash that beat down frigid Rome?
> What sacred drama through her body heaved
> When world-transforming Charlemagne was conceived?

At this point it is evident how all historical change finds its mysterious
correspondence in the secret sexual drama of adolescent lovers, of
flagellant, of passion-driven men, or of the mother of Charlemagne.

CAPTURING ECSTASY

This historical image brings us to the final poem in the sequence, 'Meru',
which is Yeats's Shakespearean sonnet to ecstasy's role in the shaping
of history. It is Shakespearean because Shakespeare, in Yeats's system,

expresses the beginning of the modern sense of fragmentation of personality. It is a sonnet because the subject is ecstasy:

> Civilisation is hooped together, brought
> Under a rule, under the semblance of peace
> By manifold illusion; but man's life is thought,
> And he, despite his terror, cannot cease
> Ravening through century after century,
> Ravening, raging, and uprooting that he may come
> Into the desolation of reality:
> Egypt and Greece good-bye, and good-bye, Rome!
> Hermits upon Mount Meru or Everest,
> Caverned in night under the drifted snow,
> Or where that snow and winter's dreadful blast
> Beat down upon their naked bodies, know
> That day brings round the night, that before dawn
> His glory and his monuments are gone.

The Apollonian peace of the historical, physical or temporal world is illusory, or at best a reflection of our desire for transcendence. Hence, more individual relationships may also be illusory, or at best nothing more than partial manifestations of the ecstatic source. This is the terror of our subjective consciousness, and it is the reason for which we seek objective primary correspondence. The Tibetan monks are able to avoid the illusion, and yet still envision the ecstatic supernatural, supersensible reality behind it, through renunciation of the world and dispossession of the self. As pure as the vision may be, however, it allows ecstasy no physical presence, and another, perhaps preferable, way to reach the ecstatic source is through the vigour of the blood, through the mingling of the sensible and supersensible. These two approaches to God represent the sacred and profane extremes of existence. The historical references in the poem and through the sequence move between the two creative aspects of our understanding of the phenomenal world – renunciation and engagement. In the context of Yeats's larger system, Egypt is identified with Ribh's pre-Romanised form of Christianity, which gives an explicit, positive place for the ecstatic vision. Following Nietzsche, Yeats places Greece in a pivotal role between Asia and Rome, one which he thinks might serve as model for Ireland in its efforts to unify Asiatic Gaelic Ireland with the Anglicised Ireland that is created after the Battle of the Boyne.

Yeats also hopes that modern Ireland might recreate the tragic sensibility of Greece, as Nietzsche hopes Germany might. For it is in Greek tragedy that sensible and supersensible, Dionysian and Apollonian are reconciled in an image of the soul's vision of positive sublimity. In fact, to Yeats, Ireland under the threat of successive Viking and English invasions is very similar to Greece under the threat of Persian invasion.

Successive invasions created a culture that became known for its conquests of mind. Their histories can be described more in the terms of tragedy and the sublime than in those of the beautiful. Rome builds on the later stages of Greek abstraction, when Greece itself becomes too 'abstract' – as Ribh states – too interrogative, too much an ancient precursor of the culture of Newton, Descartes and Locke. Yeats's attitude to late Greek abstraction is perhaps foreshadowed in Socrates's ambiguous position in *A Vision* between creative religious renunciation and sterile Roman emulation.[15] Whereas the highest Greek art celebrates tragic sublimity, Roman art has a predilection for the beautiful, the bucolic; it remains fearful of the Dionysian, as pastoral England was fearful of the French Revolution. The relationship is complicated. For, Yeats explains in *A Vision*, 'The administrative mind, alert attention [which Yeats attributes to both Rome and England], had driven out rhythm, exaltation of the body, uncommitted energy.' He continues, 'May it not have been precisely a talent for this alert attention that had enabled Rome and not Greece to express these final *primary* phases?'[16] Primary Rome prepares the way for Christ, as conversely antithetical Ireland may prepare the way for the next dispensation. Both types of cultures are necessary parts of historical change.

Yeats has such a strong preference for ecstatic cultures because he believes his age is too dry and objective, and because he views them as closer to the creative source. What he craves most is a Unity of Culture that can express both subjective ecstasy and careful objective attention. If the Dionysian means freedom for Yeats, then the Apollonian means security, and any form of human society needs both – sexuality itself expresses the need for both. Freedom, for Kant, is the basis of the experience of the sublime, while security is the basis of the shared experience of the beautiful. They combine in the tragic recognition that their separation expresses the divisions of both societies and individuals, the divisions for which ecstasy is the most powerful balm – as though its sensual

> . . . music were enough
> To make the savage heart of love
> Grow gentle without sorrowing,
> Imagining and pondering
> Heaven knows what calamity . . . (lines 108–12)

as a younger Yeats writes longingly in the narrative *Baile and Aillinn* (1903). In the end, history is a record of our attempts to capture the ecstatic 'stream that's roaring by'; it expresses each individual need to be immersed in the stream, the creative source, for the monks know that ecstatic reality is eternal as nothing we create can be, that, before dawn, 'His glory [the glory of Greece] and his monuments [the grandeur of Rome] are gone'.

14

MOVING UPON SILENCE:
ALTERNATING VISIONS
OF SUBLIMITY

> The beauty you behold indeed emanates from her,
> But it grows greater as it flows
> Through mortal eyes to its nobler abode – the soul.
> Here it becomes divine, pure, perfect
> To match the soul's immortality. It is this beauty
> Not the other, which ever outruns your vision.
>
> Michelangelo Buonarroti, *Sonnets*

For Yeats, lyric poetry must be concerned with metaphysical reality, with the conjunction of mind's spiritual coordinates and body's physical ones, with subjective imagination and objective imaginary, with desire and morality, the sensible and supersensible, otherwise poetry will lack tragic sublimity. In his last two volumes, *New Poems* (1938) and *Last Poems* (1939), these themes are placed within the formal context and questions of lyric poetry. It is a technique developed in *Words for Music Perhaps* (1932): the personal mood of the speaker finds lyric expression in an impersonal philosophical mode. This technique questions the lyric's relation to society at large, to other literary genres, and finally its part in literature's relation to religion. Is lyric poetry more suited to metaphysical questions than, say, the novel – as to some degree Yeats believes – because traditionally the latter is more concerned with society, with a cast of characters and a more logical narrative of experience? If so, how much does the lyric absorb the interaction of self and society, of the empirical narrative support? And, on the other hand, how much can fiction absorb the epiphanic structure of the lyric? Obviously, both the fictive nature and the metanarrative frames of the two genres make them very interdependent, and the lines between prose and poetry have been blurred since the Romantics.[1]

THE LASTING SUBSTANCE OF LYRIC VOICE

In an essay entitled 'Old Foes with New Faces', the American novelist William Gaddis attacks the religious zealousness of our age with an eye to these questions, an eye coloured by premises quite different from Yeats's. He admits that literature (specifically fiction) and religion are 'in the same line of business: that of concocting, arranging, and peddling fictions to get us safely through the night', but he feels that popular versions of religion have reduced the lyric moment and the Kantian transcendental idea to saccharine remedies for the widespread slaughter of contemporary life (he cites Rwanda and Bosnia).[2] 'The Priest', writes Gaddis, 'is the guardian of mysteries, the artist is driven to expose them'.[3] The effort to expose the mysterious has been at the centre of this and the last two centuries' greatest intellectual controversies. Gaddis quotes Arthur Schlesinger Jr in order to show how the current form of the examination of the mysterious is divided between postmodern relativism, which is 'concrete, pluralistic, inductive, historical, skeptical and intimately bound up with deference to experience' and a more absolutist rendition, which is 'abstract, monistic, deductive, ahistorical, solemn, and [which] is intimately bound up with deference to authority.'[4] In this broad distinction, we see a contemporary configuration of the relationship between the antithetical and primary, with the qualification that the antithetical is not 'pluralistic'; otherwise, the distinction holds. We also see the old dispute between the empiricists and the formal idealists, between Burke and Kant. There are, of course, differences in application here as well; Burke, for instance, would defer to authority, but he would hardly prefer the abstract to the concrete, or the ahistorical to the historical. Nevertheless, the categories do give a current example of a split between those who defer to the empirical (whose idea of the sublime is an experience of negativity, of the lack of origins, of the loss of metaphysics), and those who defer to formal truths (whose idea of the sublime is positive, one which affirms the existence of the transcendent).

Gaddis's point is that Kant's formal 'ball' has passed from Kant to Hegel and then to Mary Baker Eddy (the founder of the Christian Science movement), that idealist metaphysics has been popularised beyond redemption by New Age religious thinking and religious fundamentalism. On the other hand, he maintains that the relativist aporias of postmodern thought are also mystifications of the ethical dilemmas of the age; like the transcendental poetics of previous ages, they are insufficient. For Gaddis, the better position is one of ethical indeterminacy – a novelist's version of Keats's Negative Capability. Indeterminacy is at the heart of both sides of the aesthetic question, as such diverse thinkers as Kristeva and Lyotard,

Bradley and Bate have illustrated. Aesthetic fictions are meant to get us safely through the night, but they are not moral solutions. With reference to Mrs Eddy's platitudes that 'our all-powerful Father [and] our infinitely loving Mother . . . never abandon a single child. Not one is unwanted, neglected, or unloved. God is always sustaining every one of His children, young and old', the morally disappointed Gaddis replies, 'Tell it not in Bosnia, publish it not in the streets of Rwanda'.[5] Some suffering remains not only inconsolable, but unpresentable in any fashion, except the most wounded and terrifying ones. It is sublime in the simultaneous lack and necessity of morality; redemptive only, and perhaps insufficiently, along the margins of consciousness.

The practical purpose of lyric poetry is to represent images in such a way as to bear witness (although its aim for Yeats is to achieve Beatific Vision). In so doing, according to Keats, the poet must live 'in uncertainties, Mysteries, doubts, without any irritable reaching after facts & reason'.[6] The ethics of indeterminacy are the troubled grounds from which the lyric ascends, confronting on its flight the metaphysical distinctions posed by empirical and idealist reality alike, hovering between the negative and positive sublime. The lyric gathers its force from the question of whether one is bound to experience or to some higher authority. By hovering between these two positions, by interrogating the incontrovertibility of the polemic, in fact, the lyric speaks of the joy and suffering that both deference to experience and deference to authority can bring. In an article entitled 'Lyric Poetry and Society', Theodor W. Adorno writes suggestively of the reduction of Kantian formalism (and by extension of the lyric moment), and of the necessity of lyric poetry.[7] Sensitive to both claims, Adorno provides a useful transition from the American satirist of contemporary entropy to the Romantic Irish poet of the lyric moment.

The isolated lyric voice is eloquent of society's demands on the individual, and of one's need to transcend them; the ideal is not merely a revelation of Christian Science's distant conciliating force. In Adorno's terms:

> Only he understands what the poem says who perceives in its solitude the voice of humanity; indeed, the loneliness of the lyric expression itself is latent in our individualistic and, ultimately, atomistic society – just as, by contrast, its general binding validity derives from the denseness of its individuation.[8]

There is a formal, subjective need for the lyric voice as stay against the collective reifying demands of society. It is not only a way of getting safely through the night but also a way of defining the darkness. It implies the need for freedom and utopian illusion. As an apologia for the seeming mysticism of this idea, Adorno sees the lyric's impersonal expression of the personally desired object as a revolutionary alternative to purely possessive bourgeois materialism; that is, he pits the lyric against the capitalist desire to use nature to one's own mechanical or financial advantage: '. . . lyric expression, released from the heaviness of material things, should evoke images of a life free of the impositions of the everyday world, of usefulness, of the dumb drive for self-preservation.'[9] He proceeds to recount how the redemptive possibilities of the lyric (Yeats's 'changeless work of art') are based in the accursed grounds of its making (in Yeats's 'broken heart'):

> Their pure subjectivity, apparently flawless, without breaks and full of harmony, actually witnesses to the opposite, to a suffering caused by existence foreign to the subject, as much as it shows the subject's love toward that existence. Indeed, the harmony of such creations is nothing other than the mutual correspondence of such suffering and such love.[10]

Adorno's harmony and disruption owe a great deal to Kant's idea that the harmony between Imagination and Reason is found in the sublime encounter, by virtue of the contrast between the wounded Imagination and its imprecise image of the still transcendent Reason. For Kant the authority remains with Reason, for Adorno it remains with the 'ancient wound'[11] of the imagination, which art consistently seeks to redress. The Yeatsian lyric makes the consideration of self and society, of suffering and love, of wounded imagination and transcendent reason, an effort to undo the forces of entropy through alternating visions of sublimity.

'The Gyres' and 'Lapis Lazuli', from the volume *New Poems* (1938), take these questions on a grand scale. In these poems, Yeats endeavours to present a mood that can withstand the destructiveness of change, whether personal or public. This is the closing theme of 'Supernatural Songs', one that is persistent throughout the rest of the corpus. Yeats is endeavouring to move from negative to positive sublimity, from night to joy. The mood must capture the double quality inherent in the sublime. Even at its most positive, the mood must have the smell of the fire, of the negative sublime, through which it passed. This doubleness is the 'tragic joy' in 'The Gyres' and the 'tragic play' in 'Lapis Lazuli' that are experienced at the prospect of civilisation's end. While the negative aspect of such an outlook is obvious, the positive is one of Yeats's leaps of faith. The first steps were taken in the 1890s, as is shown in his fondness for Dowson's similar conflation of positive and negative sublimity in the description of poets as 'bitter and gay'. These poetic demonstrations are also the fruit of Yeats's study of Nietzsche – in some ways, they are perhaps too schematically drawn along these lines. Yeats's affirmations are not as tested by their contrary (their negation) as they are in the major poems of *The Tower* (1928) and *The Winding Stair* (1933); yet, read in light of those poems, 'The Gyres' and 'Lapis Lazuli' can be seen as the culmination of the issues at stake – as one end of the history of his attitudes towards the sublime. The works of both Yeats and Nietzsche are studies in varying attitudes.

Nietzsche's career can be said to move from faith in the power of the aesthetic ('the sublime [is that] which subjugates terror by means of art'[12]) to the unflinching materialism and ridicule of metaphysics in his middle writing (*Human All Too Human*), and then on to the belief that existence is only bearable when looked on as artistic phenomenon, that aesthetic distance is nevertheless transformative if not transcendent. The final period is his return, in *Twilight of the Idols,* to the belief that the trage-dian communicates a state of being that is 'without fear in the face of the fearful . . . [of] courage and freedom of feeling before a powerful enemy, before a sublime calamity'.[13] The stages of Nietzsche's career parallel Kant's three stages of sublimity: first positive transport at the sublime encounter, then a negative, deeply wounded sense of being overwhelmed, and finally a positive feeling that reflects the presence and power of a supersensible faculty. Yeats's career is similar, though his negative periods never com-pletely renounce transcendence as Nietzsche's negative periods do. Yeats's best poetry tends to reflect both the sublime ability and abject inability of art to subjugate terror. The chief mood is that the eternal recurrence, the repetition of the old tragedies, shall in the end result in transfiguration.

The problem remains that one must have superhuman psychic health to be able to incorporate the horrors of the world into a beautiful whole. The individual must be that marriage of the beautiful and sublime which Burke, Kant and Yeats imagine as prerequisite to Unity of Being. The rest of us are products of wounded consciousness, as many of the other poems in *New Poems* (1938) relate. This woundedness is especially true of the various songs and shorter lyrics of the late volumes. Even the oracle of 'The Gyres' is a wound or break in the rock, which is called upon to comment on the rise of philosophical doubt and on the blood shed by the revolt of the irrational. In the second stanza, Yeats sees Ledaean suffering, the rape of body and soul, as prelude to an historical shift, a violent turn of the gyres. The cry of 'What matter' in both the second and the third stanza is half ironic as it moves from question to exclamation. Yeats deplores the violence done to the sensible body and hates the coarsening of work and soul. The cry asks for aesthetic distance from suffering. The old values of beauty and worth are no longer valid in the final stanza's epistemic shift. Out of a break in the reality of death, in the tomb that grows fruitful, and between the animals of earth and air – or, in other words, amidst those opposites that have the tension of the essential antithetical and primary antinomy – will come a future form of beauty that is more congenial to body and soul. This rebirth of beauty is always accompanied by the darker, atavistic side of Yeats's economy, the reactionary return. This dangerous nostalgia, however, does not entirely diminish the transformative power of his vision.

In 'Lapis Lazuli', Yeats gives shape to the existential value of the transfigurative force. Much of the poem is familiar in light of 'Supernatural Songs'. The tragic ecstasy of the great tragic characters such as Hamlet and Lear outlasts all the destructiveness of time or war:

> Gaiety transfiguring all that dread.
> All men have aimed at, found and lost;
> Black out; Heaven blazing into the head:
> Tragedy wrought to its uttermost.

The existential aspect of the statement lies in the mind of those who create, view and act the part. The creative spirit survives the destruction of art because it resurfaces in another's hands, and because it is transmitted in a higher frame of mind, in the supersensible faculty we all possess, but to which we rarely ascend: 'All things fall and are built again/And those that build them again are gay'. The last stanza of the poem examines the role of art. The embodiment and the appreciation of art have profound possibilities. Accident and contrivance unite to show how contingent empirical reality is the substance of formal creations. The stone's 'discolouration' and 'accidental crack[s]' look like greater natural occurrences only because that aspect is highlighted by the artist's craft. The relation between the mournful quality of the scene and the gaiety of the artists who created it is another allusion to the tension between empirical, contingent truth (which Yeats calls Body of Fate) and the supersensible faculty of Reason (which Yeats calls Celestial Body). The mournfulness is for the suffering that contingency inflicts, while gaiety is born of the higher knowledge that such suffering will have meaning or reason. The assurance with which Yeats opens the volume *New Poems* (1938) is meant to emphasise the title's sense of rejuvenation. Yeats, at this point, has been rejuvenated artistically as much as physically (if not sexually) by the Steinach operation. The assurance is given various, sometimes opposing, resonances throughout the rest of the volume.

The highly masculine stoicism so valued in the opening two poems is offset by the wisdom which feminine experience next presents. It is a wise mournfulness that predicates the possibility of all tragic joy; like the subject of 'A Crazed Girl', one must be '[h]eroically lost' in order to be 'heroically found'. In many of these poems, such as 'The Three Bushes' and 'The Lady's First Song', Yeats returns to the dialectic of self and soul, of sensible and supersensible. He is aware that, for all his tragic joy, the division may be irreparable; the only hope exists in the primary principles of surrender and submission. In a sense, the synthesis is miraculous and requires a type of prayer. He uses the conventional idea of an upper-class woman as representative of the soul, and of the servant, or chambermaid, as representative of the body. The chambermaid can go to bed with the lover, while the 'Lady' and soul remain pure. The application of this basic division, one which is essential to the Marxist critique of aesthetics, is close to the Kantian domination of the sensible; only Yeats extends the pain of domination to the soul in 'The Lady's First Song' so that he highlights the correspondence between sensible and supersensible ecstasy. In 'The Lady's Third Song', he imagines a correspondence between the Lady's and servant's experience that combines body and soul in religious and erotic bliss. Such a union is entirely interpenetrating, as soul experiences physical, 'fallen' desire, and body experiences spiritual, prelapsarian pleasure. It is a reconciliation worthy of Marcuse's idea of polymorphous sexuality (albeit for Yeats the social hierarchy remains a formal necessity). In 'The Lover's Song', he imagines that the lover, loving both body and soul, is most assured of their transcendental fusion because he experiences both of its components. The two songs of the sequence, 'The Chambermaid's First Song' and 'The Chambermaid's Second Song', illustrate how, though Yeats considers religious vision erotic by nature, Eros is not necessarily religious. The sexual act is only a catalyst. Once the act is finished, the sensible bears no marks of the supersensible and, as the second song shows, is distinctly earth-bound.

In 'What Then?', Plato (Yeats's foe and friend) questions the point of the social and amorous exercise so loudly that the religious and erotic basis of Yeatsian poetics begins to appear mistaken. It is a counter-movement typical of Yeats. The volume has moved towards a sense that the formal world demands what the empirical world cannot give. The empirical world that is concrete and pluralistic, that defers to experience, is not reconcilable to the abstract and monistic authority of the formal one. Many poems such as 'Beautiful Lofty Things', 'To Dorothy Wellesley' heroically try to bridge the gap; others such as 'The Curse of Cromwell' witness the lyric drop into the divide. In the poems on Roger Casement, we see the force of the sensible world rise with a vengeance against conventional morals (which, in this case, are charges of homosexuality).[14] In the next poem, 'The O'Rahilly', we see a comparable connection between nature, the subversive sensible portion, and the Irish rebellion, only now we see the violence associated with political as well as personal freedom. This coupling makes the political poems of this volume harsh images of the revolt of the irrational, of the suppressed other. In this light, the adulterous Parnell is uncrowned king of the Irish libido. The 'coarse old man' in 'The Wild Old Wicked Man' who, on 'a woman's breast', forgets the 'stream of lightning/From the old man in the skies' and the groping 'dirty hand' of 'The Spirit Medium' also possess the profane, erotic significance of Yeats's religious vision.

YEATS'S RELIGIOUS VISION

As the volume nears its close, the question of the positive sublime's marriage of sensible and supersensible moves to the fore, though its accomplishment is difficult. In 'The Municipal Gallery Re-visited', the poem of memory, mother of the muses, Yeats recalls those moments in which the violence, the negative sublimity of Irish history attempts to reach that formal resolution which here has been named the positive sublime. The first stanza evokes both the violence of the sublime encounter ('Casement upon trial') and the moral significance of O'Higgins's act ('A revolutionary soldier kneeling to be blessed'). Like Nietzsche in his middle years, Yeats in his later years wonders if the positive quality is only an aesthetic fiction. In the last four lines of the second stanza, Yeats grasps that all beauty, even physical beauty, is potentially transcendent if it is enhanced by the artist's hand:

> Before a woman's portrait suddenly I stand;
> Beautiful and gentle in her Venetian way.
> I met her all but fifty years ago
> For twenty minutes in some studio.

In remembering the friends of youth, he is wondering if 'time may bring . . . that selfsame excellence again'. As always, his ideas of the beautiful and the positive sublime are cast in an autumnal light. Again he insists that such aesthetic power, though supersensible, is discovered in the sensible world: 'John Synge, I and Augusta Gregory thought/All that we did . . . /Must come from contact with the soil'. The chief reason for this assertion is that Yeats is looking at paintings, physical images that animate the spirit of the scene when portrayed through the formal perspective of the artist.

One may trace Ireland's history in the lineaments of such embodiments, in combinations of the empirical and ideal, the sensible and supersensible. This is how and why art is sublime and it is why the gallery is a 'hallowed place'. Nevertheless, it is difficult to say with certainty that art is finally redemptive of the sensible, of that libidinous portion of the psyche which culture, colonisation, or religion may repress. Redemption is with the 'old man in the skies' ('The Wild Old Wicked Man'); or it is with those whose eyes have been 'spiritualised by death', as Yeats infers in 'Are You Content?', the closing poem of the volume. He cannot judge if what he has done is worthy. The moral implications of the positive sublime are beyond understanding. The final stanza introduces us to the grounds for the alternating visions of sublimity which constitute Yeats's final volume, *Last Poems* (1939):

> Infirm and aged I might stay
> In some good company,
> I who have always hated work,
> Smiling at the sea,
> Or demonstrate in my own life
> What Robert Browning meant
> By an old hunter talking with Gods;
> But I am not content.

The effort of his poetry to join the sensible and supersensible too often fails. The morality of the aesthetic eludes him, and he is reduced to the indolence that has always plagued him. Yeats is left considering whether hunters are hunting truth; whether 'the lions, roaring after their prey, do seek their meat from God' (Psalms, 104: 21); whether there is any meaning or morality behind the violent struggle to 'accomplish fate'. The 'old hunter' has followed the hunt in an effort to uncover the mystery of the sensible world; does he find it in his conversation with the Gods? Yeats's discontent seems to say that he does not. Rather, he is reduced to the condition of dumbly smiling at the unplumbable sea of our sexual nature, uncertain of redemption.

The last volume, *Last Poems* (1939), is a confrontation of the negative and positive sublime as is no other. This makes sense, of course, as Yeats in old age has become a 'great tomb-haunter' who 'sweeps the distant sky', and there finds 'nothing to make [his] terror less/*Hysterica passio* of [his] own emptiness' ('A Bronze Head'). Wanting to hear an echo linger in that tomb, Yeats chooses highly violent and sexual imagery. There is sexual or violent rebirth; there is a vision of both; or there is neither. In the various preceding sections, the poems 'Under Ben Bulben', 'Man and the Echo', 'The Apparitions', 'A Nativity' and 'Politics' have been examined in terms of the moral questions of sublimity, the power of the sensible world and its potential for transcendence, and in light of Yeats's idea of the feminine. What is left to discuss is the opposition of the negative and positive sublime in 'The Black Tower' and 'Cuchulain Comforted', as well as the sexual basis for the sublime that is presented in 'The Statues', 'News for the Delphic Oracle', and 'Long-legged Fly'.

The aim of this chapter is not to resolve anything – it is impossible – but rather to leave the question in a state of uncertainty such as suits the painful basis of Yeats's lyric voice. In this, Yeats is more like Keats than either Blake or Percy Bysshe Shelley. For, unlike the elder Blake, Yeats would not opt for a personal religious vision that moves away from the violence of the sensible, that renounces some of the early intensity. Unlike Shelley, the Modernist Yeats never put his trust in the primary idea of forgiveness that frees Prometheus from the rock in *Prometheus Unbound*. Yeats's uncertainty is one of Negative Capability. The poem 'Long-legged Fly' shows how, during the uncertain aesthetic moment, one comes closest to resolution, to the positive sublime, to the harmony of reason and imagination which heals the wounded consciousness and exposes the supersensible moral sense without trying to verify its existence. In that moment, we move from negative to positive sublimity, we connect subject and object worlds; we join the wisdom, love and peace of the primary world to the knowledge, power and conflict of the antithetical one.

Throughout much of the volume, and throughout Yeats's oeuvre, antithetical and primary are in constant though varying states of strife. In 'The Black Tower' and 'Cuchulain Comforted' this opposition reaches its climax. In the former, Yeats imagines that nothing results from all that strife. In the latter, violence discovers its purpose, its final end. Cuchulain's antithetical cruelty and deceit end in primary submission and surrender. The antithetical soldiers of 'The Black Tower' are oath-bound to a King who represents the primary regenerative ideal. (The idea of sovereignty here maintains its connection to the divine, contrary to the opinion of the modern world outside the tower.) The soldiers await the millennial entrance of the King, but without much confidence in his coming. That this is Yeats's last poem, partly dictated on his death-bed, makes its nihilistic quality eerie. The chronological order of the two poems reverses the usual order of the two forms of sublimity. Negative follows and undermines positive – that is, 'Cuchulain Comforted' was written before 'The Black Tower'. The reordering of the poems for publication emphasises the affirmation; it is the poignant work of what in 'Man and the Echo' is called the 'spiritual intellect'. 'The Black Tower' ends with an image of the emptiness of death. The soldiers wait dutifully between life and death for a sign of affirmation, but the only significance is given by a liar (the cook), while the darkness of the transcendental signifier (the tomb) 'grows blacker'. The spiritual force of the winds shakes only old bones upon the mountain; it shakes the remnants of the living as sorrowful sign of an empty afterlife. There is no sign of the resurrected Passionate Body. Nevertheless, Yeats on his death-bed waits 'oath-bound'.

The resurrected body is actually seen in 'Cuchulain Comforted'. In the first two stanzas, Cuchulain still seems full of his antithetical living self as he strides into Purgatory, while the shades of the underworld peer from a distance and run. The ensuing stanzas in terza rima introduce Cuchulain to Purgatory. He is to take his place among his opposites ('convicted cowards') and engage in domestic chores. Cuchulain's limitation is that he

has not been meditative enough, as shown by his impatience in the play
At the Hawk's Well (1917). Meditating on wounds and blood, on
antithetical violence, the Celtic hero begins to understand that the
qualities of primary wisdom should be the goal of antithetical violence.
When the cowards change to birds (symbols of transmigration) and begin
to sing, we are presented with one of the central tenets of the rhetorical
sublime – that quality of sound which lies beyond rhetoric, which lies
outside of anything one could call style. We are back to the non-
discursiveness of 'fol de rol de rolly O' ('The Pilgrim'); however, instead
of being used as a mantra to ward off death, here the sounds are transmigratory songs of the soul as it prepares itself for transfiguration, for the
body which perfectly expresses it, for the reconciliation of the sensible and
supersensible that can only come in the afterlife. This is the unpresentable
aspect of the sublime. In *A Vision*, Yeats assigns this unpresentable,
exalted quality to the supernatural subjective 15th phase and the objective
1st phase of the wheel of personality. Complete subjectivity and objectivity
are impossible for the living to experience, hence they are supernatural. In
the transformation from human form to bird, the Shrouds must be aware
that, as Yeats argues in *A Vision*, 'only one symbol exists, though the
reflecting mirrors make many appear and all different'. The object (the
otherness of the bird) and the subject (the consciousness of the Shrouds)
are bound in the spherical unity of the one symbol, the Thirteenth Cone –
a sphere which to us, 'bound to birth and death', seems a cone.[15] The
mystery of such unity and revelatory perspective fully informs, but
forever eludes this volume, leaving a highly charged aporia between the
negative sublimity of 'The Black Tower' and the positive sublimity of
'Cuchulain Comforted'.

Yeats knows that the closest we may come to the mystery is through
religious and artistic expression. To be able to tap its erotic Dionysian
energy, a culture must be able to give the mystery rational, Apollonian
form. This is the crux of Yeats's religious vision; it is his ecstasy. In the
first stanza of 'The Statues' – the poem which is Yeats's call for a Greek-
like culture for Ireland – we see how the rational, indeed, mathematical
expression of sexual energy that underlies all art but especially the sculpture
of the human form, must always be the artist's aim. The miracle of art is
reflected in the artist's plan. The miracle is how anarchic, formless sexual
energy is given rational form. Art is always formed of the tension between
emotion and plastic reality, between the former's restless movement and
the latter's serene, beautiful stasis. Art is made from the pain of 'solitary
beds', as he writes in 'The Statues', from masturbation, which always left
the adolescent Yeats 'exhausted' and filled with self-loathing.[16] The urge
that rises from the sexual wound of 'imagined love' seeks the premeditated

perfection of a statue. The poem is openly a paradigm for how the historical contest between the antithetical and primary qualities should run; it is also a paradigm for how the empirical needs of selfhood and its definitions of sublime experience, based in the antithetical, are played against the formal demands of the soul, of the primary world. The historical basis for the confrontation of the Burkean and Kantian sublime is here set down. It is the confrontation between Nature (the libido, the sexual drive) and God (the moral consciousness). Art and philosophy are the great mediators; the technique of mediation is the question they must answer.

In *Swan and Shadow*, Whitaker states that 'the second stanza describes the emergence of an antithetical civilisation from the foamy sea of primary Nature'.[17] By this, he must mean the early forms of Nature, as Yeats establishes that the movement towards Nature is from phase 1 to phase 15 (from the objective to the subjective), while the movement towards God is the opposite (from subjective to objective).[18] Nature is essentially subjective, while God is essentially objective. Primary Nature is unaware of itself, and only partially realised. We see that individuals who are of these phases are so close to the supersensual rhythms of God that they have no sense of individuation. The antithetical civilisation imagined by Whitaker sloughs off a Nature of the early phases, one that is still too objective, too primary, and creates a culture that reflects it at its most antithetical and definite expression. Here we have one of those occurrences (in this case the battle of Salamis) that are designed to make humans self-conscious enough to pit themselves against divinity, to make them want to be gods. In the larger picture, that wish is also para-doxically part of the circular return from subjective humanity to objective divinity. The subjective Promethean or satanic wish to possess God-like knowledge and power is by mirror-image, as it were, the height of the human reflection of divinity and objectivity. At the apex of antithetical culture, the human body becomes emblem of divinity. The statues made according to Pythagoras's measurements glorify such a competitive image. It is a competition driven by sexual fury against too transcendental an image of its own suffering, and it is also one that will weary of not having sufficient moral form given to its actions. It will look to the objective, primary way of being, which it first cast off. This is precisely what happens in the third stanza, when a primary God rules.

In the second stanza, however, the sensible portion is supreme. It is the art in which, somewhat unconsciously, by virtue of its technical display, the terms of the beautiful (form) and those of the sublime (formlessness) are joined. There is a potential for deeper accommodation that has not the conscious frame to makes its image complete. Blake imagines the very same harmony through his philosophy of the human body: 'The Beauty proper for sublime art is lineaments, or forms and features that are capable of being the receptacles of intellect.'[19] The unity of intellect and body, of morality and desire, of natural and moral law is possible in all ages, although not permanently imaginable in any of them. The flaw of the age, the tendency to be too antithetical or too primary, inevitably casts the age towards its opposite. History is necessity when the flaw of the age grows too great; freedom is the result of the historical moment, the Salamis that drives us towards cultural or personal perfection. Referring to Berkeley's consciously Irish idealist attack on English materialism, Yeats writes: 'Berkeley's Salamis was such a conflagration, another is about us now'.[20] By 'Salamis', the victory of the Greeks over the Persians in 480 BCE, Yeats means movement towards an antithetical age. In the third stanza, he writes of the opposite move.

The antithetical multiplicity of the 'many-headed foam at Salamis' is revealed by an image of Buddha crossing it to be mere flux. It is revealed to be sexual instinct grown so turbulent that the age has begun to crave a moral form, a rational aim, has begun to crave some meaningful release from the horror of its own desire. Hamlet, like Buddha, though crazed rather than transcendent before such unchecked desire, tries unsuccessfully to cleanse the rotten body politic of Denmark. The sensible portion is now so unrepresentative of the spirit, so volatile, that Shakespeare calls Hamlet fat, although he makes him agile. Yeats was very sensitive to this contradiction, and saw in it the beginnings of the Cartesian sacrifice of the body. Appearance has now ceased to represent reality in the higher ideal sense. Knowledge only increases the division between them. Ironically, the more one emphasises the empirical, sensible world as the only reality, the more it seems a hall of smoke and mirrors. The nothingness behind the wall of the physical world echoes in the mind and creates the ghosts and goblins, the taste for Gothic horror, for Grimalkin (the witches' cat in *Macbeth*), that followed the loss of origins from the definition of the sublime. Hamlet insists on making sense of the turbulence of desire and the mad multiplicity of meaning; he consequently grows 'thin from eating flies', that is from trying to derive sustenance where there is none – the body of desire is corrupted because it does not know what is its object. The stanza closes with an image of the horror of the negative sublime being subsumed by a primary, transcendental ethos. The sensible portion grown monstrous, Grimalkin is given supersensible form and meaning in Buddha's emptiness.

In the last stanza, Yeats imagines a return to Greek antithetical civilisation as a result of both Berkeley's Salamis and the present great battle between the primary modern tide and the Cuchulain-like Pearse who has come to fight the time's authority:

When Pearse summoned Cuchulain to his side,
What stalked through the Post Office? What intellect,
What calculation, number, measurement, replied?
We Irish, born into that ancient sect
But thrown upon this filthy modern tide
And by its formless spawning fury wrecked,
Climb to our proper dark, that we may trace
The lineaments of a plummet-measured face.

The mystery of numbers lies in their ability to reply to our deepest urges. When Pearse was planning and staging the rebellion, something of that mysteriousness replied. As it gave definite shape to what had been a formless longing for independence, it turned motley into green. It changed the aesthetic as well as the political nature of Irish society. For all of its anti-heterogeneity, its proto-fascist or fascist rhetoric, Yeats's dream of an Irish nation that could find moral form through violent desire – and thereby free antithetical desire from its bondage to an outmoded primary law – is nevertheless quite liberating in its coupling of the sensible and supersensible.

To Yeats, the 'people stare' because of this miracle, this sublime intermingling that gives shape to turbulent sexual instinct, and synthesises freedom and authority. The 'formless spawning fury' of modern heterogeneity is going to find shape in the statue's lineaments. 'Lineaments', it must be remembered, is Blake's word for the marriage of the beautiful and the sublime, the sensible and the supersensible. With this word, he identifies a form of reason that has sufficient energy to soothe the pain of sexual loneliness, of modern individuation. The 'dark' horror of the negative sublime has a higher positive dimension, a 'proper dark' which can give the violence of desire a conciliatory shape. The poem itself is an effort to drop the plummet that will measure the face of future Ireland. In its antithetical cruelty and its ignorance of the causes of the 'filthy modern tide', it spawns its own fury, and one that too lacks definition. The waters of sexual purification must flow over the wounds before they can heal. Yeats performs this feat of positive sublimity in 'News for the Delphic Oracle' with skilled Modernist irony. The Greek miracle is as elusive for Yeats as it was for Marx,[21] and a certain playfulness is appropriate. The heavy subject of death glances off the jocular sexual tenor of 'News for the Delphic Oracle'.

THE EROTIC BASIS OF THE
SUBJECT–OBJECT MYSTERY

For all of its playfulness, 'News for the Delphic Oracle' is still concerned with the distress of becoming; this is especially true of the last part. The poem begins with an ironic pastoral scene that is peopled by characters from Yeats's poetry. Paradise, it appears, is full of 'golden codgers'. Niamh is colloquially referred to as 'Man-picker'. The images reflect a certain comic boredom at having transcended the Heraclitean strife of existence. Plotinus, dominator of the sensible (at least in Yeats's mind), has been made aware of the splendours of the body. He climbs out of the sensually purifying waters with 'salt flakes' still clinging to him. He too lays 'sighing like the rest', but only after having 'stretched and yawned awhile'. Does he sigh from boredom or desire? The open-endedness of the sighs reflects the impossibility of imagining a desire that is not tied to strife; even the desire that means to transcend strife is fuelled by it. The scene definitely is one of harmony, as it contains primary philosophers and antithetical heroes. The low style of the description makes one wonder whether such harmony leaves the imagination slack. The conflict of life must be registered. The second part of the poem does just that.

In part II, there is a scene of sensual purgation which is very similar to that described in 'Byzantium' and to that implied in 'The Second Coming'. Now the murder of the innocents becomes the object of purification, of the bloodshed marking a divine advent – as in the original scene of the coming of the Messiah. The bloodshed of the entrance of divinity into human affairs ('The Second Coming' and 'Leda and the Swan') is here matched by the bloodshed of human mingling with the divine. As in 'Byzantium', the dolphin is the sexual fish of transmigration. Its fin is phallic object and guide. The 'ecstatic waters' laugh at the Baroque cherubic entrance of human innocence. The cries of the murdered innocents are 'sweet and strange' because the death of innocence is so rare, is such virgin transport. The innocents have moved from torture to sweet cries in their growing awareness of tragic ecstasy or tragic joy, that doubled version of sublime consciousness. The murdered innocents are carried by the 'brute dolphins' (images of the sensible and natural law) to the place where antithetical, pagan lovers and heroes and primary philosophers have been reconciled and have formed the 'choir of love'. The judges from Hades, Rhadamanthus and Minos, are conspicuously absent from this version of the Isle of the Blessed. The 'salt blood' that blocked their judgement in 'The Delphic Oracle upon Plotinus', unknown to them, is the emblem of the desire that they chose to repress, when instead they should have ridden its waves. It is the force of the sensible, empirical world that carries the self towards the quarter of the soul.

The innocents are received in a ritual of Apollonian illusion. They are offered the 'sacred laurels' that Apollo takes from Daphne's denial of his desire. It is the leaf that crowns the poet's disappointed sense of the ideal – disappointed, because entry into the world of permanent forms destroys the desired ephemeral beauty. Daphne's transformation into a laurel tree proves that the only way to escape reality is to lose the original shape, is, in poetic terms, to use metaphor. In a purely empirical vision, the metaphorical capacities of the leaf, however, are purely illusionary; matching two objects does not change either's constitution. In this poem of surpassing reality, the illusion and the metaphor are real; sensible form becomes supersensible reality only through the act of comparison. Yeats's persistent irony registers the nagging doubt that there is no transcendence, that metaphor accomplishes nothing, that the move from metaphor to meaning is not so much reductive or escapist as it is impossible.

In the third part, the intercourse between immortal and mortal beings is significant for Yeats. At this juncture, he can imagine a higher world; it is a moment of threshold consciousness. In the description, we see both the brutality of the antithetical, of Nature, and the primary gentleness and love of the divine:

> Slim adolescence that a nymph has stripped,
> Peleus on Thetis stares.
> Her limbs are delicate as an eyelid,
> Love has blinded him with tears;
> But Thetis' belly listens.
> Down the mountain walls
> From where Pan's cavern is
> Intolerable music falls.
> Foul goat-head, brutal arm appear,
> Belly, shoulder, bum,
> Flash fishlike; nymphs and satyrs
> Copulate in the foam.

The mortal Peleus and immortal Thetis conceive Achilles; her 'belly listens' to what he will be like. All she hears is '[i]ntolerable music' from the world of demi-gods, the nymphs and satyrs who personify the brutality of Nature. The wounding hearts of these threshold beings traditionally remain immortal and unwounded, as opposed to wounded and wounding mortal hearts. Their copulation provides the link, the coupling, between mortal and immortal worlds; it is the purifying threshold. The delicacy of one part of the stanza contrasts sharply with the coarseness of the other. They are not unrelated, however; quite the contrary. Thetis gives birth to violent Achilles as Mary inversely gives birth to gentle Christ. The coming of Christ meant the death of Pan and of the Greek world Achilles represented. Now, the return of Pan will mean the death of Christ. The turning of the gyres is either marked by gentleness or violence.

In a similar type of interconnection, the significance of the lovemaking between Peleus and Thetis is not wholly lost in the description of the nymphs and satyrs. The latter 'fish-like . . . [c]opulate in the foam', that is, their sexual interplay has the same transmigratory capacity as the dolphins' fins. This part bears the pain and ecstasy of becoming. It is both 'delicate' and 'blinded with tears', on the one side, and '[i]ntolerable' and 'brutal' on the other. Thetis is like Leda and Mary, in that she is sublime mother to the turning of the gyres; she is representative of the coming of the antithetical age, of a violent tincture. Yet, she does not express the violence. In her act of creation, she transcends it. Throughout all of Yeats's work, there are visions of beauty that give moral expression to the perfected sensible portion of our being. By bringing beauty to this realm, the visions become examples of positive sublimity which, though still with the smell of the fire about them, still singed by the negative, nevertheless manage to move beyond the empirical world of their making. They reconcile the formal idealist pure mind, whence inspiration came, to the various debris of the street out of which the work was made. They sing with Self and Soul. That Nicholas Poussin's *Acis and Galatea* (significantly called *The Marriage of Peleus and Thetis* during Yeats's lifetime) is seen as Yeats's source makes this poem an assuaging image of negative sublimity and the beautiful. 'Learned' Poussin was considered by eighteenth-century aestheticians to be a link between sublime Salvator Rosa and beautiful Claude Lorraine; as such, Poussin was a painter of the religious sublime.[22]

'Long-legged Fly' is the description of the process underlying that link in terms of political, social, artistic and religious inspiration. Each stanza describes creation in one or a pair of these forms of inspiration and show how interrelated are the terms of Unity of Culture and Unity of Being. Highlighting the metaphysical basis of these lyric moments, each character involved is solitary and silence-inspired. The moments of inspiration are situated in the historical conflict of antithetical and primary qualities. They will have a strong, sometimes violent, sometimes soothing influence, one which either way belies the impassiveness, the aesthetic distance of creation. They are written in tragic joy; the mixed quality is not surprising. The antithetical subjective movements and the primary objective ones are joined in the subject–object interrelation that underlies the act of creation. This healing combination is the aim of the Byzantine worker: the glory which the walls of Coole helped the Irish Literary Renaissance to beget; the unity which artists labour to produce; the terms of the beautiful in society and history which the feminine represents; and the force of faery in Yeats's early otherworldly aesthetic. The combination heals the division between God and individual, individual and society, divisions in society's idea of itself, and in the individual process of becoming.

Yeats begins the poem with an image of Caesar, the antithetical counterpart to Christ, although the secular world which he represents (in a complicated Yeatsian twist) becomes antithetical only upon Christ's birth. Prior to the Advent, Caesar is a primary administrative influence, and meditative as well as active in character. In the poem, he is contemplating the strategy that is required to extend the Roman Empire, and consequently to change the course of European and North-African history. His surgical and harsh decisions will replicate themselves throughout the known world in Classical times; importantly, the process by which he makes these decisions also possesses something of the transcendental. Yeats uses a dialectic of barbarism and civilisation as his historical aesthetic. Antithetical cultures crush primitive and unselfconscious barbaric peoples so that they can civilise them and appropriate their powers. The much discussed place of violence is brought into subtle play in this poem. We are presented with it through the vehicle of the supersensible mind that, moving upon the silence, implicitly knows the goals of violence. Rather than finding his inspiration looking at maps, flipping through minutiae, Caesar is described as gazing at the subject–object mystery, the source of creative energy: the waterfly which Coleridge sees as symbolic of the answer to that mystery. Reality is neither subjective nor objective; it is their interrelation. At the battlefield, the reality (the interaction of subject and object) becomes a clash of arms. Yeats views something in Caesar as higher than the administrative Empire which he began. Caesar is parallel to Christ as well as Christ's antipode. He is the end of an era, for 'the Roman State was from his day to the end a dead thing, a mere mechanism'.[22] In his creative transport, Caesar knows something of the positive sublime of metaphysical thought as well as of the negative, terrible sublime of war.

In the next stanza, Yeats examines the basis of the beautiful in the feminine, how it can be both terrible and propitiating, how it needs protection to be able to exert its world-transforming influence. There is an irony in his description that is reminiscent of 'News for the Delphic Oracle'. It is as if all the images of the terrible beauty of Helen and of Maud Gonne, of the violence they inspired, were revealed to be caused by the sheer vulnerability and dangerous desirability of the beautiful. We are warned to move gently near the Chaplinesque moment of loneliness, pathos and insecurity, lest the power of this unusual and unselfconscious moment within beauty's sphere be dispelled. The image is quite the opposite of that of Helen on the ramparts of Troy explaining with her beauty to the old men of the city why they went to war; it is opposite to that of Athena-like Maud Gonne in the part of Cathleen Ni Houlihan, or waiting arrogantly at Howth Station. Yeats is presenting one of his best implicit images of the supersensible world in this poem. The 'tinker shuffle' is informed by its opposite, as the empirical is informed by the ideal. Grace is implied in the woman's every awkward gesture, as primary wisdom is implied in every one of Caesar's acts of power. Throughout the poem, the ideal trope is in the refrain, which presents the mingling of mind and body, of perceiver and perceived, and which contains the creative force that precedes the existence of either subject or object. The subject–object mystery is incarnate even in a 'tinker shuffle'. The low style is appropriate here, for where does the transcendent wish come from if not from poverty, from social outcasts and the street? The very emblem of beauty knows this best of all, and in a secret moment expresses its bitter truths; moved by instinct, being 'three parts child', she (the subjective antithetical vision of the body's power) expresses the reality of her deformed mask, of her opposite – a tinker woman marred by the difficulty of her circumstances. She unites the deformed life of the subject and the objective reality of the ideal.

If the Helen-like figure of the second stanza takes a private moment for vaudevillian pleasure, in the third stanza Michelangelo – the artist of *la terribilità*, of the sublime (as Raphael is one of the beautiful) – shows how the splendour of his religious vision inversely stems from the most basic and profane of desires:

> That girls at puberty may find
> The first Adam in their thought,
> Shut the door of the Pope's chapel,
> Keep those children out.
> There on that scaffolding reclines
> Michael Angelo.
> With no more sound than the mice make
> His hand moves to and fro.
>
> *Like a long-legged fly upon the stream*
> *His mind moves upon silence.*

Yeats's erotic vision tries to remake religion even as he bars its representatives from the Sistine Chapel, where sacred and profane are joined in the 'profane perfection of mankind' ('Under Ben Bulben'). Here we are given the sublime occasion for the combined expression of religion and art. This is the aim of Yeats's 'sacred book'. He knows that it is dangerous, so he ironically advises us to 'keep the children [and the clergy] out'. This act provides Unity of Culture and Being. His historical, philosophical, religious, aesthetic, and personal outlooks come down to the act of creation, to the mystical connection between sexual ecstasy and all other types of inspiration. Although Yeats has found it difficult to give the simple, empirical realities (such as the sound the mice make) any higher formal meaning since the days of 'The Stolen Child', he has never ceased endeavouring to do so. In 'Long-legged Fly' the mundanities of the fallen world are equated with sublime inspiration. In the last stanza, the force of Adam's beauty itself is shaped by the sinfulness of the empirical. This profane mundane force is given sacred expression.

Michelangelo, in his poetry, is also aware of the need to accord violent, profane desire some sacred expression, rather than giving sacred reality a profane expression, as Yeats does. Peace is not something an object of beauty can confer, although it promises that peace. Peace comes from surrender to the beyond, to the primary force of the soul – the force of 'One who assails me with love like His own'. Only then can the antithetical desire of the sensible world find supersensible shape. Only then can the needs of the self meet the demands of the soul. Michelangelo's sweet error is that he surrenders to the flesh without thinking of how his perception of beauty can express metaphysical reality; he forgets his own belief that 'sensual desire kills the soul' and that 'love does not'.[24] It is the perceiver's attitude to the object of his gaze that provides transcendence, that moves towards the eternal form. The power of the beautiful object flows into subjective eyes, and there achieves its noblest expression through the mediation of the soul. In the act of love, the soul becomes abject, suffering, cast out of subjective and objective realms – overrunning the vision of the perceiver – because it is too ideal, but, in that abjection, it holds the solution to their relationship.

What Michelangelo is describing is the process underlying Yeats's refrain. The literary origin of the refrain is Coleridge's famous description of the 'water-insect' in the *Biographia Literaria*.[25] In his description, Coleridge explores a possible solution to the question occupying the minds of aestheticians and philosophers over the relation between subjective and objective realities. In his description of the 'water-insect', Coleridge raises the question of philosophy, aesthetics and the sublime:

> Most of my readers will have observed a small water-insect on the surface of rivulets which throws a cinque-spotted shadow fringed with prismatic colours on the sunny bottom of the brook; and will have noticed how the little animal wins its way up against the stream, by alternate pulses of active and passive motion, now resisting the current, and now yielding to it in order to gather strength and a momentary fulcrum for a further propulsion. This is no unapt emblem of the mind's self-experience in the act of thinking. There are evidently two powers at work which relatively to each other are active and passive; and this is not possible without an intermediate faculty, which is at once both active and passive. (In philosophical language we must denominate this intermediate faculty in all its degrees and determinations the *imagination*. But in common language, and especially on the subject of poetry, we appropriate the name to a superior degree of the faculty, joined to a superior voluntary controul [*sic*] over it).[26]

The latter faculty, ascribed to poetry, is like that which apprehends the sublime. For Yeats, this intermediate aspect of mind works both in the subjective and the objective realms; it is what interconnects them; it is at the heart of the creative act and is that which may make the void between the realms grow fruitful. Theoretically, the aesthetic does so by mediating between active and passive, antithetical and primary currents, and by uniting the sensible and the supersensible. When Yeats writes '*Like a long-legged fly upon the stream/Her mind moves upon silence*', he imagines that every organism, weaving its way through the turning gyres of subjective and objective reality, occasionally experiences a sublime moment that 'pre-supposes the power [which] by perceiving creates it'.[27] If the silence prove absolute, if the sublime prove to be negative, the roaring stream has run dry. Yet, in order to move upon the silence, Caesar, Helen, Michelangelo, Yeats, among the cast of humanity, rely on the sense of something more.

NOTES

1 INTRODUCTION

1 I have dated the authors who are central to this book, that is, Burke, Kant and Yeats, as well as their works. For the sake of simplicity, and because they are either not as essential or are easily referenced, other authors and their works have not been dated. Burke's and Kant's works are dated when they first appear, as are Yeats's prose works, where it is deemed necessary. His volumes of poetry, on the other hand, are dated throughout in order to keep the most important chronology present in the reader's mind.

2 See the beginning of chapters 3 and 12 for more detailed analysis of the contemporary positions, and for a more detailed argument in favour of the necessity of transcendence in Yeats's poetry.

3 David L. Sedley, 'Sublimity and Skepticism in Montaigne', *PMLA* 113 (1998): 1079–92.

4 W. B. Yeats, 'Modern Poetry', *Essays and Introductions* (London: Macmillan, 1968 [contains essays dating from 1903 to 1937]), pp. 502–3.

5 All the references to Yeats's poems are taken from *The Poems of W. B. Yeats*, ed. Daniel Albright (London: Dent, 1990).

6 Yeats, *A Vision* (New York: Macmillan, 1966), p. 296. All citations are from the revised edition (1937), but it should be noted that many concepts have been developed in the first edition (1925) and formally conceived as far back as the essay *Per Amica Silentia Lunae* (1917). One of the critical assumptions of this study is that many ideas of *A Vision* are found in incipient form in Yeats's early work.

7 Critical practice is somewhat split on whether to follow Yeats's habit of italicising aspects of his system in *A Vision* – Whitaker and Bloom, for instance, do, while Ellmann and Vendler do not. I have chosen the latter course for the sake of simplicity and have italicised only when quoting Yeats or when using his Latin phrases. As the terms primary and antithetical are used quite often before the chapter of this book entitled 'The Language of Illusion', which explains *A Vision*, it may be helpful to offer a working definition. Yeats schematically renders the difference between the two dispensations thus: 'the primary dispensation look[s] beyond itself towards a transcendent power, [it] is dogmatic, levelling, unifying, feminine, humane, peace its means and end'. Its characteristics are 'necessity, truth, goodness, mechanism,

science, democracy, abstraction, peace'. The antithetical dispensation 'obeys imminent power, [it] is expressive, hierarchical, multiple, masculine, harsh, surgical'. Its characteristics are 'freedom, fiction, evil, kindred, art, aristocracy, particularity, war'. *A Vision*, pp. 52, 263.

8 Yeats, *A Vision*, p. 279.
9 Yeats, *Autobiographies* (London: Macmillan, 1980 [first published in 1926]), p. 519.
10 Ibid., p. 501.
11 Ibid., p. 296.
12 Yeats, *Explorations* (London: Macmillan, 1973 [a collection of essays that date from 1901 to 1939 and which George Yeats published together in 1962]), p. 332.
13 Immanuel Kant, *Prolegomena to any Future Metaphysics*, trans. J.P. Mahaffy (London: Macmillan, 1915), p. 36.
14 Edward O'Shea, *A Descriptive Catalogue of W.B. Yeats's Library* (New York: Garland, 1985), pp. 46–7.
15 In a note to his edition of the *Enquiry*, Boulton remarks that *The Famous and Delectable History of Don Bellienis of Greece* (1673) by Francis Kirkman 'was probably Burke's source. H. Thomas, *Spanish and Portuguese Romances of Chivalry* (Cambridge, 1920, pp. 256–62) gives an account of the history of the romance and says that the English versions were popular in Ireland in the eighteenth century.' See Edmund Burke *A Philosophical Enquiry into the Origin of our Ideas of the Sublime and the Beautiful* , ed. James T. Boulton (Oxford: Blackwell, 1987), pp. 20–1, n.7.
16 Anne Yeats, personal interview, 6 August 1999.
17 Nietzsche, whose aesthetics is in many ways more central to Yeats, is not examined in the passage because, for the German philosopher, aesthetics is only part of a much larger project. Croce's book, on the other hand, has ideas of art as its main subject and it contains such very specific references to the history of aesthetics, Burke and Kant included, that it provides a frame from Yeats's reading for the present discussion.
18 William Blake, *The Works of William Blake, Volume 2*, ed. Edwin Ellis and W.B. Yeats (London: Bernard Auaritch, 1893), p. 341.
19 Blake, *Works*, p. 339.
20 Ibid., p. 328.
21 Ibid., p. 325.
22 Ibid., p. 342.
23 Ibid., p. 329.
24 Benedetto Croce, *Aesthetics as Science of Expression and General Linguistics*, trans. Douglas Ainslie (London: Macmillan, 1922), p. 417.
25 Ibid., p. 345.
26 Ibid., p. 84.
27 Ibid., p. 4.
28 Quoted in Richard Ellmann, *The Identity of Yeats* (Oxford: Oxford UP, 1964), p. 234.

2 MERCURY SUBLIMATE

1 See Ernest Lee Tuveson, 'The Imagination in the New Epistemology', *The Imagination as a Means of Grace: Locke and the Aesthetics of Romanticism* (New York: Gordian, 1974) p. 172.

2 Though the sublime is considered Hebrew by birth, the history of the criticism of sublimity begins with the Greek Pseudo-Longinus's *Peri Hypsous*, written in the first century A.D. See Longinus, *On the Sublime*, trans. W. Rhys Roberts. *Classical Literary Criticism* (London: Penguin, 1965), pp. 97–158. For more on Longinus's ideas see M.H. Abrams, *The Mirror and the Lamp* (London: Oxford, 1953), passim; Neil Hertz, 'A Reading of Longinus', *The End of the Line: Essays on Psychoanalysis and the Sublime* (New York: Columbia UP, 1985), pp. 1–20; Lyotard, 'The Sublime and the Avant-Garde', *The Inhuman: Reflections on Time*, trans. Geoffrey Bennington and Rachel Bowlby (Stanford: Stanford UP, 1991), pp. 89–108. For more on John Dennis, see David Morris, *The Religious Sublime* (Lexington: U of Kentucky P, 1972), passim; and for more on Addison see Tuveson, *Imagination*, passim.

3 For the history of ideas on this subject, see Marjorie Hope Nicolson, *Mountain Gloom and Mountain Glory* (Ithaca: Cornell UP, 1959).

4 For a study of Burke's influence on such authors of the Gothic as Ann Radcliffe, see Malcom Ware, *Sublimity in the Novels of Ann Radcliffe* (Copenhagen: Lundequistska Bokhandeln, 1963).

5 See Burke, *A Philosophical Enquiry into the Origins of our Ideas of the Sublime and Beautiful*, ed. Adam Phillips (Oxford: Oxford UP, 1990), p. 117; all references to Burke's *Enquiry* will be to this edition unless otherwise stated.

6 Ibid., p. 58.

7 Ibid., p. 67.

8 Ibid., p. 30.

9 Ibid., pp. 63, 65.

10 Ibid., p. 59.

11 Ibid., p. 62.

12 Ibid., p. 62.

13 Ibid., p. 63.

14 Ibid., p. 64.

15 See Ibid., p. 64.

16 Ibid., p. 64.

17 Ibid., p. 83.

18 See Tom Furniss, *Edmund Burke's Aesthetic Ideology: Language, Gender, and Political Economy in Revolution* (Cambridge: Cambridge UP, 1993), pp. 4–7; Isaac Kramnick, *The Rage of Edmund Burke: Portrait of an Ambivalent Conservative* (New York: Basic, 1977), p. 109.

19 Burke, *Enquiry*, p. 57.

20 See Ibid., pp. 75–6.

21 In a footnote (p. 382, n. 36) to his edition of the *Reflections on the Revolution in France* (London: Penguin, 1968), Conor Cruise O'Brien notes that 'Burke's horror of regicide does not prevent him from seeing merits in Cromwell: "Cromwell had delivered England from anarchy. His government, though military and despotic, had been regular and orderly. Under the iron, and under the yoke, the soil yielded its produce." (*Letter to a member of the National Assembly*, 1791: Works II, p. 544)'. Yet what is quite indicative of Burke's contradictory attitudes towards Cromwell and revolution, is that he

also attacked Protestant titles to Irish land as products of Cromwell's betrayal of the English Parliament. See Conor Cruise O'Brien, *The Great Melody: A Thematic Biography* (London: Sinclair-Stevenson, 1993), p. 484.

22 Burke, *Reflections*, p. 137.
23 Ibid.
24 Cruise O'Brien, *Great Melody*, p. 96.
25 See Ibid., p. xxvi.
26 Burke, 'A Letter on the Affairs of Ireland', *Letters, Speeches and Tracts on Irish Affairs* (London: Macmillan, 1881), p. 389.
27 Burke, 'A Letter to Richard Burke, Esq.', *Irish Affairs*, p. 368.
28 See Declan Kiberd, *Inventing Ireland: The Literature of the Modern Nation* (London: Cape, 1995), p. 18.
29 'Where there is property there will be less theft; where there is marriage there will always be less fornication'. Burke, 'A Letter to Sir Hercules Langrishe, MP, 1792', *Irish Affairs*, p. 222.
30 Burke, 'A Letter to Richard Burke, Esq.', *Irish Affairs*, p. 350.
31 Burke, 'On the Penal Laws against Irish Catholics', *Irish Affairs*, p. 201.
32 Burke, 'A Letter to Sir Hercules Langrishe, MP, 1792', *Irish Affairs*, p. 265.
33 Ibid., p. 268.
34 Peter de Bolla, *The Discourse of the Sublime* (Oxford: Blackwell, 1989), p. 64, n. 6.
35 C. B. Macpherson, *Burke* (Oxford: Oxford UP, 1980), pp. 64–5.
36 Furniss, *Burke's Aesthetic*, p. 39.
37 See *Enquiry*, p. 83; and *Reflections*, p. 135.
38 Burke, *Enquiry*, p. 105.
39 'As they [women] have inverted order in all things, the gallery is in place of the house'. Burke, *Reflections*, p. 165.
40 Ibid., p. 161.
41 Ibid., p. 124.
42 Quoted in O'Brien, *Great Melody*, pp. 64–5.
43 See Anne K. Mellor, *Romanticism and Gender* (London: Routledge, 1993), p. 108.
44 Burke writes of the effects of revolutionary subversion: 'on this scheme of things, a king is but a man; a queen is but a woman; a woman is but an animal; and an animal not of the highest order. All homage paid to the sex in general as such, and without distinct views, is to be regarded as romance and folly'. *Reflections*, p. 171.
45 Burke, *Reflections*, pp. 169–70.
46 Seamus Deane, 'Edmund Burke', *The Field Day Anthology of Irish Writing* (Derry: Norton, 1991), p. 808.
47 Kiberd, *Inventing Ireland*, p. 18.
48 Daniel Corkery, *The Hidden Ireland: A Study of Gaelic Munster in the Eighteenth Century* (Dublin: Gill, 1924), p. 176.
49 Seamus Heaney, *New Selected Poems, 1966–1987* (London: Faber, 1987), p. 74.
50 Burke, *Reflections*, p. 170.
51 Mary Wollstonecraft, *A Vindication of the Rights of Men*, ed. Eleanor Louise Nicholes (Gainesville: Scholars' Facsimiles and Reprints, 1960), p. 115.
52 Wollstonecraft, *A Wollstonecraft Anthology*, ed. Janet Todd (Oxford: Blackwell, 1989), p. 78.
53 Furniss, *Burke's Aesthetic*, p. 193.
54 Burke, *Enquiry*, p. 101.

3 THE SMELL OF THE FIRE

1 Samuel H. Monk, *The Sublime: A Study of Critical Theories in Eighteenth-Century England* (Ann Arbor: U of Michigan P, 1960), p. 11.
2 Frances Ferguson, *Solitude and the Sublime: Romanticism and the Aesthetics of Individuation* (London: Routledge, 1992), pp. 5–6.
3 Ibid., p. 21.
4 Ibid., p. 22.
5 Thomas Weiskel, *The Romantic Sublime: Studies in the Structure and Psychology of Transcendence* (Baltimore: Johns Hopkins UP, 1976), pp. 23–4
6 Ibid., p. 56.
7 See Paul Crowther, *The Kantian Sublime* (Oxford: Clarendon, 1989), pp. 131–2.
8 Jean-François Lyotard, *Lessons on the Analytic of the Sublime*, trans. Elizabeth Rottenberg (Stanford: Stanford UP, 1994), p. 137.
9 See Weiskel's brilliant consideration of the confrontation of negative and positive sublimity in the 'Simplon Pass' episode in 'Wordsworth and the Defile of the Word: Crossing the Threshold', *The Romantic Sublime*, pp. 195–204.
10 A.C. Bradley, *Oxford Lectures on Poetry* (London: Macmillan, 1914),   pp. 51–2.
11 For discussion of Elohim and Yahweh, see Rudolf Otto, 'The Numinous in the Old Testament', *The Idea of the Holy: An Inquiry into the Non-rational Factor in the Idea of the Divine and its Relation to the Rational* (New York: Oxford UP, 1923), pp. 72–82. See also pp. 62–3 for discussion of the analogy between the 'grandeur' and 'dread' of sublime experience and those characteristics of the religious experience of God.
12 Immanuel Kant, *The Critique of Judgement*, trans. James Creed Meredith (Oxford: Clarendon, 1928), p. 22.
13 Jacques Derrida, 'The time of the thesis; punctuations', *Philosophy in France Today*, trans. Kathleen McLaughlin and ed. Alan Montefiore (Cambridge: Cambridge UP, 1983), pp. 37–8.
14 Roger Scruton, *Kant* (Oxford: Oxford UP, 1982), p. 94.
15 Immanuel Kant, *Critique of Pure Reason*, trans. Norman Kemp-Smith (London: Macmillan, 1929), p. 8.
16 See Scruton, *Kant*, p. 32.
17 Kant, *Critique of Judgement*, p. 88.
18 Ibid., p. 225.
19 See Richard Kearney, *The Wake of the Imagination: Ideas of Creativity in Western Culture* (London: Hutchinson, 1988), p. 176.
20 Kant, *Critique of Judgement*, p. 98.
21 Scruton, *Kant*, pp. 55–7.
22 See Kant, *Critique of Judgement*, p. 109.
23 Ibid., pp. 123–4.
24 Ibid., pp. 124–5.
25 Crawford is both unconvinced of the bridge between aesthetics and morality and of the universality of either judgement. Donald Crawford, *Kant's Aesthetic Theory* (Madison: U of Wisconsin P, 1974), pp. 149–52.
26 See Kant, *Critique of Practical Reason*, trans. Lewis White Beck (London: Macmillan, 1956), pp. 75–8.
27 Crowther, *Kantian Sublime*, pp. 152–74.
28 Patricia M. Matthews, 'Kant's Sublime: A Form of Pure Aesthetic Reflective Judgement', *Journal of Aesthetics and Art Criticism* 54: 2 (1996): 169.

29 Matthews, 'Kant's Sublime', p. 171.
30 Kant, *Critique of Judgement*, p. 107.
31 Lyotard, *Lessons on the Analytic of the Sublime*, p. 239.
32 J. M. Bernstein, *The Fate of Art: Aesthetic Alienation from Kant to Derrida and Adorno* (Cambridge: Polity, 1992), p. 18.
33 Kant, *Critique of Judgement*, pp. 190–1.
34 Ibid., pp. 191–2.
35 Ibid., p. 100.
36 Hans-Georg Gadamer, *The Relevance of the Beautiful and Other Essays*, trans. Nicholas Walker and ed. Robert Bernasconi (Cambridge: Cambridge UP, 1986), p. 168.
37 Kant, 'Critique of Teleological Judgement', *Critique of Judgement*, p. 97.
38 Stuart Hampshire, 'The Social Spirit of Mankind', *Kant's Transcendental Deductions*, ed. Eckart Förster (Stanford: Stanford UP, 1989), pp. 150–1.
39 Kant, *Observations on the Feeling of the Beautiful and the Sublime*, trans. John T. Goldthwait (Berkeley: U of California P, 1960), p. 66; cf. Edmund Burke, *A Philosophical Enquiry into the Origin of our Ideas of the Sublime and Beautiful*, ed. Adam Phillips, part III and part I, sections ix and x, pp. 38–40.
40 Kant, *Observations*, p. 77.
41 Ibid., p. 79.
42 Ibid., p. 82.
43 Ibid., p. 87.
44 Ibid., pp. 76–7.
45 Ibid., pp. 95–6.
46 Yeats, *Explorations*, 316.

4 NIGHT OR JOY

1 Walter Pater, *The Renaissance* (Oxford: Oxford UP, 1986), p. 80.
2 Burke, *Reflections*, p. 165.
3 Yeats, *Explorations*, p. 393.
4 Yeats, *Explorations*, p. 399.
5 Quoted in Patrick J. Keane, *Yeats's Interactions with Tradition* (Columbia: U of Missouri P, 1987), p. 77.
6 Quoted in Richard Ellmann, *Identity of Yeats*, p. 307.
7 Yeats, *A Vision*, p. 112.
8 Ibid., p. 279.
9 Corinna Salvadori, *Yeats and Castiglione: Poet and Courtier* (Dublin: Allen, 1965), pp. 4–19.
10 Yeats, *A Vision*, p. 52.
11 Ibid., p. 187.
12 Ibid., p. 70, n. 2.
13 Quoted in Ellmann, *Identity of Yeats*, p. 234.
14 Yeats, *Mythologies* (London: Macmillan, 1969 [mostly contains publications dating from 1890s, but the last essay *Per Amica Silentia Lunae* was published in 1917]), p. 332.
15 Yeats, 'Modern Poetry', *Essays and Introductions*, pp. 502–3.
16 Burke, *Enquiry*, p. 77.
17 Kant, *Critique of Judgement*, p. 149.

18 The connection between Schiller's view that the sublime is not merely a destructive agent but can complement the beautiful, and the attempt by Irish writers to restore some of beauty's harmony and humanity to a history marked by destruction and terror has been noted before in regard to James Clarence Mangan. Interestingly, the nineteenth-century Irish poet was seen in turn by Yeats as an important example. See David Lloyd, 'Oversettings from the German: Dissembling the Sublime', *Nationalism and Minor Literature: James Clarence Mangan and the Emergence of Irish Cultural Nationalism* (Berkeley: U of California P, 1987), pp. 129–58, for a discussion of the relationship between Schiller's aesthetics, Mangan's travails and translations, and the larger problems of Irish identity.

19 Friedrich von Schiller, *The Philosophical and Aesthetic Letters and Essays of Schiller*, trans. J. Weiss (London: Chapman, 1854), p. 259.

5 ETERNAL BEAUTY

1 For a discussion of the famine and the sublime, see Chris Morash, *Writing the Irish Famine* (Oxford: Clarendon, 1995) and his essay entitled 'Literature, Memory, Atrocity' in Richard Hayes and Chris Morash (eds), *Fearful Realities: New Perspectives on the Famine* (Blackrock: Irish Academic P, 1996).

2 Edward Said, 'Yeats and Decolonization', *Culture and Imperialism* (London: Chatto, 1993), pp. 274–5.

3 See Roy Foster, 'Protestant Magic: W. B. Yeats and the Spell of Irish History', *Paddy and Mr Punch: Connections in Irish and English History* (London: Penguin, 1993), pp. 212–33; see also *W.B. Yeats: A Life: I: The Apprentice Mage, 1865–1914* (Oxford: Oxford UP, 1997), passim.

4 Seamus Deane, *Celtic Revivals: Essays in Modern Irish Literature, 1880–1980* (London: Faber, 1985), p. 49.

5 Theodor W. Adorno, *Aesthetic Theory*, trans. C. Lenhardt (London: Routledge, 1984), p. 196. 'Utopia' will be used here because of its transcendent connotations. The later Yeats (not the earlier escapist Utopian Yeats) has famous reservations about the term and its political uses. He sees the 'vague Utopia' ('In Memory of Eva Gore-Booth and Con Markiewicz'), of which Eva Gore-Booth dreams, as hostile to artistic embodiment of the beautiful. Similarly, in the essay 'The Holy Mountain' contained in *Essays and Introductions*, Yeats believes that Balzac's *Comédie Humaine* 'will cure the world of all Utopias' (p. 468) because Balzac's work reminds him 'of [his and its] preoccupation with national, social, personal problems . . .' (p. 448). The later Yeats sees Utopian thinking as an escapist reminder of his former self; and yet his engagement, as well as his visions of the unalienated labour and transcendental freedom of Byzantium, Greece and Urbino, accord well with the Frankfurt School's conception of Utopia. The word is used here with this idea, and this relationship, in mind.

6 Denis Donoghue, *William Butler Yeats* (New York: Viking, 1971), p. 36. In later work, Donoghue is very specific about the need for an ethical aesthetics of the object, and of the limits of will, especially against what he states is Harold Bloom's erroneous contention that the 'will' must 'maintain itself against every object of experience'. *The Pure Good of Theory* (Oxford: Blackwell, 1992), p. 98.

7 See Donoghue, *Yeats*, p. 24. See Donoghue's development of Blackmur's idea into a taxonomy of the imagination that operates in three modes: the Franciscan, or objective, in which 'imagination lavishes attention upon natural forms'; the Promethean, or dialectical mode, in which 'imagination proposes to set against the natural world a rival fiction'; and the mode of negation, or subjectivism, in which the 'mind repudiates its dependence on objects' *The Sovereign Ghost* (London: Faber, 1978), pp. 40–4. Yeats would not have much to do with the third category, but obviously his imagination is very Promethean. The present contention is that it is not Promethean to the exclusion of the Franciscan mode.

8 See Richard Ellmann, *The Man and the Masks* (London: Penguin, 1979), p. 69.

9 See Donoghue, *Yeats*, p. 37.

10 See Yeats, *A Vision*, pp. 82–3.

11 Donoghue, *Yeats*, p. 37.

12 See Ellmann, *Identity of Yeats*, p. 163.

13 Yeats, *A Vision*, p. 83.

14 Yeats, *A Vision*, pp. 82–3.

15 Yeats, *A Vision*, p. 105.

16 Yeats, 'Moods', *Essays and Introductions*, p. 195.

17 Although this quotation moves ahead in time (1917), the ideas it presents were previously evident in his poetry; the quotation and ones like it serve to highlight the incipiency of these ideas as they appear in his work.

18 Yeats, *Per Amica Silentia Lunae*, *Mythologies*, p. 359.

19 See Yeats, *A Vision*, pp. 45–50.

20 Yeats, *Mythologies*, p. 277.

21 Yeats, *Autobiographies*, p. 123.

22 Ibid., p. 364.

23 For the relationship of Donne, Yeats and the thinking body, see Frank Kermode, *Romantic Image* (New York: Vintage, 1964), p. 49; see also Yeats, *Autobiographies*, pp. 292–3 for a comparative description of paintings by Strozzi and Sargent which also explains Yeats's concept.

24 Yeats, *Explorations*, p. 308.

25 Thomas R. Whitaker, *Swan and Shadow: Yeats's Dialogue with History* (Washington: Catholic UP, 1989), p. 89.

26 See Wayne K. Chapman, *Yeats and English Renaissance Literature* (London: Macmillan, 1991), pp. 185–218.

6 THE LABOUR TO BE BEAUTIFUL

1 Yeats, *A Vision*, p. 187.

2 Burke, *Enquiry*, p. 73.

3 For a discussion of the Romantic misreading of Locke, see R.S. Crane's 'Notes on the Organization of Locke's Essay', *The Idea of the Humanities and Other Essays Critical and Historical: Vol. I* (Chicago: U of Chicago P, 1967), pp. 288–301.

4 Burke, *Reflections*, p. 170.

5 See Kant, *Critique of Judgement*, pp. 46–50.

6 See Arthur Symons, *The Symbolist Movement in Literature* (New York: Haskell, 1971), p. 7. He writes that 'the desire to bewilder the middle class is itself middle class'.

7 George Moore, *Vale, Hail and Farewell*, 3 vols: *Ave, Salve, Vale* (London: Heinemann, 1947 [first published 1914]), pp. 113–15.

8 Yeats, *A Vision*, p. 83.

9 Friedrich Schiller, 'The Sublime', *Philosophical and Aesthetic Letters*, p. 254.

10 See Terry Eagleton, 'The Marxist Sublime', *The Ideology of the Aesthetic* (Oxford: Blackwell, 1990), pp. 196–234.

11 Yeats writes of this cause quite tellingly, citing Kropotkin as his source: 'the [French] Revolution by sweeping away old communal customs and institutions in the name of equal rights and duties left the French peasant at the mercy of the capitalist'. *Explorations*, p. 316. Though one might argue elsewhere with his somewhat sweeping condemnation of equality, the condemnation of the effect of too complete a loss of tradition seems very accurate indeed and also very relevant to the costs of the modernisation that is taking place in Ireland today.

12 See Yeats, *Memoirs*, ed. Denis Donoghue (London: Macmillan, 1972 [contains the suppressed autobiography from 1915–16 and a more complete version of the journal begun in 1908]), pp. 81–3.

13 See Burke, *Enquiry*, p. 100.

7 LIVING BEAUTY

1 In Yeats's work there is a complicated relationship between Protestant 'taste', something which he felt Catholics lacked, and Catholic mythological and spiritual power, a quality which in Protestants he felt was vitiated by the obsession with 'getting on'. These basic ideas were pivotal in Yeats's changing attitude towards the two aspects of Irish society. By the time of *The Wild Swans at Coole*, any hopes for the Irish Catholics that the Rebellion of 1916 might have renewed have long since dimmed with the controversy over the Hugh Lane bequests.

2 See Roy Foster, 'Yeats's progress from the twilight of Ascendancy to the new nation', *Times Literary Supplement* 27 Sept. 1996: 9–10.

3 Francis Bacon, 'On Beauty', *The Essays of Francis Bacon*, ed. John Pitcher (New York: Penguin, 1985), p. 181.

4 'Tread', *Oxford English Dictionary*, 1989 ed.

5 Yeats, *Mythologies*, p. 332.

6 J.M. Bernstein, *The Fate of Art*, p. 8.

7 See Lionel Johnson, 'Mystic and Cavalier', *Poetical Works of Lionel Johnson* (London: Elkin, 1915), p. 35.

8 See Ian Fletcher's introduction to *The Complete Poems of Lionel Johnson* (London: Unicorn, 1953), pp. ii–xxxiv.

9 Yeats, 'The Death of Synge', *Autobiographies*, p. 509.

10 W. B. Yeats, ed., *The Oxford Book of Modern Verse* (Oxford: Oxford UP, 1936), p. xxvii.

11 Elizabeth Butler Cullingford's chapter on Crazy Jane contains a good discussion of Yeats's changing ideas; see 'Crazy Jane and the Irish Episcopate', *Gender and History in Yeats's Love Poetry* (Cambridge: Cambridge UP, 1993), pp. 227–44. For a good discussion of Burke's relationship to the

228NOTES TO PP. 96–110

gender constructions just delineated above, see Linda Zerilli, 'Text/Woman as Spectacle: Edmund Burke's Revolution', *The Eighteenth Century* 33: 1 (1992): 47–72.

12 Quoted in Kenneth S. Lynn's review of Laura E. Skandra-Trombley, *Mark Twain in the Company of Women* (Philadelphia: U of Penn. P, 1996) in *Times Literary Supplement* 17 May (1996): 3–4. Throughout her recent biography, *George's Ghosts: A New Life of W. B. Yeats* (London: Picador, 1999), Brenda Maddox details the rich role of women in this period of Yeats's life.

13 Yeats writes: 'Men have set up a great mill called examinations to destroy the imagination. Why should women go through it?' *The Letters of W. B. Yeats*, ed. Allen Wade (New York: Macmillan, 1955), p. 123.

14 Yeats states of Symons: '. . . he could listen as a woman listens, never meeting one's thought as a man does with a rival thought, but taking up what one said and changing, giving it as it were flesh and bone'. Yeats, *Memoirs*, p. 87.

15 See Yeats, *Letters on Poetry to Dorothy Wellesley from W.B. Yeats*, ed. Dorothy Wellesley (London: Oxford UP, 1940), p. 110.

16 See Yeats, *Memoirs*, p. 40.

17 Lyotard, *Lessons on the Analytic of the Sublime*, p. 4.

18 Kant, *Judgement*, p. 123.

8 THE LANGUAGE OF ILLUSION

1 Yeats, *A Vision*, pp. 52, 263.

2 It must be noted that the connection between the feminine, the scientific, and the mechanical belies Yeats's other treatment of the feminine as more in touch with the instinctual, the physical, etc. It would be helpful to separate these ideas into feminine, for the cultural construction, and female for the biological construction of the term, although Yeats is not consistent enough in his usage to allow this to work. Instead, the contradictions must be noted as they appear.

3 Yeats, *A Vision*, p. 105.

4 Ibid., p. 105.

5 Friedrich Nietzsche, *The Birth of Tragedy and The Genealogy of Morals*, trans. Francis Golffing (New York: Doubleday, 1956), p. 247.

6 Yeats, *A Vision*, p. 81.

7 Ibid., p. 110.

8 Ibid., p. 110.

9 Ibid., p. 108.

10 Yeats, *Per Amica*, *Mythologies*, pp. 344–5.

11 Ibid., p. 349.

12 Yeats, *A Vision*, p. 136.

13 Ibid., p. 135.

14 Ibid., p. 82.

15 Ibid., p. 181.

16 Ibid., p. 189; see also *Per Amica*, *Mythologies*, p. 336.

17 Kant, *Judgement*, p. 100.

18 Yeats, *A Vision*, p. 187.

19 Ibid., p. 187.

20 Ibid., p. 289.

21 Ibid., p. 230.
22 Ibid., p. 230.
23 Ibid., p. 232.
24 Ibid., p. 236.
25 Ibid., p. 279.
26 Yeats, ed., *Oxford Book of Modern Verse*, p. xxxvi.
27 Lyotard, 'The Inhuman', *The Inhuman: Reflections on Time*, trans. Geoffrey Bennington and Rachel Bowlby (Stanford: Stanford UP, 1988), p. 2.
28 Kant, *Judgement*, pp. 175 and 180.
29 Yeats, *A Vision*, p. 82.
30 Ibid., p. 79.
31 Ibid., pp. 136–7.
32 Ibid., pp. 136–7.
33 Yeats, *Explorations*, 425.
34 Lyotard, 'God and Puppet', *The Inhuman*, 163.
35 Lyotard, 'Obedience', *The Inhuman*, p. 167.
36 Yeats, *A Vision*, p. 208.
37 Yeats, 'A General Introduction for my Work', *Essays and Introductions*, p. 514.

9 THE FRIVOLOUS EYE

1 Yeats, *A Vision*, p. 105.
2 Lyotard, *Lessons on the Analytic of the Sublime* 180; Julia Kristeva, *Powers of Horror: An Essay on Abjection*, trans. Leon S. Roudiez (New York: Columbia UP, 1982), p. 55.
3 Kristeva, *Powers of Horror*, p. 210.
4 Otto, *The Idea of the Holy*, p. 28.
5 Paul Verlaine, 'Cupid Fallen', *Paul Verlaine: Selected Poems*, trans. C.F. MacIntyre (Berkeley, U of California P, 1948), p. 15.
6 Yeats, *A Vision*, pp. 52–3.
7 See Yeats's poem 'The Mother of God' for this version of positive sublimity.
8 Yeats, *A Vision*, p. 53.
9 Burke, *Enquiry*, p. 63.
10 Nathaniel Hawthorne, *The Scarlet Letter* (New York: Penguin, 1983), p. 191.
11 Otto, *The Idea of the Holy*, p. 28.
12 Burke writes: 'The horse in the light of an useful beast, fit for the plough, the road, the draft, in every social useful light the horse has nothing of the sublime; but it is thus that we are affected with him *whose neck is cloathed with thunder, the glory of whose nostrils is terrible, who swalloweth the ground with fierceness and rage, neither believeth that it is the sound of the trumpet?' Enquiry*, p. 60.
13 Yeats, 'Modern Poetry', *Essays and Introductions*, p. 502–3.
14 Kant, *Critique of Judgement*, p. 107–8.
15 Ibid., p.108.
16 The significant difference between Yeats's poem and Woolf's novel is that instead of placing the violent conceptual change in a remote historical setting as does Yeats, Woolf ends domestically with Mrs Swithin (a merely accidental player in the remembered newspaper rape-scene) coming in with hammer in hand and therefore becoming the archetypal female revenger, 'entering

through the Arch of Whitehall', the seat of the British civil service, the bastion of male power. See *Between the Acts* (London: Penguin, 1992), p. 13.

17 Seamus Heaney, 'Punishment', *New Selected Poems* (London: Faber, 1990), p. 72.

18 See M.H. Abrams, *The Mirror and the Lamp* (London: Oxford, 1953), p. 73.

19 Longinus, *Sublime*, 108. There is a Longinian treatment of 'Leda and the Swan' by Hoyt Trowbridge entitled '"Leda and the Swan": A Longinian Analysis', *Modern Philology* 51, Nov. (1953): 118–29. It nevertheless seems inadequate, as the author maintains, quite remarkably (on pp. 121 and 123 in particular), that sublimity and terror are not reconcilable (that they most definitely are is, of course, Burke's famous contention), and that sublimity is not carnal experience (when the Yeatsian sublime is profoundly carnal). I follow some of Trowbridge's very fine Longinian insights into the poem in order to illustrate how, on the contrary, the terror and grotesqueness of the poem are found in its very rhetoric.

20 Longinus, *Sublime*, p. 129.

21 Ibid., p. 129.

22 Ibid., p. 110.

23 Harold Bloom, *Yeats* (London: Oxford, 1970), p. 365.

24 I make this point to counter Yvor Winters's view that Yeats did not believe in such systems, and to counter recurring like beliefs that Yeats had not the philosophical depth to give them credence. Winters's opinion is cited in Bloom, *Yeats*, p. 365.

25 Yeats, *A Vision*, p. 295.

26 Ibid., p. 296.

27 For a criticism of the position that Yeats assumes, see Geoffrey Hartman, *Criticism in the Wilderness: the Study of Literature Today* (New Haven: Yale UP, 1980), p. 21.

28 Yeats, *The Variorum Edition of the Poems of W.B. Yeats*, ed. Peter Allt and Russell Alspach (London: Macmillan, 1957), p. 828 .

29 See Burke, *Enquiry*, p. 43; and Kant, *Critique of Judgement*, p. 112.

30 See, for example, Shakespeare's long narrative poem *The Rape of Lucrece*, Carew's poem 'A Rapture', and Nashe's prose narrative, *The Unfortunate Traveller*.

31 Yeats, *Autobiographies*, p. 349.

32 Yeats, *A Vision*, p. 53.

33 See Brian Davies, 'Good and Evil', *An Introduction to the Philosophy of Religion* (Oxford: Oxford UP, 1993), pp. 32–55. For a source in Yeats's reading, see Alfred North Whitehead, *Science and the Modern World* (Cambridge: Cambridge UP, 1927).

34 Among the many critics who make this acknowledgement, see Elizabeth Butler Cullingford, *Gender and History in Yeats's Love Poetry*, pp. 151–64, for one of the most recent and well known. Though hesitant to read the poem as an epiphany (for example, she quotes the American poet Mona Van Duyn's rejection of the validity of any epiphanic basis in the poem 'To See, To Take'), she nevertheless does acknowledge that Yeats's poem 'exposes the brutality of the male or divine exercise of force' (p. 164) – which surely means she does read it, at least nominally, as an epiphany. For a reading aligned with mine, but more concerned with the postmodern aspects of the poem's epiphany than purely aesthetic ones, see William Johnsen, 'Textual/Sexual Politics in

Yeats's "Leda and the Swan"', ed. Leonard Orr, *Yeats and Postmodernism* (Syracuse: Syracuse UP, 1991), pp. 80–90.

35 Kristeva, *Powers of Horror*, p. 127.

36 Ibid., p. 208. For a poetic example of the 'Crisis of the Word' in a less violent setting, see Medbh McGuckian's 'Sky-Writing', *Marconi's Cottage* (Meath: Gallery, 1991), p. 79.

37 John Donne, 'The Ecstasy', *The Norton Anthology of English Literature*, ed. M.H. Abrams, et al. (New York: Norton, 1986), pp. 1095–6.

38 Roland Barthes, *A Lover's Discourse: Fragments*, trans. Richard Howard (London: Penguin, 1979), pp. 188–9.

39 For this reading see Leo Spitzer, 'On Yeats's poem, "Leda and the Swan"' *Modern Philology* 51, Nov. (1953): 275.

40 See William Wordsworth, *Selected Prose*, ed. John O. Hayden (Harmondsworth: Penguin, 1988), p. 269.

41 See Curtis B. Bradford, *Yeats at Work* (New York: Ecco, 1978), p. 101.

42 Yeats, *A Vision*, p. 286.

43 Barthes, *Lover's Discourse*, p. 189.

44 For a depiction of Leda's revenge see June Jordan, 'The Female and the Silence of Man (cf. W.B. Yeats's "Leda and the Swan")', *Naming Our Destiny: New and Selected Poems* (New York: Thunder's Mouth, 1989). There are other poems in response (or analogous) to Yeats's, but none that I have found matches Yeats in the intensity and violence of its depiction as does Jordan's. For example, H.D.'s 'Leda' is openly erotic; Van Duyn's 'To See, To Take' is a rejection of the epiphanic basis. Adrienne Rich's poem, 'Rape', is more of an attack on the patriarchal state apparatus than it is a depiction of the actual violation.

45 Yeats, *Autobiographies*, p. 123.

46 See Bradford, *Yeats at Work*, pp. 104–5.

47 Yeats, *Letters on Poetry*, p. 192.

48 Quoted in Evelyn Underhill, *Mysticism* (New York: Doubleday, 1911), p. 376.

49 Ibid., p. 377.

50 Yeats, *A Vision*, p. 53.

10 DESIRE AND THE FASCIST DREAM

1 Yeats writes of the relation between individual and society: 'A civilisation is a struggle to keep self-control . . . it is like some great tragic person, some Niobe who must display an almost superhuman will or the cry will not touch our sympathy', *A Vision*, p. 268.

2 Ibid., p. 279.

3 See Otto Bohlmann, 'Conflict, Will, Power', *Yeats and Nietzsche* (London: Macmillan, 1982), pp. 19–40.

4 Yeats, *Uncollected Prose of W. B. Yeats: Vol I*, ed. John P. Frayne (London: Macmillan, 1975), p. 87.

5 Theodor W. Adorno, *Minima Moralia*, trans. E.F.N. Jephcott (London: Verso, 1974), p. 193.

6 Adorno, *Minima Moralia*, p. 192.

7 Friedrich Nietzsche, *A Nietzsche Reader*, ed. and trans. R. J. Hollingdale (London: Penguin, 1977), p. 75.

8 Yeats, *Explorations*, p. 441.

9 Ibid., p. 332.

10 Ibid., p. 332.

11 See Adorno, *Negative Dialectics*, trans. E.B. Ashton (New York: Continuum, 1992), p. 400.

12 Yeats, ed., *Oxford Book of Modern Verse*, p. xxxiv.

13 See Weiskel, *Romantic Sublime*, pp. 99–103.

14 For a discussion of the maternal sublime, see Patricia Yaeger, 'Towards a Feminist Sublime', *Gender and Theory*, ed. Linda Kaufman (London: Blackwell, 1986), pp. 191–210.

15 According to Anne Yeats, her mother did not like starlings – 'stare' is a Sligo word for starling – because they were always fighting amongst themselves. The poet obviously equates the character of the birds with the nature of the Civil War in Ireland (Anne Yeats, personal interview, 6 August 1999).

16 See René Girard, *Violence and the Sacred* (Baltimore: Johns Hopkins UP, 1972), p. 34.

17 Edmund Spenser, *The Fairie Queene: Book I, The Norton Anthology of English Literature* ed. M.H. Abrams et al., 6th edn (New York: Norton, 1986), p. 519.

18 Adorno, *Minima Moralia*, p. 163.

19 See Girard, *Violence*, pp. 5–13.

11 HEART'S VICTIM AND ITS TORTURER

1 See Burke, *Enquiry*, p. 35.

2 Yeats, *Essays and Introductions*, p. 502.

3 See Kant, *Judgement*, pp. 92–7.

4 Lyotard, *Lessons on the Analytic of the Sublime*, p. 137.

5 Richard Crashaw, 'The Flaming Heart', *Norton*, p. 1398.

6 Ibid., p. 1398.

7 Yeats, *A Vision*, p. 237.

8 See Yeats, *A Vision*, pp. 237–9. Also, see *Essays and Introductions*, pp. 522–3 and *Explorations*, p. 163.

9 Lyotard, *The Inhuman*, p. 2.

10 Yeats, *Mythologies*, p. 287.

11 For a similar description of the dangers of love and courtship, but one made along opposite gender lines, see the previous lyric in the same sequence, section III, entitled 'The Mermaid'.

12 Adorno, *Minima Moralia*, p. 105.

13 See Yeats, *Autobiographies*, p. 55.

14 See Yeats, *Letters on Poetry*, p. 120.

15 Adorno, *Minima Moralia*, p. 63.

16 See Max Horkheimer, *The Eclipse of Reason* (New York: Continuum, 1947), pp. 92–115.

17 Yeats, ed., *Oxford Book of Modern Verse*, p. xxxv.

18 Ibid., p. xxxiv.

19 Adorno, *Minima Moralia*, p. 105. Though I employ Adorno's phrase in order to illustrate how Yeats's ideas could be fascist in the worst sense, the 'manic gaze' being prelude to acts of barbarism, I also intend to illustrate how, inversely, Yeats finds the sensitive spot in our consciousness and recognises the part that violence and the irrational can play in our imaginative life.

20 See Yeats, *Per Amica, Mythologies*, p. 347.

21 See Evelyn Underhill, *Mysticism*, pp. 109–11.

22 See part II of Yeats's lyric sequence 'Supernatural Songs'.

23 Adorno, *Minima Moralia*, p. 190.

12 STARLIT AIR

1 Jahan Ramazani, *Yeats and the Poetry of Death: Elegy, Self-Elegy, and the Sublime* (New Haven: Yale UP, 1990), p. 106.

2 Yeats writes: 'When the image of despair departed with poetical tragedy the others could not survive, for the lover and the sage cannot survive without that despair which is a form of joy and has certainly no place in the modern psychological study of suffering'. *Explorations*, p. 296. Of course, more recent psychological ideas such as that of *jouissance* do indeed have a place for this sublime, doubled experience of joy and despair.

3 Ramazani, *Yeats and the Poetry of Death*, p. 113.

4 I have capitalised 'Soul' and 'Self' only when specifically discussing 'A Dialogue of Self and Soul' as I am referring to Yeatsian personifications; otherwise when considering the self and soul as concepts I have used lower case. Yeats sets the standard in the poem itself by using the upper case for the personifications and the lower case for the concept.

5 Ramazani, *Yeats and the Poetry of Death*, p. 112.

6 Ibid., p. 110. Although privileging the empirical realm of the self and distrustful of the mystical, Ramazani writes insightfully of what many might consider to be mystical self-sacrifice: 'Yeats's theory of the mask is a theory of self-transformation through imitation of the not-self, a theory cognate with the sublime in both privileging the subject and violating its integrity', p. 111. His understanding of the transcendental nature of the sublime, if not its necessity, is also profound: 'The transcendental impulse of the sublime is ultimately apocalyptic and self-destructive – a rage not only against formal order but also against the self and language', p. 125. Here, again, the present contention is that Yeats's idea of positive sublimity is emphatically one of self-realisation that is achieved by passing through the apocalyptic threshold.

7 Yeats, *A Vision*, p. 237.

8 Italo Calvino, *Six Memos for the Next Millennium*, trans. Patrick Creagh (London: Vintage, 1996), p. 87.

9 Ramazani also makes a strong case for not using other names for death: 'In my view, death precipitates the emotional turning called the sublime, although theorists of the sublime often refer to death by other names, or by what Kenneth Burke terms "deflections": castration, physical destruction'. *Yeats and the Poetry of Death*, p. 109.

10 Ellmann, *Identity of Yeats*, p. 55.

11 Kant, *Critique of Judgement*, p. 148.

12 Ibid., p. 148.

13 Ibid., pp. 175, 180.

14 Quoted in Ellmann, *Identity of Yeats*, p. 97.

15 Burke, *Enquiry*, p. 71.

16 Quoted in Scruton, *Kant*, p. 10.

17 Kant, *Critique of Judgement*, p. 175.

18 See Ellmann, *Identity of Yeats*, p. 97.
19 Yeats's emotional dependence on Lady Gregory cannot be underestimated. Upon hearing that Lady Gregory is ill, he writes in his journal: 'I thought my mother was ill and that my sister was asking me to come at once; then I remembered that my mother died years ago and that more than kin was at stake. She [Lady Gregory] has been to me mother, friend, sister and brother. I cannot realise the world without her'. Yeats, *Memoirs,* pp. 160–1. See also Brenda Maddox, 'The Silent Woman', *George's Ghosts* for a discussion of Yeats's relationship with his mother and of Lady Gregory's place therein. See also, *Yeats and Women,* ed. Deirdre Toomey (London: Macmillan, 1992).
20 See Monk, *The Sublime*, p. 87.
21 *W.B. Yeats and T. Sturge Moore: Their Correspondence, 1901–37,* ed. Ursula Bridge (New York: Oxford, 1953), p. 162.
22 See Burke, *Enquiry*, p. 158.
23 Yeats, *A Vision*, p. 279.
24 Yeats, *Explorations*, p. 290.
25 Yeats, *Memoirs*, pp. 356–7.
26 See Yeats, *Per Amica, Mythologies*, pp. 364–5.
27 Ibid., pp. 364–5.
28 Ibid., pp. 364–5.
29 Yeats, *Letters* ed. Kelly, p. 132.

13 THE STREAM THAT'S ROARING BY

1 Quoted in Brian Arkins, *Builders of my Soul: Greek and Roman Themes in Yeats* (Gerrards Cross: Colin Smythe, 1990), p. 148.
2 Roy Foster, 'Protestant Magic', p. 212.
3 For the connection between Ireland and Asia see Yeats, *Explorations*, pp. 400–1; and for the connection between Ribh's Gaelic world and the East see *The Variorum Edition of the Poems of W. B. Yeats*, pp. 837–8.
4 See Yeats, *A Vision*, p. 146.
5 See Kant, *Critique of Judgement*, p. 190; also, see Burke, *Enquiry*, p. 71.
6 Friedrich Nietzsche, *The Birth of Tragedy*, p. 102.
7 Yeats, *Autobiographies*, p. 471.
8 See Christopher Norris, 'Kant Disfigured', *The Truth about Postmodernism* (Oxford: Blackwell, 1993), pp. 182–257.
9 Yeats, *Explorations*, p. 336.
10 See Yeats, *Essays and Introductions*, p. 241.
11 Yeats, *Letters on Poetry*, p. 192.
12 See Kristeva, *Powers of Horror*, pp. 1–2.
13 Yeats, *A Vision*, pp. 295.
14 Ibid., pp. 150–1.
15 Cf. Socrates's position in Phase 27 of Yeats, *A Vision*, pp. 180–1.
16 Yeats, *A Vision*, p. 276.

14 MOVING UPON SILENCE

1 Yeats's attitudes towards novels are mixed; he read Joyce's *Ulysses* in the same way that he read poetry, which perhaps reflects his sense of the connection between the stream of consciousness and the lyric point of view. Balzac's example is also worth noting, for his novels comprise worlds whose nature the lyric can only inflect: '. . . whenever I have been tempted to go to Japan, China, or India for my philosophy, Balzac has brought me back, reminded me of my preoccupation with national, social, personal problems, convinced me that I cannot escape from our *Comédie humaine* . . .' *Essays and Introductions* (New York: Macmillan, 1968), p. 448.

2 William Gaddis, 'Old Foes with New Faces', *The Yale Review* 83: 4 October (1995): 2.

3 Gaddis, 'Old Foes', p. 3.

4 Quoted in ibid., p. 4.

5 Ibid., p. 4.

6 Keats, *Selected Poems and Letters*, p. 261.

7 Adorno, 'Lyric Poetry and Society', *Telos* 20 (1974): 55–71.

8 Ibid., p. 57.

9 Ibid., p. 58.

10 Ibid., p. 59.

11 Adorno, *Minima Moralia*, p. 63.

12 Nietzsche, *The Birth of Tragedy*, p. 52.

13 Nietzsche, *Twilight of the Idols*, *The Portable Nietzsche*, trans. W. Kaufmann (New York: Vintage, 1966), p. 24.

14 Though the charge of homosexuality has proved to be true, Yeats did not know it at the time because the charge had seemingly been refuted. Furthermore, as champion of Wilde during and after the time of his trial for 'indecency', Yeats would hardly have condemned Casement.

15 Yeats, *A Vision*, p. 246.

16 Yeats, *Memoirs*, p. 71–2.

17 See Whitaker, *Swan and Shadow*, p. 241.

18 Yeats, *A Vision*, p. 104.

19 Quoted in Whitaker, *Swan and Shadow*, p. 243.

20 Yeats, *Explorations*, p. 336; for Yeats's comments on Berkeley's Salamis, see *Explorations*, pp. 333–4, where he writes: 'Between Berkeley's account of his exploration of certain Kilkenny laws which speak of the "natives", came that intellectual crisis which led up to the sentence in the Commonplace Book: "We Irish do not hold with this". That was the birth of the national intellect and it caused the defeat in Berkeley's philosophical secret society of English materialism, the Irish Salamis'. [The 'Kilkenny Statutes', p. 1366, prohibiting Anglo-Normans from wearing Irish dress, among other prohibitions, meant to stop them from becoming 'more Irish than the Irish themselves', from becoming Hiberno-Normans; see Katharine Simms, 'The Norman Invasion and the Gaelic Recovery', R.F. Foster, ed., *The Oxford History of Ireland* (Oxford: Oxford UP, 1989), p. 75].

21 See Henri Arvon, *Marxist Esthetics*, trans. Helen Lane with intro. Fredric Jameson (Ithaca: Cornell UP, 1973), p. 8.

22 James Thomson writes: 'Whatever Lorraine light-touched with softening hue/Or savage Rosa dash'd, or learned Poussin drew'. Quoted in Andrew

Wilton, 'The Landscape Sublime', *Turner and the Sublime* (Chicago: U of Chicago P, 1980), p. 27.

23 Yeats, *A Vision*, p. 245.

24 Quoted in Anthony Blunt, *Artistic Theory in Italy, 1450–1600* (Oxford: Oxford UP, 1962), pp. 67–8.

25 W. E. Rogers notes this in *Concerning Poetry* 8 (1975): 11–21.

26 Samuel Taylor Coleridge, *Biographia Literaria*, p. 72.

27 Ibid., p. 68.

SELECT BIBLIOGRAPHY

Abrams, M.H. *The Mirror and the Lamp*. London: Oxford, 1953.

Ackroyd, Peter. *William Blake: A Biography*. New York: Knopf, 1996.

Adorno, Theodor W. *Aesthetic Theory*. Trans. C. Lenhardt. London: Routledge, 1984.

——. 'Lyric Poetry and Society'. *Telos* 20 (1974): 55–71.

——. *Minima Moralia*. Trans. E.F.N. Jephcott. London: Verso, 1974.

——. *Negative Dialectics*. Trans. E.B. Ashton. New York: Continuum, 1992.

Appignanesi, Lisa, ed. *ICA Documents 4/5: Postmodernism*. London: Institute of Contemporary Arts, 1986.

Arkins, Brian. *Builders Of My Soul: Greek and Roman Themes in Yeats*. Gerrards Cross: Colin Smythe, 1990.

Armstrong, Tim. 'Giving Birth to Oneself: Yeats's Late Sexuality'. *Yeats Annual* 8 (1991): 39–58.

Arvon, Henri. *Marxist Esthetics*. Trans. Helen Lane and intro. Fredric Jameson. Ithaca: Cornell UP, 1973.

Bacon, Francis. *The Essays of Francis Bacon*. Ed. John Pitcher. New York: Penguin, 1985.

Barthes, Roland. *A Lover's Discourse: Fragments*. Trans. Richard Howard. London: Penguin, 1979.

Bataille, George. *Inner Experience*. Trans. and intro. Leslie Anne Bolt. New York: State Univ. of New York, 1988.

Bate, W. Jackson. *The Burden of the Past and the English Poet*. London: Chatto, 1971.

Bernstein, J. M. *The Fate of Art: Aesthetic Alienation from Kant to Derrida and Adorno*. Cambridge: Polity, 1992.

Blackmur, R.P. *A Primer of Ignorance*. Ed. Joseph Frank. New York: Harcourt, 1967.

Blake, William. *The Selected Poetry and Prose of William Blake*. Ed. Northrop Frye. New York: Random House, 1953.

Bloom, Harold. *Agon: Towards A Theory of Revisionism*. New York: Oxford, 1982.

——, ed. *Poets of Sensibility and the Sublime*. New York: Chelsea, 1986.

——. *The Visionary Company: A Reading of English Romantic Poetry*. Ithaca: Cornell UP, 1961.

——. *Yeats*. London: Oxford UP, 1970.

Blunt, Anthony. *Artistic Theory in Italy, 1450–1600*. Oxford: Oxford UP, 1962.

Bohlmann, Otto. *Yeats and Nietzsche*. London: Macmillan, 1982.

Bornstein, George. *Yeats and Shelley*. Chicago: U of Chicago P, 1970.

Bradbury, Malcolm and James McFarlane. *Modernism: A Guide to European Literature, 1890–1930*. London: Penguin, 1976.

Bradford, Curtis B. *Yeats at Work*. New York: Ecco, 1978.

Bradley, A. C. *Oxford Lectures on Poetry*. London: Macmillan, 1914.

Brown, Terence. *Ireland: A Social and Cultural History, 1922–79*. London: Fontana, 1981.

——. *Ireland's Literature: Selected Essays*. Mullingar: Lilliput, 1988.

Brownmiller, Susan. *Against Our Will: Men, Women and Rape*. London: Secker & Warburg, 1975.

Burke, Edmund. *Letters, Speeches and Tracts on Irish Affairs*. London: Macmillan, 1881.

——. *A Philosophical Enquiry into the Origin of Our Ideas of the Sublime and the Beautiful*. Ed. James Boulton. Notre Dame: U of Notre Dame P, 1958.

——. *A Philosophical Enquiry into the Origin of our Ideas of the Sublime and Beautiful*. Ed. Adam Phillips. Oxford: Oxford UP, 1990.

——. *The Political Philosophy of Edmund Burke*. Ed. Iain Hampsher-Monk. London: Longman, 1987.

——. *Reflections on the Revolution in France*. Ed. Conor Cruise O'Brien. London: Penguin, 1968.

——. *Selections From Burke*. Ed. and intro. Bliss Perry. New York: Holt, 1896.

Calvino, Italo. *Six Memos for the Next Millennium*. Trans. Patrick Creagh. London: Vintage, 1996.

Chandler, James K. *Wordsworth's Second Nature: A Study of the Poetry and Politics*. Chicago: U of Chicago P, 1984.

Chapman, Wayne K. *Yeats and English Renaissance Literature*. London: Macmillan, 1991.

Coleridge, Samuel Taylor. *Biographia Literaria*. Ed. and intro. George Watson. London: Dent, 1993.

Corkery, Daniel. *The Hidden Ireland: A Study of Gaelic Munster in the Eighteenth Century*. Dublin: Gill, 1924.

Crawford, Donald. *Kant's Aesthetic Theory*. Madison: U of Wisconsin P, 1974.

Cronin, John. *The Anglo-Irish Novel: Volume 1, The Nineteenth Century*. Totowa: Barnes & Noble, 1980.

Crowe, Ian, ed. *Edmund Burke: His Life and Legacy*. Dublin: Four Courts, 1997.

Crowther, Paul. *The Kantian Sublime*. Oxford: Clarendon, 1989.

Cullingford, Elizabeth Butler. *Gender and History in Yeats's Love Poetry*. Cambridge: Cambridge UP, 1993.

——. *Yeats, Ireland and Fascism*. London: Macmillan, 1981.

Davies, Brian. *An Introduction to the Philosophy of Religion*. Oxford: Oxford UP, 1993.

Day, Aidan. *Romanticism*. London: Routledge, 1996.

De Bolla, Peter. *The Discourse of the Sublime*. Oxford: Blackwell, 1989.

De Luca, Vincent Arthur. *Words of Eternity: Blake and the Poetics of the Sublime*. Princeton: Princeton UP, 1991.

De Man, Paul. *Blindness and Insight: Essays in the Rhetoric of Contemporary Criticism*. London: Methuen, 1983.

——. *The Resistance to Theory*. Minneapolis: U of Minnesota P, 1986.

Deane, Seamus. *Celtic Revivals: Essays in Modern Irish Literature, 1880–1980*. London: Faber, 1985.

——, ed. et al. *The Field Day Anthology of Irish Writing*. Derry: Norton, 1991.

——. *A Short History of Irish Literature*. London: Hutchinson, 1986.

Derrida, Jacques. 'The time of the thesis: punctuations'. Trans. Kathleen McLaughlin. *Philosophy in France Today*. Ed. Allan Montefiore. Cambridge: Cambridge UP, 1983.

Donoghue, Denis. *The Arts Without Mystery*. London: BBC, 1983.

——. *The Pure Good of Theory*. Oxford: Blackwell, 1992.

——. *The Sovereign Ghost*. London: Faber, 1978.

——. *William Butler Yeats*. New York: Viking, 1971.

Eagleton, Terry. 'Aesthetics and Politics in Edmund Burke'. *Irish Literature and Culture*. Ed. Michael Kenneally. Savage: Barnes & Noble, 1992.

——. *The Ideology of the Aesthetic*. Oxford: Blackwell, 1990.

Eliade, Mircea. *The Sacred And The Profane: The Nature of Religion*. Trans. Williard R. Trask. London: Harcourt, 1959.

Eliot, T.S. *Selected Essays*. New York: Harcourt, 1932.

Ellmann, Richard. *The Identity of Yeats*. Oxford: Oxford UP, 1964.

——. *The Man and the Masks*. London: Penguin, 1979.

Engelberg, Edward. *The Vast Design: Patterns in W. B. Yeats's Aesthetic*. Toronto: U of Toronto P, 1964.

Engstrom, Timothy H. 'The Postmodern Sublime? Philosophical Rehabilitations and Pragmatic Evasions'. *Boundary 2*: 20 (1993): 190–204.

Ferguson, Frances. *Solitude and the Sublime: Romanticism and the Aesthetics of Individuation*. London: Routledge, 1992.

Finneran, Richard J., ed. *Critical Essays on W.B. Yeats*. Boston: Hall, 1986.

Fletcher, Ian. '"Leda and the Swan" as Iconic Poem'. *Yeats Annual* 1 (1982): 82–113.

Foster, Hal, ed. *The Anti-Aesthetic: Essays on Postmodern Culture*. Seattle: Bay P, 1983.

Foster, R.F., ed. *The Oxford History of Ireland*. Oxford: Oxford UP, 1989.

——. *Paddy and Mr Punch: Connections in Irish and English History*. London: Penguin, 1993.

——. *W.B. Yeats: A Life: I: The Apprentice Mage, 1865–1914*. Oxford: Oxford UP, 1997.

——. 'Yeats's progress from the twilight of Ascendancy to the new nation'. *Times Literary Supplement* 27 September 1996: 9–10.

Furniss, Tom. *Edmund Burke's Aesthetic Ideology: Language, Gender, and Political Economy in Revolution*. Cambridge: Cambridge UP, 1993.

Gadamer, Hans-Georg. *The Relevance of the Beautiful and Other Essays*. Trans. Nicholas Walker and ed. Robert Bernasconi. Cambridge: Cambridge UP, 1986.

Gaddis, William. 'Old Foes with New Faces'. *The Yale Review* 83: 4 (October 1995): 1–16.

Gallagher, Michael Paul, SJ. *Struggles of Faith*. Dublin: Columba, 1990.

Gibbons, Luke. 'Topographies of Terror: Killarney and the Politics of the Sublime'. *The South Atlantic Quarterly* 95: 1 Winter (1996): 23–44.

Girard, René. *The Scapegoat*. Trans. Yvonne Freccero. London: Athlone, 1986.

——. *Violence and the Sacred*. Trans. Patrick Gregory. Baltimore: Johns Hopkins UP, 1972.

Goodson, A. C. 'Burke's Orphics and Coleridge's Contrary Understanding'. *The Wordsworth Circle* XXII: 1 (1991): 52–8.

Hartman, Geoffrey. *Criticism in the Wilderness: The Study of Literature Today.* New Haven: Yale UP, 1980.

Hassan, Ihab. *The Dismemberment of Orpheus.* Madison: Wisconsin, 1982.

Hassett, Joseph. *Yeats and the Poetics of Hate.* Dublin: Gill, 1986.

Havel, Václav. 'An Opportunity to create a New and Lasting Order in Europe'. *The Irish Times* 9 November 1994.

Hawthorne, Nathaniel. *The Scarlet Letter.* New York: Penguin, 1983.

Hayes, Richard, and Chris Morash, eds. *'Fearful Realities': New Perspectives on the Famine.* Blackrock: Irish Academic P, 1996.

Heaney, Seamus. *New Selected Poems, 1966–1987.* London: Faber, 1987.

——. *The Redress of Poetry.* London: Faber, 1995.

Henn, T.R. *Last Essays.* Gerrards Cross: Colin Smythe, 1976.

Hertz, Neil. *The End of the Line: Essays on Psychoanalysis and the Sublime.* New York: Columbia UP, 1985.

Hone, Joseph. *W.B. Yeats, 1865–1939.* London: Macmillan, 1965.

Horkheimer, Max. *The Eclipse of Reason.* New York: Continuum, 1947.

Howes, Marjorie. *Yeats's Nations: Gender, Class and Irishness.* Cambridge: Cambridge UP, 1996.

Jay, Martin. *Adorno.* London: Fontana, 1984.

——. *The Dialectical Imagination: A History of the Frankfurt School and the Institute of Social Research, 1923–1950.* Berkeley: U of California P, 1996.

Jeffares, A. Norman and Anna MacBride White, eds. *The Gonne–Yeats Letters, 1893–1938.* London: Pimlico, 1992.

——. *W.B. Yeats: Man and Poet.* New Haven: Yale UP, 1949.

Jefferson, Ann and David Robey, eds. *Modern Literary Theory.* London: Batsford, 1982.

Johnsen, William. 'Textual/Sexual Politics in Yeats's "Leda and the Swan"'. *Yeats and Postmodernism.* Ed. Leonard Orr. Syracuse: Syracuse UP, 1991.

Johnson, Lionel. *The Complete Poems of Lionel Johnson.* Ed. Ian Fletcher. London: Unicorn, 1953.

Johnson, W.R. *The Idea of the Lyric: Lyric Modes in Ancient and Modern Poetry.* Berkeley: U of California P, 1982.

Jones, John. *The Egotistical Sublime: A History of William Wordsworth's Imagination.* London: Chatto, 1964.

Jordan, June. *Naming Our Destiny: New and Selected Poems.* New York: Thunder's Mouth, 1989.

Kant, Immanuel. *The Critique of Judgement.* Trans. James Creed Meredith. Oxford: Clarendon, 1928.

——. *Critique of Practical Reason.* Trans. Lewis White Beck. New York: Macmillan, 1956.

——. *Critique of Pure Reason.* Trans. Norman Kemp-Smith. London: Macmillan, 1929.

——. *Observations on the Feeling of the Beautiful and the Sublime.* Trans. John T. Goldthwait. Berkeley: U of California P, 1960.

Kaufman, Linda, ed. *Gender and Theory.* London: Blackwell, 1986.

Keane, Patrick J. *Yeats's Interactions with Tradition.* Columbia: U of Missouri P, 1987.

Kearney, Richard. *The Wake of the Imagination: Ideas of Creativity in Western Culture.* London: Hutchinson, 1988.

Keats, John. *Selected Poems and Letters of John Keats*. Ed. Douglas Bush. Boston: Houghton, 1959.

Kelly, Theresa. *Revisionary Aesthetics*. Cambridge: Cambridge UP, 1988.

Kermode, Frank. *Lawrence*. London: Fontana, 1973.

——. *Romantic Image*. New York: Vintage, 1964.

Kiberd, Declan. *Inventing Ireland: The Literature of the Modern Nation*. London: Cape, 1995.

——. *Men and Feminism in Modern Literature*. London: Macmillan, 1985.

Kramnick, Isaac. *The Rage of Edmund Burke: Portrait of an Ambivalent Conservative*. New York: Basic, 1977.

Kristeva, Julia. *In the Beginning was Love: Psychoanalysis and Faith*. Trans. Arthur Goldhammer. New York: Columbia UP, 1987.

——. *Powers of Horror: An Essay on Abjection*. Trans. Leon S. Roudiez. New York: Columbia UP, 1982.

Leighton, Angela. *Shelley and the Sublime: An Interpretation of the Major Poems*. Cambridge: Cambridge UP, 1984.

Levinas, Emmanuel. *The Levinas Reader*. Ed. Seán Hand. Oxford: Blackwell, 1989.

Lewalski, Barbara. *Protestant Poetics and the Seventeenth-Century Religious Lyric*. Princeton: Princeton UP, 1979.

Lindley, David. *Lyric*. London: Methuen, 1985.

Lloyd, David. *Nationalism and Minor Literature: James Clarence Mangan and the Emergence of Irish Cultural Nationalism*. Berkeley: U of California P, 1987.

Longinus. *On the Sublime*. Trans. W. Rhys Roberts. *Classical Literary Criticism*. London: Penguin, 1965.

Louth, Andrew. *Denys The Areopagite*. London: Chapman, 1989.

Lyotard, Jean-François. *The Differend*. Trans. G. Van den Abbeele. Manchester: Manchester UP, 1990.

——. *The Inhuman: Reflections on Time*. Trans. Geoffrey Bennington and Rachel Bowlby. Stanford: Stanford UP, 1988.

——. *Lessons on the Analytic of the Sublime*. Trans. Elizabeth Rottenberg. Stanford: Stanford UP, 1994.

——. *The Postmodern Condition*. Trans. Geoffrey Bennington and Brian Massumi. Minneapolis: U of Minnesota P, 1984.

McDonagh, Thomas. *Literature in Ireland: Studies in Irish and Anglo-Irish*. Dublin: Talbot, 1916.

McGann, Jerome. *The Romantic Ideology: A Critical Investigation*. Chicago: U of Chicago P, 1983.

McGuckian, Medbh. *Marconi's Cottage*. Meath: Gallery, 1991.

MacNeice, Louis. *The Poetry of W.B. Yeats*. London: Faber, 1967.

Macpherson, C. B. *Burke*. Oxford: Oxford UP, 1980.

Mahon, Derek. *The Selected Poems of Derek Mahon*. London: Viking, 1991.

Marcuse, Herbert. *An Essay on Liberation*. Boston: Beacon, 1969.

Martin, Augustine. 'Hound Voices Were They All: An Experiment in Yeats Criticism'. *Yeats, Sligo and Ireland*. Ed. A. Norman Jeffares. Gerrards Cross: Colin Smythe, 1980.

Matthews, Patricia M. 'Kant's Sublime: A Form of Pure Aesthetic Reflective Judgement'. *The Journal of Aesthetics and Art Criticism* 54.2 (1996): 165–78.

Meaney, Gerardine. *(Un)Like Subjects: Women, Theory, Fiction*. London: Routledge, 1993.

Mellor, Anne K. *Romanticism and Gender*. London: Routledge, 1993.

Meyer, Linda C. et al. *The Aftermath of Rape*. Lexington: U of Kentucky P, 1979.

Monk, Samuel Holt. 'A Grace beyond the Reach of Art'. *Journal of the History of Ideas* 5: 2 (1944): 131–50.

——. *The Sublime: A Study of Critical Theories in Eighteenth-Century England*. Ann Arbor: U of Michigan P, 1960.

Morash, Chris. *Writing the Irish Famine*. Oxford: Clarendon, 1995.

Morris, C.R. *Locke, Berkeley, Hume*. Oxford: Oxford UP, 1931.

Morris, David. *The Religious Sublime: Christian Poetry and Critical Tradition in Eighteenth-Century England*. Lexington: U of Kentucky P, 1972.

Nicolson, Marjorie Hope. *Mountain Gloom and Mountain Glory: The Development of the Aesthetics of the Infinite*. Ithaca: Cornell UP, 1959.

Nietzsche, Friedrich. *The Birth of Tragedy and The Genealogy of Morals*. Trans. Francis Golffing. New York: Doubleday, 1956.

——. *A Nietzsche Reader*. Ed. R. J. Hollingdale. London: Penguin, 1977.

——. *Twilight of the Idols, The Portable Nietzsche*. Trans. and ed. W. Kaufmann. New York: Vintage, 1966.

Norris, Christopher. *The Truth about Postmodernism*. Oxford: Blackwell, 1993.

——. *Uncritical Theory, Postmodernism, Intellectuals and the Gulf War*. London: Lawrence, 1992.

O'Brien, Conor Cruise. *The Great Melody: A Thematic Biography of Edmund Burke*. London: Sinclair-Stevenson, 1992.

——. *Passion and Cunning: Essays on Nationalism, Terrorism and Revolution*. New York: Simon & Schuster, 1988.

Otto, Rudolf. *The Idea of the Holy: An Inquiry into the Non-rational Factor in the Idea of the Divine and its Relation to the Rational*. Trans. John W. Harvey. Oxford: Oxford UP, 1923.

Page, Judith W. *Wordsworth and the Cultivation of Women*. Berkeley: U of California P, 1994.

Pater, Walter. *The Renaissance*. Oxford: Oxford UP, 1986.

Paulson, Ronald. *Representations of Revolution*. New Haven: Yale UP, 1983.

Paz, Octavio. *The Labyrinth of Solitude*. Trans. Lysander Kemp. New York: Penguin, 1965.

Prophet, Jane. 'Sublime Ecologies and Artistic Endeavors'. *Leonardo* 29: 5 (1996): 339–44.

Ramazani, Jahan. *Yeats and the Poetry of Death: Elegy, Self-elegy, and the Sublime*. New Haven: Yale UP, 1990.

Renan, Ernest. *Poetry of the Celtic Races and Other Studies*. Trans. William G. Hutchison. Port Washington: Kennikat, 1970.

Roberts, Cathy. *Women and Rape*. New York: Harvester, 1989.

Said, Edward. *Culture and Imperialism*. London: Chatto, 1993.

Salvadori, Corinna. *Yeats and Castiglione: Poet and Courtier*. Dublin: Allen, 1965.

Schiller, Friedrich. *On the Aesthetic Education of Man*. Trans. Reginald Snell. Bristol: Thoemmes, 1994.

——. *The Philosophical and Aesthetic Letters and Essays of Schiller*. Trans. J. Weiss. London: Chapman, 1854.

Scruton, Roger. *Kant*. Oxford: Oxford UP, 1982.

Sedley, David. 'Sublimity and Skepticism in Montaigne'. *PMLA* 113 (1998): 1079–92.

Spitzer, Leo. 'On Yeats's poem, "Leda and the Swan"'. *Modern Philology* 5: 1 (1954): 217–76.

Sturrock, John. *Structuralism and Since: From Lévi-Strauss to Derrida*. Oxford: Oxford UP, 1979.

Symons, Arthur. *The Symbolist Movement in Literature*. New York: Haskell, 1971.

Tabbi, Joseph. *Postmodern Sublime: Technology and American Writing from Mailer to Cyberpunk*. Ithaca: Cornell UP, 1995.

Teresa, St of Avila. *Interior Castle*. Trans. E. Allison Peers. New York: Doubleday, 1989.

Torchiana, Donald T. *W.B. Yeats and Georgian Ireland*. Evanston: Northwestern UP, 1966.

Trowbridge, Hoyt. "'Leda and the Swan': A Longinian Analysis'. *Modern Philology* 5: 1 (1953): 118–29.

Tuveson, Ernest Lee. *The Imagination as a Means of Grace: Locke and the Aesthetics of Romanticism*. New York: Gordian, 1974.

Underhill, Evelyn. *Mysticism*. New York: Doubleday, 1911.

Vendler, Helen. *Yeats's Vision and the Later Plays*. Cambridge: Harvard UP, 1963.

Verlaine, Paul. *Paul Verlaine: Selected Poems*. Trans. C. F. MacIntyre. Berkeley: U of California P, 1948.

Ware, Malcolm. *Sublimity in the Novels of Ann Radcliffe*. Copenhagen: Lundequistska Bokhandeln, 1963.

Weil, Simone. *The Simone Weil Reader*. Ed. George A. Paniches. New York: McKay, 1977.

——. *Waiting For God*. Intro. Leslie Fiedler and trans. Emma Craufurd. New York: Harper, 1973.

Weiskel, Thomas. *The Romantic Sublime: Studies in the Structure and Psychology of Transcendence*. Baltimore: Johns Hopkins UP, 1976.

Whitaker, Thomas R. *Swan and Shadow: Yeats's Dialogue with History*. Washington: Catholic UP, 1989.

White, Stephen K. *Edmund Burke: Modernity, Politics and Aesthetics*. London: Sage, 1994.

Whitehead, Alfred North. *Science and the Modern World*. Cambridge: Cambridge UP, 1927.

Wilde, Oscar. *The Critic as Artist*. Ed. Richard Ellmann. London: Allen, 1970.

Willey, Basil. *The Seventeenth-Century Background: Studies in the Thought of the Age in Relation to Religion and Poetry*. New York: Doubleday, 1935.

Wilton, Andrew. *Turner and the Sublime*. Chicago: U of Chicago P, 1980.

Wlecke, Albert. *Wordsworth and the Sublime*. Berkeley: Berkeley UP, 1973.

Wollstonecraft, Mary. *A Vindication of the Rights of Men*. Ed. Eleanor Louise Nicholes. Gainesville: Scholars, 1960.

——. *A Wollstonecraft Anthology*. Ed. Janet Todd. Oxford: Blackwell, 1989.

Woolf, Virginia. *Between the Acts*. Ed. Gillian Beer. London: Penguin, 1992.

Wordsworth, William. *Selected Poems and Prefaces of William Wordsworth*. Ed. Jack Stillinger. Boston: Houghton, 1965.

——. *Selected Prose*. Ed. John O. Hayden. London: Penguin, 1988.

Yeats, W.B. *Autobiographies*. London: Macmillan, 1980.

——. *The Collected Letters, Vol. III (1901–1904)*. Ed. John Kelly and Ronald Schuchard. Oxford: Oxford UP, 1994.

——. *The Collected Plays*. London: Macmillan, 1982.

——. *Essays and Introductions*. London: Macmillan, 1968.

——. *Explorations*. London: Macmillan, 1973.

Yeats, W.B. (*cont.*)
——. *John Sherman & Dhoya*. Ed. Richard Finneran. Detroit: Wayne State UP, 1969.
——. *The Letters of W. B. Yeats*. Ed. Allen Wade. London: Macmillan, 1955.
——. *Letters on Poetry from W.B. Yeats to Dorothy Wellesley*. Ed. Dorothy Wellesley. London: Oxford UP, 1940.
——. *Letters to New Island*. London: Oxford UP, 1934.
——. *Memoirs*. Ed. Denis Donoghue. London: Macmillan, 1972.
——. *Mythologies*. London: Macmillan, 1969.
——, ed. *The Oxford Book of Modern Verse*. Oxford: Oxford UP, 1936.
——. *The Poems of W. B. Yeats*. Ed. Daniel Albright. London: Dent, 1990.
——. *Uncollected Prose of W. B. Yeats (Vol I)*. Ed. John P. Frayne. London: Macmillan, 1975.
——. *The Variorum Edition of the Poems of W. B. Yeats*. Ed. Peter Allt and Russell Alspach. London: Macmillan, 1957.
——. *A Vision*. New York: Macmillan, 1966.
——. *W.B. Yeats and T. Sturge Moore: Their Correspondence 1901–37*. Ed. Ursula Bridge. Oxford: Oxford UP, 1953.
Zerilli, Linda. 'Text/Woman as Spectacle: Edmund Burke's Revolution'. *The Eighteenth Century* 33: 1 (1992): 47–72.

INDEX